# Working with Chakras for Belief Change

"This book is simply marvelous. It is the epitome of the perfect read in terms of a healing modality and can be accessed straight away. Thoroughly researched information, inspirational lessons, healing tools, channeled guidance, and the whole truths about the author's own spiritual journey and how she healed herself are all part of the rich tapestry that will have you intrigued on every page. Nikki gives you a complete sense of understanding why she was divinely inspired to create this healing system that empowers people to heal themselves. The depth of her knowledge and experiences, plus her high intuitive nature, will have you captivated. A must-read, this book is life-changing."

— **DENISE DEVLIN**, author of *The Untold Story: Peter and Jesus–The Gap Years* and founder of Positive Parties: Training with a Difference

"Nikki Gresham-Record draws from her own personal healing journey from incurable lupus to full recovery and her extensive experience working with clients as a psychologist, counselor, empath, and intuitive healer to help the reader understand the steps needed for healing to occur. The Healing InSight method utilizes great sources of wisdom, giving us a way to identify the limiting beliefs that prevent healing. It encourages us to face our fears and to listen to our body's pain as a cry for help that when heard will lead us to wholeness. Readers will be encouraged to take responsibility for the creation of health, happiness, and healing in their own lives and will be left with the feeling that they are powerful creators of their own reality."

— **RICHARD ELLIS**, author of *Reiki and the Seven Chakras* and *The Heart of Reiki*

"You are holding in your hand a skillfully crafted masterpiece. Nikki is a mistress of top-level energy work, with years of research and successful practical application. Here, she asks you to pay attention to the finer details of your life: what are you putting up with that you know is not really you? Using specific techniques to uncover unconscious blocks, this Healing InSight method asks what disturbance you would like to shift and where it feels locked at a chakra level. Nikki shows you how you can move past this for good.

"This superbly clear, compassionate, fired-up, wise guide is a complete system and has links to a range of supporting material. You are not on your own. The integration key that makes sure you actually receive the adjustments uses classical qigong movements to embody the change. Genius! This component is often overlooked in not-so-successful talk-based therapies. Change is hugely possible, and necessary, when you harmonize body, mind, and soul. Your gifts then have a clear channel to manifest through for you and to influence the field of energy that links each and every one of us."

— **CLARA APOLLO**, director of New Forest Elemental Qigong and Conscious Living Events, founding member of the Alliance of Tai Chi Qigong UK, and presenter of *Chi Time Radio*

"Occasionally a book comes along from someone who can offer hands-on advice that we can learn from. It is a book where the language and content is very clear. Thank you, Nikki, for shining a light and sparking my interest once again into mind, body and spirit. It is my pleasure to recommend this excellent book."

— **JOE DALTON**, host of *Breakthrough Brands* radio show

# Working with Chakras for Belief Change
## The Healing InSight Method

Nikki Gresham-Record

FINDHORN PRESS

Findhorn Press
One Park Street
Rochester, Vermont 05767
www.findhornpress.com

Findhorn Press is a division of Inner Traditions International

**Disclaimer**

The information in this book is given in good faith and is neither intended to diagnose
any physical or mental condition nor to serve as a substitute for informed medical
advice or care. Please contact your health professional for medical advice and treatment.
Neither author nor publisher can be held liable by any person for any loss or damage
whatsoever which may arise directly or indirectly from the use of this book or any of the
information therein.

Cataloging-in-Publication data for this title is available from the Library of Congress

ISBN 978-1-62055-902-4 (print)
ISBN 978-1-62055-903-1 (ebook)

Printed and bound in the United States by Versa Press, Inc.

10 9 8 7 6 5 4 3 2 1

Edited by Nicky Leach
Text design, layout by Damian Keenan
This book was typeset in Adobe Garamond Pro, Calluna Sans, Museo Sans
with Telegraph Light and Boho Sans used as display typefaces.
Artwork by Lucy Record, Jo Davey and Rob Record

To send correspondence to the author of this book, mail a first-class letter to the
author c/o Inner Traditions • Bear & Company, One Park Street, Rochester,
VT 05767, USA, and we will forward the communication, or contact the author
directly at **www.healinginsight.co.uk**

# Contents

# Preface

Many of us are seeking more from life than our current experiences. We carry emotional and physical pain and are trapped by insecurities and limitations from our past, uncertain of how to shift these deeply entrenched patterns of conditioning. This book seeks to make real the idea that healing is possible. Using real-life examples of that healing in action, it offers reassurance and insights, tools, and methods that guide self-directed transformational healing.

The importance of diet, detox, exercise, and mindfulness for health has been well established. The new consciousness revolution of science and spirituality shows us that healing is possible when we understand the mechanisms of what it is to be human—that we are light/energy beings at varying vibrational densities connected to a wider field of consciousness. If we are to heal we must remember who we are. It is time to free ourselves from the negative beliefs and emotions that keep us limited, fearful, powerless, and separate.

I write to share my learning, understanding, and wisdom as a counselling psychologist, healer, intuitive, and empath. I have journeyed from the tough, industrial North of England through a painful adolescence into womanhood, from chronic "incurable" autoimmune disease into health, and from ignorance into blissful spirituality and love. I have witnessed magic unfolding as I surrendered to my inner calling and came to trust and work with the flow of the universe. A lover of life, light, integrity, and creativity, I have and will continue to walk my talk, which requires the courage to step through the darkness of the birthing canal in order to transform and innovate.

On my journey, I discovered how we can heal lower vibrational emotions, such as hurt, sadness, hopelessness, anger, and fear, and live in the vibration of love for self, our beautiful planet, and our brothers and sisters throughout life, with its many twists and turns. Evolution requires us to clear our karma and lower vibrations so that we can resonate with and restore the natural world. The time is now for big change to occur. We must start that process by first healing ourselves if we are to heal our Earth.

The beginnings of this book, though derived from my life's work and inspired in part by the therapies I have practised, were conceived in 2014 as seven simple affirmations representing the seven chakras. Three years later, those affirmations had developed into a comprehensive and transformative healing system, with a set of channelled beliefs in a 56-card deck (available as an app) and this book. The cards, which are included as images in this book, are designed to bring you into resonance with the vibration of the chakra aspects they represent. The colour frequencies, animals, deities, and words shown on the cards hold a unique vibration, directing your attention towards your intended alignment whilst rebalancing the overall health of your body, mind, and spirit.

The innovative method utilizes qigong, whole-brain hemispheric integration, and visualization, which together help to align the body, mind, and spirit with the vibration a helpful new belief. This shift affects our vibrational field(s), which allows more joy, love, connection, and expansion in our reality.

My gift to you is a unique healing system that not only reprogrammes the subconscious mind with healthy, life-affirming beliefs but also identifies and clears vibrational patterns that previously prevented resonance with these beliefs. The result is transformation and awakening to the inner truth of your being, supporting healing in the direction of your desires.

This work has a momentum all its own. Its intent is to bring healing and help unite us. It is time for personal empowerment, and this system provides just that: a self-help healing system that offers powerful transformation. All you have to do is play and let things be easy. Commit to yourself. Choose love over fear. Honour yourself and your truth, and be of service to the greater good. Together, we can create "Heaven On Mother Earth" (HOME).

I begin by offering insights from my own life story and follow this with information about the science of consciousness and evidence that shows our potential to affect our realities, for healing or otherwise. I lay out what you need to know to use the Healing InSight system, including qigong and muscle testing, and follow with the method itself. The book contains channelled beliefs for your exploration and alignment and is supported by case studies, meditation and qigong practices, and a forgiveness and manifestation protocol. Further support can be found in the Resources in the Appendices at the end of the book.

I give you my sincere blessings. Go for it. It might just transform your life!

# PART ONE

# Development of Healing InSight:
# My Personal Journey

AS A PSYCHOLOGIST AND HEALER, I run a full practice in both the small West Sussex town of Midhurst and Richmond, southwest of London, integrating counselling psychology with energy psychology and healing methods. I teach qigong and reiki, along with my own Healing InSight self-help belief realignment method.

Like all healers, I went on my own painful journey of self-discovery to find my true self, heal my wounds, and awaken to deep compassionate love and joy, the great spiritual essence of life.

In the following three chapters, I take you on my own journey of personal and professional discovery, mind-body-spirit connection, and understanding of myself as a spiritual being, connected to God, Oneness, or Source energy. I share the how-tos of my path and purpose: to bring the magic of healing and fulfilment to my own and others' lives. If I had not experienced adversity, pain, separation, sickness, and desperation and learnt how to transform them into their polar opposites—joy, connection, health, and possibility—I would never have discovered the pathways to transformation. Along the way, I share important aspects of my life story, weaving in personal insights and how I came to develop this system of practice-based evidence. In a world full of possibility, I hope to demonstrate that all truly is possible.

I trust that my story will resonate with you on some level, readying you to further your own healing journey with the help of the Healing InSight method. I have witnessed many transformations in others, so it is with great pleasure that I offer my insights into how healing can be "in sight".

# Chapter 1

# My Awakening

I grew up north of Nottingham, one of two children. Mum was a home-maker, and Dad ran a precision engineering company. There was a lot of love in our home, but as I became more aware, I began to experience an inner discomfort. My mother was a gentle home-maker, but when I saw British Prime Minister Margaret Thatcher on television, I realized that women could be powerful, have careers, and make a difference. I knew from an early age that I wanted more from life than what I could see. Discord and injustices deeply bothered me.

I developed a progressively difficult relationship with my dad, a critical Virgo perfectionist type who always knew best. My dad and I are both wise old souls, but there was not much room at our dinner table for more than one opinion, and as a sensitive and empathic teenager, I felt worn down by this. Eventually, I stopped speaking up and often skulked away to my bedroom, feeling hopeless, frustrated, and disconnected, pushing down emotions, and pretending to the outside world that I was okay.

I enjoyed the community college school my brother and I attended, and did well academically, but my outer and inner light faded as a result of bullying, family dynamics, and existing in a culture where it was not okay to shine. I hid for two years at school and couldn't seem to get it right at home, either, so although spirited and strong willed, I lost confidence in my ability to be present and express myself.

Lifelong patterns were set up during this time, and I believe it was these trapped, unexpressed emotions, belief patterns, sensitivity and self-rejecting thoughts that led me to develop an autoimmune disease: Systemic Lupus Erythematosus (SLE).

## Systemic Lupus Erythematosus

At age 18, while studying for my A Levels, I started to experience a dull, aching pain in my hips and legs, which moved to my arms and shoulders. Two years later, whilst at Leeds University studying for my BSc in Psychology, I was diagnosed with SLE.

SLE is an autoimmune disease in which the immune system mistakenly attacks the skin, joints, or organs, causing inflammation, as it does not recognize the body as self. It is a serious chronic condition that is said to be incurable.

I felt sad that I would have this condition for life, suffered in silence, but carried on regardless, taking 800mg of Ibuprofen three times a day to deal with the pain. I was unable to sit for any length of time and woke frequently in the night with such severe pain it left me breathless. During exam time, I remember being unable to walk downstairs in the morning, my feet in agony and inflexible on waking. I would be hit by occasional sudden and severe chest pain and had to lie still and shallow-breathe until the pain subsided. I tried to hide these symptoms and be a normal 20-year-old. I did not tell my flatmates half of what I was experiencing, but my boyfriend's support was a breath of fresh air for me.

Chest x-rays revealed nothing, so I was mostly ignorant about how this disease was playing out in my life. I discovered years later that I had inflammation of the rib joints, not suspected heart problems. It was scary and challenging trying to navigate these huge changes in my body during my university years.

I was determined that SLE would not become the focus of my life. I had to come to terms with it and battled through like a warrior, making sure it did not define who I was or what I was capable of. I persevered, remained positive, and good things happened. I made friends, fell in love, enjoyed my studies, and began dancing again. Looking back, dancing was the one activity where I was fully in my body and free to express myself. Although I could barely walk downstairs in the morning, I won the Intervarsity Ballroom Dancing Competition for the quickstep in 1994. I received support from the Psychology Department and was given special dispensation in sitting exams as I was only able to sit still for an hour without pain. The determination paid off, and I achieved a good honours degree in Psychology in 1996.

## Falling into Therapeutic Work

After university, I moved to London to take up a temporary opening in the Occupational Therapy department of a North London mental health hospital. I found an advert in a local post office window for a room to rent and, within the space of one week, my boyfriend and I had moved in with a French couple and my helping career had begun.

I think that my physical being became a separate entity to me at this point. Disowned, abandoned, and treated with painkillers, I pushed through without listening to my body or my unresolved emotions. There was some easing of my lupus symptoms, perhaps because I felt more relaxed and a sense of purpose and connection to my work, clients, and colleagues.

In my work as an occupational therapy assistant, I did my best to engage with patients, either through talking, relaxation classes, or activities like art and music. I remember vividly an elderly Greek lady who had been depressed and mute for months. Each day I would go onto the ward where she was sitting, her eyes filled with sadness. She was on medication and undergoing a course of electroconvulsive therapy. It seemed that her condition was deteriorating, and she had begun to lose urinary function.

I sat with her every day for two weeks, speaking a little, but mostly we just sat together. It was agreed that I could take her outside, and we would sit on a bench. She had come to trust me and would hold my hand as we sat, looking at me once in a while. Her pained expression seemed to convey something she was unable to express verbally.

By week three, I took her into a music therapy class to see if she could break her silence through instruments. In her second class she beat a drum, and then, as if the heavens were opening, she started to sing. A hauntingly beautiful song escaped her lips and as the sound of despair and sadness transmuted into more joyful sounds, a cautious smile began to crinkle her eyes. She cried tears of joy and sadness that day. It felt profound and beautiful, as if her spirit reconnected with her physical body.

She looked into my eyes, held my hands, and said, "Thank you. You made me talk again." I was, young, naïve, and completely humbled. I have tears in my eyes as I write this, remembering how the power of simple human compassion and connection transformed her hopelessness. That was my first taste of the power of love and compassion to heal dark despair. I believe that it began the journey that has shaped me over the years.

**Lesson no. 1**
The power of human compassion and connection transforms and heals—the simple art of being in loving kindness with what is.

## New Beginnings

After this, I spent time living and working abroad and began a new relationship, but I realized that I had become depressed. I was prescribed antidepressants, which helped lift my mood, but they did nothing to change my thoughts, beliefs, limiting self-talk, and patterns of aloneness and helplessness. At work, I was surrounded by mental health difficulties, hopelessness, isolation, depression, and anxiety, which were challenging as I didn't have much to give, but I began to cope again on a daily basis.

My time overseas offered the time and space to see that without my usual crutches of friends, family, and a secure relationship I felt lost. I finally had to admit to myself that I was unhappy. My heart was not singing a joyous song. On my return home, I became determined to discover a future pathway into personal happiness.

I took up a community outreach post in London serving those with mental health difficulties. I enjoyed the clients but hated the system, which I felt could not meet the needs of the clients. A weathered psychologist told me that I had on "rose-tinted spectacles" and it was better to remove them. My clients' stories were dismissed, even rejected as lies at times. The system I experienced felt too impersonal and absent-hearted to me, and again I moved on.

I trained as a counselling psychologist and began working in a charity sector residential drug dependency rehabilitation unit. I started a new relationship with an old friend from university who would become my husband and father to my two eldest boys. Although working with this new client group was challenging, I loved my work and was good at it. I started my MSc and felt part of something meaningful for the first time in years. I planned a big white wedding from our little flat in South Clapham, and we had grand plans. I still had to push through lupus daily, and began taking immune modulators (anti-malarials) and steroids to help with the aches and pain.

I was a naturally gifted therapist, and 90 percent of my clients stayed clean and completed the six-month residential programme (a success rate of less than 50 percent is typical, so I realized that something I was doing was getting results). I worked in the rehabilitation unit, facilitating groups and counselling, whilst doing other work experience in a women's therapy centre. I also completed the research component of my MSc, writing my thesis on "The Process of Recovery from Drug Dependency in a Residential Rehabilitation Unit" and passed with distinction. I recognized that I had a gift for therapeutic work.

## Empowerment

Three years into the job and training, now married and pregnant with my first son, I encountered a new life challenge: I became very sick with hyperemesis (chronic and acute pregnancy sickness), and lupus was now causing inflammation in my brain. I was exhausted and being bullied at work by an angry colleague who considered me too inexperienced to help this client group and resented my success.

As part of my training, I was in therapy with a great Gestalt therapist, and this proved to be a lifeline. I began to face my past demons and saw how those patterns were repeating in my present work situation. I was supported to honour my being, find my voice, and step into my power. It was terrifying, going through this transition, but I could not continue with the pattern of hiding, playing small, and allowing myself to be victimized any more. It was vital, now that I had a beautiful innocent being growing inside me.

I found the courage to write up my grievance against this work colleague, which led to a long process of dispute and his suspension. He was eventually reinstated with a final warning. His return to work was challenging, but this situation and his behaviour towards me was a gift. It enabled me to get in touch with my anger, my voice, and my personal power and to set and hold acceptable boundaries and begin to heal important relationships.

**Lesson no. 2**
Addressing our hurts and fears brings healing rewards—find the gift in your life challenges.

## The Golden Key of Personal Responsibility

I completed the loose ends of my post-MSc in Counselling Psychology and welcomed into the world the light of my life, my dear son Jackson. Nine months later, when I was thinking about beginning to see clients, a gift from God arrived, and I became pregnant with the second light of my life, Benjy. I again suffered from hyperemesis, and having one baby already to look after made the pregnancy hard. My husband would go to work and leave me and Jackson in the playpen with food supplies, nappies, and sick bowl. If I ate, I threw up. If I moved, I threw up.

After becoming dehydrated from vomiting, I was put on 30 mg of steroids by the specialist. This helped the sickness, but perhaps had a consequence:

poor Benjy was born with chronic reflux, intolerant of many proteins, and screamed most of the day and night. I did my best as a mother of two with the awareness I had at the time, but it was devastating being unable to ease Benjy's suffering and having to ply his tiny body with drugs. My unresolved health issues took hold again, and I could no longer ignore them and push on through.

I began my healing journey and connection to spirituality when Benjy was four months old. We were holidaying in Cirencester, and my husband had taken the babies off for a few hours. Knowing that I needed something to change, I found myself sitting on the bed, meditating, and repeating the statement "I open myself up to the healing energies of the universe" over and over again. Amazingly, two hours later, I came across a leaflet for a healer. With a mixture of curiosity and trepidation, I booked a healing session with her later that afternoon. I was physically exhausted when I saw her, my ribs and hips were hurting, and I had not been able to breathe properly for over a month due to the inflammation in the rib joints.

The first thing the healer said to me when she saw me was "You know that you're a healer?" I smiled in confusion. I had been asked in rehab a few times, "Are you a white witch, a healer?" and had no idea what this meant. That world was alien to me. I was good at reading people, compassionate, and seemed to bring comfort through my being and words, but healers were mystical, almost Jesus-like, and I couldn't align myself comfortably with the idea of being "super-powered" at that time. Of course, now I recognize that we are all super-powered!

I was surprised that the healer didn't want to know anything about me. I was desperate to tell her about the pain in my hips and ribs, but she cupped my jaw for most of the session and then we were done. The session was relaxing, but I left with the feeling that I had not got what I needed. However, when I awoke the next morning, I was astounded to find that I could breathe and the pain in my ribs and chest had gone. I felt a pang of excitement. Maybe healing was possible after all.

In time, what I now understand to be universal guidance led me to a healer in Surrey, who I began to visit once a fortnight. I started to process my inner world in a new way, and each session finished with 20 minutes of hands-on healing. I cleaned up my diet and started to use herbs and supplements and my health started to improve, but consumed with my busy toddler and poorly baby, and still getting very little sleep each night due to his screaming, it was all I could do to focus on getting through each day.

Benjy's health issues resulted in two solid years of worry, continuous sleepless nights, numerous hospital visits, and interventions. I had lost faith in Western medicine. I was in less pain, had cleared the underlying low-level depression and some of the lower vibrational energies through the healing work, but I was exhausted by the continuing stress, worry, and lack of sleep and was at an all-time low.

I was producing very little cortisol and no DHEA in my adrenals, no growth hormone, and my baby boy was being traumatized with drugs, needles, and tubes. After one blood test too many for my baby, I decided to put a stop to all of the invasive investigations and went into protective mother mode. I realized that if I didn't attend to my own recovery, I would never ride a bike with my boys or see them grow old. This was scary but true. I guess that until that point I was still waiting for something outside of me to come to the rescue. I realized that our lives and health are in our own hands. Health and happiness are an inside job. So I took responsibility for my current reality and the one I wanted to create. This was life lesson number three!

**Lesson no. 3**
We are powerful creators of our own reality, and we benefit from taking responsibility for our own health, happiness, and healing!

# Chapter 2

# Let the Healing Begin

I threw myself into healing. I cut out dairy, gluten, most sugar, anything chemical or artificial, and started taking supplements and herbs. I took Benjy to see a naturopath who used "muscle testing" to find out which foods he could not tolerate. Remarkably, within two weeks, the screaming, arching, and diarrhoea had stopped. After a two-year marathon, finally he was able to sleep!

> We can use the body's energy system to "muscle-test", with reasonable accuracy, if something weakens or strengthens us. The body's feedback provides a response, giving us a "yes" or a "no". We can muscle-test our compatibility with substance and for the presence or absence of beliefs in the subconscious mind.

Gradually, I substituted anti-inflammatory herbs such as turmeric and boswellia for painkillers and immune-modulating (adaptogenic) herbs such as astragalus and schissandra for steroids to aid my recovery. I also did a 12-week course of acupuncture, which helped rebalance my energy flow. I noticed the biggest shifts, however, through energy psychology and healing work, and excited by the results I was getting, began to train in these techniques. My health and vitality improved, and my body became largely free from pain and illness. I increased my client intake and set up a practice in Richmond.

My husband was understandably preoccupied with his daily work challenges as the family provider, and our marriage began to feel the strain, so we decided to move to the countryside to enjoy more space, freedom, and nature. My husband and I had both settled away from our families and were craving the security of a closer village community. In the hope of a new start we moved to Haslemere, Surrey. It was here that I began to immerse myself in energy healing and energy psychology work.

As you start working with energy flow, you recognize its wisdom and desire for expression and the way it reveals a unique pathway for healing.

A brief introduction to several therapy modalities and my learning and experience with them follows. Each offers great value and possibility for healing.

## The Emotional Freedom Technique

Emotional Freedom Technique (EFT) works by tapping on various acupuncture points related to the meridians, or energy lines, in our bodies whilst allowing emotions to be explored and expressed. I found this technique profound, particularly Matrix Re-imprinting, and went on to train in it. I started to play with emotion as energy, and it was easy to follow the expression of energy back to where it was experienced earlier in life.

The key shifts within EFT often occur through what is called a "cognitive shift". Very often we perceive events through the eyes of the child we once were and make decisions or form beliefs about ourselves, the world, or others according to specific incidents in childhood. Healing comes not only from releasing the emotion but also from shifting our perception (story and beliefs) of the difficult event. With Matrix Re-imprinting, we often ask "What does the inner child need?" and then give the child the understanding and resolution they had needed (and not received) energetically at that time.

On Day One of my training, I nervously volunteered for a demonstration with EFT Master Karl Dawson. We worked through my lost voice and frustration with myself and my dad at the dinner table. This was my first understanding of how I had developed lupus. Lupus is a disease in which the immune system attacks the body indiscriminately, and here I was, angry with myself and my dad for not being able to communicate my frustrations or to express myself at all. In the echo of myself as that 14-year-old, I saw how lonely she was then, bullied at school, misunderstood, and helpless.

Four years later, my physical body expressed all of the internal pain and anger I was unable to express as that 14-year-old girl. As I energetically released the anger and hurt, the physical pain and inflammation in my body began to ease. Clearing the emotion heals the physical pain.

> **Lesson no. 4**
> Unexpressed emotions and associated beliefs cause chronic injury within the body. Our bodies express our dis-ease!

## The Lightning Process

By the time my youngest child was three years old, I needed fewer herbs and vitamins and was drug free and pain free, but I was still exhausted and couldn't shift the adrenal fatigue or balance my glandular system. My hormones were still underfunctioning, and I had been offered growth hormone injections for life.

I had been told about the Lightning Process for Myalgic Encephalomyelitis (ME), a form of chronic fatigue syndrome (CFS), and decided to take a one-to-one course. Within a week, I experienced transformation. I learnt about neuro-linguistic programming (NLP), the power of the mind, our focus of attention, and how tangibly our thoughts impact our mood and behaviours.

I had learnt this through cognitive behavioural therapy (CBT), but this new insight was profound. I had been paying attention to my symptoms of fatigue, and that in turn maintained the fatigue and low energy. The Lightning Process is really about mind over matter, actively choosing and focusing on how we want to feel. I came to understand the power of visualization and imagination (both positive and negative), and how borrowing energy from nature, including the animal kingdom, can be a valuable vision-focusing tool.

The Lightning Process made a difference to my physical energy levels and mood. It needs to be followed to the letter to assist in unwinding unhelpful habitual thoughts and refocusing them into helpful ones. It also helps to develop your inner personal coach, which aids you on the journey to self-love.

**Lesson no. 5**
Visualization and focus are powerful. If we use our mind and visions wisely, we can directly impact the health of our bodies. We can choose to focus upon and create health!

## Psych-K and the Power of Belief Change

I understood very clearly from my psychology training that negative thinking creates negative emotions, but what I had not really understood was the power of the subconscious mind running the show behind the scenes. The renowned epigenetic scientist Bruce Lipton, author of the 2005 book *The Biology of Belief*, describes the subconscious mind as a tape player. I find this to be a helpful analogy and use it with my clients. When we learn to tie our shoelaces or drive, we concentrate until we learn how to do it. Once we've learnt, the subconscious mind plays back past responses like a tape player, informing our behaviours so that we do not have to consciously think about them. Our subconscious mind drives our thoughts. For example, if we have a belief that says "I am not good enough", our self-talk and filter (our focus of attention) will work on finding and/or expressing what we did that was wrong or not good enough, rather than what we did right. This in turn makes us feel inadequate. We like to affirm our beliefs, whether they serve us or not. I see this as an unhelpful organization system.

We exist largely in theta brainwave state for our first six to seven years of life, absorbing the world like a sponge and forming beliefs about self, others, and the world. Unfortunately, this is a stage of our lives when we are often rather egocentric, with partially developed empathy. We can therefore come to the conclusion that the lack of attention we may be experiencing (because of Mum's depression or Dad's busyness) is because we are not important or good enough, rather than understanding and seeing the bigger picture.

If we want to shift the pattern and self-talk that we are not good enough, we have to change the belief. Affirmations are not enough. We can tell ourselves that we are good enough over and over, but unless the belief is reprogrammed in the subconscious mind, we will still unconsciously be looking for evidence to support the unhelpful belief, even though it doesn't serve us.

> **Lesson no. 6**
> The subconscious mind is an unconscious tape player, pattern-matching triggers in the environment to experiences and beliefs from our past. We must change beliefs in the subconscious mind if we are to successfully think, feel, and behave differently.

Psych-K facilitates belief change by using left and right hemispheric brain integration on a basic level and more complex energetic systems at the advanced level. Muscle testing is used for exploration and feedback to show that the beliefs have changed within the subconscious mind. I love Psych-K because it is effective, and I use and highly recommend it. I have helped many people make incredible shifts in their lives through changing their beliefs using advanced Psych-K methods. The system continues to be developed and extended by its creator, Rob Williams, to help with allergies, relationships, and other life domains.

> **Lesson no. 7**
>
> Changing our beliefs about ourselves, others, and the world transforms our experience of reality.

## Theta Healing

Theta Healing is another system that changes beliefs in the subconscious mind but through more esoteric methods. The practitioner is taught how to connect to Source, or Creator, and from this place, with the client's permission, command a change. When we connect to Source, we often go into a slower theta brainwave state, hence the name.

We live our lives predominantly in beta brainwave state and when our brainwaves slow down, such as in meditation, we move into the alpha range of brainwave frequencies. Theta is the brainwave state associated with healing and is the dreamlike state we pass through before falling into delta brainwaves, which are experienced in deep sleep. It feels beautiful and profound as one tunes in to this state—a different level of consciousness, which feels peaceful, easy, loving, and expansive.

I remember a big shift in my relationship to religion during my training session when I aligned with the belief that I was "worthy of God's unconditional love". I had been christened as a baby but was not brought up a practising Christian. Perhaps semi-aware of a higher benevolent power that I had felt as a child on occasion, I was buying into some kind of story that I was "letting God down" or not following the righteous path. Religion, particularly Catholicism, teaches that we are sinners, unworthy of the blessings of God in our default state, creating more separation from our soul, or spiritual selves.

Many of us carry the guilt and powerlessness that have been instilled in us by such religious doctrines. Unworthiness breeds helplessness and prevents us from receiving good things. I remember leaving that day and ordering the most divine chocolate éclair from Paul's Patisserie because, if I was worthy of God's unconditional love, I was worthy of a chocolate éclair! It was so delicious.

Theta Healing was an eye-opener for me. I connected with my true, gentle, personal power and saw myself as a spiritual being in a human body. This work added depth to my life and felt both tangible and magical. Surrendering to the flow of healing as a witness and observing a meaningful energetic shift offered lessons in magic and possibility. Soul and heart healing, body scanning, and removal of negative energies are also taught in Vianna Stibul's Theta Healing. Her work continues to develop and help many people across the globe.

> **Lesson no. 8**
> God/Source Energy loves each of us unconditionally—magical blessings are possible.

## Geneline Therapy

Geneline Therapy is a practitioner-led healing system that addresses how to clear feelings from deep in the body. Empaths like myself are highly sensitive to and aware of emotions, and are able to sense other people's feelings and emotions through our own bodies. These feelings are viscerally felt as our own energy when we are connecting with another. Many people struggle in their earlier years if they are not aware that they have empathic gifts. I say "gifts" because that is what they are: an ability to be highly perceptive and match how other people are feeling. Being an empath enables me to connect deeply and compassionately to others in order to uncover the source of an issue quickly.

At first, many of my reiki students feel that being empathic is a curse. They carry the burden for other people and are unsure of how to shake off the negative feelings or vibrations of others. Being a skilled empath means being able to notice feelings (and perhaps thought forms and resistance to the release of these) without attaching to the emotion or drama within the story.

The first step involves knowing yourself well and distinguishing whether what you are feeling is yours or someone else's. When I hear people say "I don't feel like myself" or "I don't know where this feeling came from", this is a good indication, particularly if they have just been with other people who are struggling, that the feelings they are carrying are not their own. We feel other people's feelings in order to help release them / help them to release them and bring ease, but we are not responsible for making others feel better, which can lead to burnout. We always have a choice: we can help with compassion, but each individual must remain responsible for their own process.

Once you have learnt how to recognize others' emotional resonances within you, the next step involves learning how to be at ease experiencing emotion, how to listen by paying attention, acknowledge (releasing resistance and allowing the emotion to be so), and release. We must become skilled at letting go. This means embracing change, loosening, lightening, and surrendering. The divine always helps us with this.

For empaths, or indeed anyone struggling with managing emotional regulation, I recommend familiarizing yourself with Geneline or Reference Point Therapy. This therapy teaches how to allow and acknowledge emotion in its energetic form and enable it to express itself. It is hugely powerful and deeply clearing for us. We must tend to and release trapped and stored emotions. Belief work does help shift emotional patterns, but if you have kept traumas and pain hidden, it may be advisable to work with a therapist, healer, or journal to help with self-expression and begin the process of healing.

Geneline Therapy teaches that feeling comes before belief. Many of the vibrations of emotion that run through our lives have been created in our ancestors' lives and passed down as some sort of warning or protection against re-experiencing the same. Sadly, if the vibration is there, then, in a manner of speaking, the "elephant in the room" is already in our subconscious awareness, ready to be avoided.

I found Geneline to be a valuable and therapeutic tool for deep ancestral and soul-level healing. If we can manage to remove the elephant from our subconscious awareness, we no longer need to remain in protective mode, which is hugely healing for the body's glandular and immune systems. Always scanning for or being triggered by old vibrations of fear keeps us in a protective, restricted mode of being and can attract more of the same experiences. If we clear our old fears that are often not relevant in our lives today, we can realign with new vibrations of love, trust, safety, faith, and possibility.

**Lesson no. 9**
What we resist, persists. We must access our deepest fears and hurts in order to clear them vibrationally in our bodies, soul, and minds.

## Recognizing the Loving Wisdom of the Universe

We had five reasonably happy years living in Haslemere. I had begun to integrate the healing work into my psychology practice, which was working really well. I had moments of truly seeing the beauty in life, of peace and possibility. I loved my work, the meaningful connections I had with clients, and their transformed lives. I felt alive through my work and recognized that Spirit was working through me. I increasingly found that the feelings I picked up on in sessions actually belonged to my clients and could be named, cleared, and healed. I enjoyed using my empathic skills and developed a love for the universal energy and wisdom that flowed through me in a session. I came to trust my experiences, learnt lesson number 10, and once again, the universe stepped in and I was guided to the next level of my journey.

**Lesson no. 10**
We are never truly alone and are connected to a loving, intelligent wisdom far greater than ourselves and our current "knowing". This is guidance; it exists for everyone when we open and listen.

# Chapter 3

# Honouring the Calling: Qigong

Qigong and Taoist philosophy allowed me to awaken and fully experience surrender and flow. Through qigong practice, I recognized myself as an energetic being and learnt the importance of energy regulation, movement, and stillness. Movement had been missing from my life since my dancing and sporting days at school. Although my health was 90 percent improved, when I found qigong the missing piece of the puzzle restored me to full health.

On a visit to my grandmother's house, I noticed a 1986 *Readers' Digest* on her shelf entitled "The Complete System of Self-Healing, Internal Exercises" by Dr S. T. Chang. Drawn to this old book, I discovered the ancient Chinese wisdom and art of qigong, which was to change my life. After a week of devouring the book, I was sure that this form of exercise was exactly what I needed to do to fully restore my health and nurture me as my boys got older and my practice began to grow.

Not long afterwards, while I was running a stall at a Mind Body Spirit fair, I met a qigong teacher who was to become a dear friend, Clara Apollo, who had travelled from the New Forest recruiting students for her qigong teacher training course. I tried her workshop and found myself settling happily in my body and enjoying the gentle movements. I trusted that the universe had brought this to me and signed up to train one weekend a month over the year.

I felt nervous on my way to the first day of training, having never practised qigong before, and filled with doubt about the commitment I had made for the next year. I stopped off at the service station to use the bathroom, grabbed a cup of tea, and returned to my car to find that I had forgotten my car keys. I darted back, remembering I had put them on the toilet roll holder. As I hesitated, looking at the long line of identical toilet doors in front of me, I heard my keys suddenly fall on the floor in one of the stalls. I knew then that I was on the right path. This was a sign that my guides, or angels, were with me and I was doing the right thing by embarking upon this course. Indeed, that day, my life was to change forever.

I was greeted by Clara and several other smiling faces, one being the reiki master and author Richard Ellis. As we began our practice, my nerves disappeared, and I found myself experiencing a truly deep connection to myself and the earth. The work was profound, instinctual, and my body bathed in the *qi* (chi), or energy, as though drinking nectar from a universal well. Having danced so much throughout my childhood, my body had missed the focused awareness and movement that qigong now offered.

Qigong's predominant teachings involve learning to let go and become empty. It is from emptiness that *qi* is born and can begin to flow. In qigong (as explained in Chapter 7) we become an empty vessel between Heaven and Earth and move universal *qi* through the main energy channels of the body, clearing, gathering, and distributing *qi* to the energy reservoirs, and through the meridians to the organs. It is a wonderful practice, which I highly recommend, connecting us more deeply with our physical and energy bodies, quieting our minds, and connecting us to the universal *qi* field that extends beyond us.

A friend and student of Richard's, Dave, was also taking the training course, and during a break the two men gave each other what I can only describe as a heart-centred hug. It lasted several moments, and from my understanding now, I imagine that their heart resonances had expanded so greatly that I became part of their *qi* field. I connected with their open-hearted expression of love and, in the next breath, became filled with an unbearable sadness; my mind loudly saying, "I don't have that". It was a daunting realization, and the underlying sadness I had been pushing away bubbled up like a fountain. I found myself witnessing this truth like a cymbal clashing in my head and feared for my marriage.

> **Lesson no. 11**
> Open-hearted love exists at our core—love is our foundational truth.

## Divorce

My husband and I loved each other dearly, but his inability to express to me the kind of love I had witnessed on the qigong course shook me. I recalled noticing this lack of heartfelt affection at the end of our first date, through our early relationship and marriage—seeing it as an opportunity to be more sovereign. Now, it was like a dagger in my heart, which I could withstand no longer. The more I came into my truth, light, and awareness, the more distant and problematic our relationship became. I knew that I wanted heartfelt love in my life and to develop as an open-hearted intuitive and healer. It was painful and difficult, but my wings were clipped and that felt unbearable.

Distance grew between us. I allowed my intuition and truth to move me along, and we eventually divorced. The sadness and desperation I felt were overwhelming. Apart from my mother and one or two close friends, no one seemed to understand what I was doing leaving a beautiful home and a man who seemed to love me, in full knowledge of the devastation it could cause to my two children.

We managed the separation as consciously as possible, but the divorce served as a catalyst for the anger that had been suppressed over the years. My youngest child, who is psychically gifted, was always one step ahead of what was happening, and my eldest, an empath, unknowingly picked up on all the sadness and anger around him. There was plenty of heartache involved, but there was also much love, and we navigated our pathways forward.

We live with many judgements that cause us pain and distress. Many come from religious doctrines, parents, grandparents, and so on, while others come from self-judgement. My husband judged that I was mentally unstable, rather than awake to my truth, and, as happens to a lot of people who separate, many of my friendships also disappeared. It was a blessing to escape once a month to my qigong training course, connect with the Tao, the universal *qi* field, and be around other like-minded beings, and just "be", without judgement and with my truth. It was around this time that I had my most profound spiritual experience.

> **Lesson no. 12**
> Facing our deepest truths and our deepest hurts, although not easy, brings transformational healing.

## Enlightenment

It began with a trip to Glastonbury in the summer of 2013. I did my usual trek up the Tor with my diary, met a good friend, and visited the Chalice Well, a world peace garden. We paddled in the freezing red well, thought to be the *yin*, or divine feminine, waters, and to possess healing qualities. Within moments, I had slipped and fallen over, fully clothed. Submerged in the water, my baptism into the healing energy of the divine feminine took place. We laughed about it, as I stood there freezing and without a change of clothes, but it was a perfect "now" moment in which to accept myself as a woman, empowered, and able to be with what was.

In Glastonbury, I was drawn to the work of artist Ioanis Antoniadis, and in particular, a painting of a woman with a dove entering the crown of her head. The artist approached me as I was viewing the painting and told me that it represented the Holy Spirit and that this would happen to me as part of my own journey, then left. I bought several prints, inspired by the high vibration of these paintings.

I knew the importance of clearing emotion, so I decided to release my emotions the following morning using the Geneline Therapy technique whilst taking a bath. I focused on my heart and, like the story of the Glastonbury Thorn, which is said to have taken root from Joseph of Arimathea's staff in the earth in Glastonbury's Wearyall Hill, I released all resistance, quietly observing as I allowed intense pain to pierce my heart.

As I experienced this, with eyes closed, I suddenly became flooded with a pink-and-white light that was brighter and warmer than anything I had ever experienced before. It was the energy of pure love, of ecstasy penetrating my heart and entire being. Tears of joy streamed down my face, and I felt awe. I had a vision of being carried beyond the sky by two doves on a silvery-golden thread in the bright light, and I stayed there in this almost orgasmic state of bliss for what turned out to be three hours!

I was conscious of what was happening and reminded of the artwork and message that had been conveyed to me. I perceived this experience as the Holy Spirit or Great Spirit entering my entire being and healing my broken heart. I became unstuck, unbroken, and brightly filled with wondrous light.

This was my own deep awakening and experience of enlightenment. I declared myself to be of service during that process. I was humbled and felt myself to be God's servant; I now knew that I was not, and could never again, feel alone. I was a part of, and connected to, this great consciousness, and I knew in that moment that there is more to our universe than what we can see, understand, or explain.

I had always believed that there was more to life than we generally experienced, a greater good and an unquantifiable magic to the universe. When I was a teenager, I remember telling my dad that I was eternal and could not die. This incredible experience was my confirmation that there was a beautiful, strong, all-encompassing love available to us all—a divine love so powerful that it heals all in its path. This energy stayed with me for weeks, and I re-experienced glimpses of divine love in my healing sessions with clients, for by then, I had become a clear channel, trusting Spirit to guide me in my life and work.

> **Lesson no. 13**
> There is a universal divine love whose immense power can transform pain and suffering.

One message came to me in a dream before I woke up. I was sitting with a Native American woman in circle, and was shown myself as a man transmitting intelligence in Morse code during wartime. After being discovered, I then experienced my life ending violently, even as I frantically radioed for help, with the words "There is no help" echoing in my soul.

I had lived most of my life believing that I must go it alone and that "there was no help for me". After this re-connection, or healing from Spirit, I woke up and within the space of five minutes had received two texts and a telephone call, all offering help. So I wish to convey that, yes, there *is* help! The universe wants and needs us to evolve, to come into our greatest expressions of love and trust, and when we pledge to do so, we will be guided and supported. The question is whether we can allow our mind to quieten enough, stop the stories, and allow the help and love through? Will we choose to do what it takes to transform the suffering into forgiveness and joy?

There is much suffering in this universe of limitless possibility, but there is also love and joy, and my experience tells me that we can choose which we align with, once we learn how to clear the old vibrations and align with something new.

## Soulmate Uniting

Nine months after this experience, I met my soulmate, Rob. I was told that I was going to meet him during an intuitive reading practice group several months beforehand, that he was in France and making his way to me. One week after this reading, my dear qigong teacher and friend, Clara Apollo, told me she had met somebody interested in qigong training who she thought I should meet, even though he was living in France at the time! A little flabbergasted, I waited patiently, curious of course, but very grateful that I had been given the messages. Although I was willing to live a purposeful life alone, I wanted reciprocal love in my life.

When I first met my dear Rob, I would never have put two and two together. He was very attractive, but six and a half years younger than me and without a home or penny to his name. He travelled extensively, helping others with their business ventures, had no commitments, and was content to not know where his next meal was coming from. He lived in the world of exchanging the gift of time and experience for a meal or temporary home. I was working hard for a living, figuring out how I would pay my mortgage and look after my children. I was both confused and intrigued!

After our second meeting, that was it. We were inextricably bound. He was and still is the kindest, most gentle soul, and has loved and nourished me in a way I never dreamed possible. Things were challenging in the first few years, mainly due to our differences, but we know how to come back to love when our egos, fears, and beliefs take over. He moved in with me and my children fairly quickly. They loved his lightness, and our house again filled with love and laughter.

> **Lesson no. 14**
> Love is important. We can find love in strange places. Believe in good things coming!

## The Healing Voice Mandala Ceremony

Another universal alignment led to the birth of our baby boy, Phoenix. As a Christmas gift, I bought tickets for Rob and myself to Jill Purce's Healing Voice Mandala Ceremony in May 2016. The mandala is a spiritual symbolic representation of the circular nature of the universe, and the gift was to help Rob to find his voice and confidence instead of the conditioned programmes of unworthiness he had been running internally for many years. This was a retreat I had wanted to attend for years. My parents babysat for the week, and we went off with our tent to Glastonbury.

The mandala was an amazing experience—an energy and momentum of vibrational healing incorporating Tibetan overtone chanting, song, and Family Constellation therapy. Rob and I were welcomed into a beautiful tribe of about 80 people that week. We chanted for seven days, turning around the human mandala, clearing our attachments to fears and hurt, honouring and embodying the light deity Green Tara, mother of the Buddhas, who embodies fearless action.

## Kundalini Rising

I had another profound spiritual experience during the mandala ceremony, as my *kundalini* (universal life energy) rose. The energy of the mandala was so high, I started to feel overwhelmed. During one of our short breaks, I felt that I needed to place my forehead on the earth to help ground myself. As people moved back inside, Rob came over to me, but I was barely capable of words. I knew from my reading that kundalini was rising and that I should allow it. I was vaguely able to mutter "kundalini" to him, half-conscious, before the energy took hold.

I writhed on the grass for a while, toning vocally as the energy birthed through me. I saw beautiful deities around me, and Jill standing among this circle (although she was actually inside the building facilitating the mandala), and a crooked man with a staff merging with the image I had of Jill from time to time. My mouth repeated the words "Rinpoche, Rinpoche", not knowing much about Tibetan Buddhist practices or the significance of Guru Rinpoche, but I was aware that this god-like figure or deity was overseeing this experience.

Although kundalini is a feminine universal energy, this felt like an intense masculine rush up my spine, to which I had no choice but to surrender. In hindsight, it was a purge or cleanse, readying me for the conception of my third child the following day.

Rob and I had spoken of consummating our love with a child, and indeed, it was something we both wanted and felt called to do, but with our current financial situation, my need to work and parent my boys, it made no sense.

We were invited to represent the May King and Queen for the group's Beltane ceremony the following and final day and, delighted to do so, were adorned with earthly spiritual May Day dress and floral crowns. On what felt like our wedding day, with dew collected to the sound of the harp at sunrise from the Glastonbury hills, we ceremonially led a cauldron of fire to the maypole, where we sang and danced, before returning to the final day of the mandala. At the end of the day under the full moon—with me ovulating, of course—exhausted and elated by the week's happenings, we were carried by the momentum of Spirit and universal love; the peacock in the field sang, the sheep chanted, and we lovingly allowed the conception of our magical child.

> **Lesson no. 15**
> Surrender to the flow of energy. There is a higher consciousness inside us and a universal benevolent consciousness that knows exactly what it is doing. We just need to get our protective ego minds and fears out of the way, and allow.

## Through Adversity Be in the Now

I was the main earner, and all-day morning sickness made work difficult. I loved being pregnant and knew that this was the right thing for us, trusting in Spirit's calling, but it was a challenging pregnancy, which put strain on our relationship.

I became resentful that I had to work, throwing up during and between client sessions for most of the pregnancy. I lay awake most nights, wondering how we were going to make this work. It took a toll on Rob, too, as he cared for and fed me and my older boys and tried to make his new business work financially.

Love and faith got us through, and exactly to the day, nine months later, we had a wonderful hypno-birthing experience. At 9.09 pm on the 1st February 2016, whilst holding open the blue portal as I had been told to do by both my guides and my dear friend Louisa, our son Phoenix was born. My older children were now 10 and 12 years old, respectively, so this really was a new beginning. We all welcomed this being of pure joy and light into our life and hearts.

The day after Phoenix was born, Rob went to see the doctor about a growth in his testicle. Soon after, amid the fullness of baby-dom, we discovered that his lump was cancer, which had vigorously spread to around 40 tumours in his lungs. Here was another ride to endure.

Had we not heard the call of Spirit to bring Phoenix into the world, it is possible that Rob would never have become a father, and without our joyous babe, the world would certainly not be the same.

We researched and did what was needed to heal Rob of his old psychological and emotional patterns of unworthiness, passivity, and insufficiency. Rob had chemotherapy, took herbs, juiced, cut out sugar and the usual suspects, and ate organic foods, whenever possible. Almost three years on, we believe that he is out of the woods. Lessons are still being learnt, fears and insecurities being released, but life has gained momentum. I am optimistic for our future together. No matter what happens, I have no regrets and will always be grateful for each exchange of love we share.

> **Lesson no. 16**
>
> Always be in the "now". When in adversity, we can usually handle the current moment and, if not, we have the power to change this perception.

Like most of us, I have spent far too much time fearing unwanted circumstances. CBT defines this as "Having a bad case of the what-ifs". When I was pregnant, I spent a lot of time fearing how I would cope with a new baby—how I would be able to take enough time away from work to nurture and breastfeed him, give enough time and attention to my older boys, and earn enough to pay my mortgage, alongside everything else that having a house, car, pets, and career demands. But I found that when I stayed in the "now", everything was okay.

If we can cope with the demands in the "now", minute by minute, hour by hour, we can cope with the future as we experience it unfold. In this intensely demanding time, I remained physically and mentally well and optimistic, with no signs of the return of autoimmune disease. For this, I give thanks to the work I did on myself and to my connection with a universal supreme energy. I recognize my own light, and trust my ability to manage my emotional and physical health, taking responsibility for creating a reality I am happy to experience.

Two years on, I have a fully booked full-time practice and have developed this healing system, which I teach alongside qigong and reiki. I am building the foundations of a tribe and therapeutic healing and creative centre—Heaven On Mother Earth (HOME)—to help liberate and empower others into awakening, healing, and love. I look forward to sharing with you the principles by which I have come to find health, joy, trust, and love, and the amazing healing system that will enable you, too, to lift your own vibration to that of love, empowerment, and ease. With gratitude to all of those mentioned and unmentioned along my path, thank you for journeying alongside me.

## The Healing InSight Belief Realignment Method

What follows are the golden keys to harmony and healing, which have informed the development of the Healing InSight belief change system.

### 1. Choose Love

Love is the fundamental energy of the universe. It exists at our core; we all desire to return to love. The journey of love begins with kindness to self and others. Be kind above all else. True love is safe, and it is kind. It needs no introduction and adds meaning and riches to our lives.

So many of my clients ask how they can begin to love themselves. I suggest that it begins with kindness. This means moving away from self-deprecation and anything that constricts or limits your identity or possibilities. It means listening to yourself and your needs, developing a caring and understanding relationship with yourself, and stepping into action to support and honour your needs. We all are worthy of love. You must recognize and align with this. Love breeds love; following your joy and desire attracts more of the same into your life. Love and compassion heal, and when we offer that gift to ourselves, we develop a healthy inner relationship, which strengthens and supports us to become independent, interconnected beings. When we have a loving, supportive relationship with ourselves, we move away from loneliness and are happy in our own company and free to give love to others.

## 2. Personal Responsibility – Self-Help

We cannot wait for the world to change, for our circumstances to change, or for someone to come and fix us. Our realities are largely shaped by our own beliefs, expectations, focus of attention, and behaviours. If something is not working, we have to take responsibility for changing it ourselves. There is help. We are affected by the physical and emotional toxicity in our environment, and must clean it up. We do not have to be victims of our past or expect our future to be dictated by our past. Start a little at a time, but just start and continue to take responsibility (without any blame or shame) for your own thoughts, beliefs, behaviours, and experiences. It is both empowering and rewarding, and you will be supported in your endeavours.

## 3. Understanding the Mind-Body-Spirit Connection

Our bodies do not exist separately from our mental processes or spiritual selves. The mind, body, and spirit affect one another and are best considered as a whole. I have never met a well-rounded, happy, healthy, balanced person who does not tend to the mind, body, and spiritual self. Visualization is a powerful way to harness the mind-body-spirit connection. As we visualize with intention, our imagination can fill us with good or bad scenarios. Corresponding beliefs and emotions (inner-sights) can come into our awareness. We feel in our bodies, we hear stories in our minds, and we receive guidance in the form of thoughts, impulses, and imagination from our higher self. When these are experienced as a whole, we can become aware of our subconscious patterns and programmes and our deeper truth, which may otherwise have been hidden from us.

## 4. Opening Up to Spirituality

We are spiritual beings in a human body having a human experience. There may be things we do not fully understand spiritually, but there is much we can learn from others who have experienced something greater than themselves. We once believed that the world was flat, but that did not make it true. Germs cannot be seen by the naked eye, but that does not mean they do not exist. The same goes for spiritual energies or beings in contact with us on this earthly plane. Quantum physics demonstrates that subtle energy does exist and can be both measured and, to some extent, explained.

We have been taught by religion to mistrust or fear spirituality without a religious basis, but to embrace spirituality is to embrace a desire for reconnection to love, meaning, and purpose. Without it, we are adrift. I have seen many depressed or anxious people recover quickly once reconnected to their true self and soul's purpose. Many of us have questioned our faith and moved away from religious institutions, but when we deny our spirituality we deny our essence, and this can lead to pain and disease. All you need is curiosity, openness, and desire, and the universe will do the rest—if you ask and allow it to be so. As a healer, I see and experience the love that Spirit has for everyone. There is no judgement from Spirit, no withholding of love or healing. Spirit can be found anywhere, but especially in nature, in sacred sites, in one's heart, in quietening, and through music and creativity.

## 5. Releasing Judgement

Judgement of ourselves, others, and the world around us causes separation and pain. There is judgement everywhere in our world. Even some of the most popular spiritual teachers and authors tell us that certain ideas are wrong and deny the multifaceted truths that exist on this polarized Earth. I am concerned when I find this duality and ideas of right or wrong, which focuses on dividing us into separate camps rather that searching for the universal truth that unites us. It is only when we connect to the whole and practise acceptance of what is, right now, that we can pour love into every corner and create the magic of oneness.

I talk about this with clients as needing to find the "and" rather than the "or". When we judge or deny another's truth or perspective, we create separation. Even judging someone to have more knowledge, skill, or ability than us encourages us to see them as separate. Real empowerment comes when we accept that we are all different, we are all unique: no one is better or less than us. Life is our greatest teacher and will always bring experiences to facilitate our expanding consciousness.

Accepting our own behaviours and emotions without judgement, simply as expression and experience, allows the lightness needed for our state of mind and energetic resonance to be altered. This practice of non-judgement and non-attachment—being with what is, in the now. This is freedom.

## 6. Mindful Movement

It is no coincidence that the year after I stopped dancing regularly, I developed lupus. I think that the regular dancing kept it at bay by clearing my body of stuck energy and emotion. For me, qigong is the most powerful form of mindful movement; as I can attest, practising regularly offers multiple health benefits. Like yoga, qigong helps clear stagnant energy, strengthen mind and body, and utilize the power of the breath and intention for health and healing. For people who struggle with mobility, the benefits of qigong can be experienced even when it is performed whilst seated.

## 7. Energy Clearing and Maintenance

We must first acknowledge and accept that we are energetic beings, with electrical activity along circuits throughout our bodies. These energy pathways can become disrupted or stagnant, and if we don't clear these old blockages, our physical bodies begin to suffer, underperform, or become prone to disease. Many energy-clearing modalities are available, including reiki, EFT, Zero Balancing, the Bowen Technique, massage, yoga, qigong, acupuncture—and I know many people who swear by a good run. Paying attention to the body's energy system and clearing the body of stagnant energy and stress-holding patterns is essential for physical health. An energetically free-running body is a healthy body.

## 8. Emotional Understanding and Expression

Unexpressed emotional upset and turmoil are held in the body by the breath and can tighten and constrict the muscles and mind. If emotion is left to express itself freely, it will happily do so until the process is complete.

Understanding that emotions are a normal, healthy, natural, and useful feedback system is a necessary component of healing the mind and body. Trapped and unexpressed emotion causes us disease and actual physical inflammation and pain over time. It helps to simply be curious as an observer when we feel emotional.

What is the feeling? Name it, and understand why you're feeling it through taking responsibility for how you are judging and perceiving the unfolding event. When we look with curiosity, we see things that help us to make sense of events differently. We do actually have a choice in how we feel about something. Most of our current emotional responses were created from early-life, ancestral, or soul experiences. We can witness the bigger picture by inviting in our non-judgemental observer self.

### 9. Using the Earth's Medicine – Plants, Herbs, and Nutrition

We are what we eat, and our food sources are being poisoned with hormones, insecticides, chemicals, and toxins. We must not only think consciously but act and choose consciously when it comes to food and drink. This is particularly important if you are in recovery from ill health. Nature gave us powerful food and herbs to help the body heal; slowly, these are disappearing from our shelves in favour of pharmaceutical drugs, which are reported by many eminent alternative health care physicians to be the biggest killer in the Western world.

I am not a nutritionist, herbalist, or homeopath, but my personal experience has been that replacing daily doses of steroids and anti-malarial drugs with natural remedies healed my body without the side effects I experienced with pharmaceuticals. In addition, cutting out chemical-containing cosmetics, cleaning agents, and foods lessens the toxic load for our bodies and saves our environment. Natural products are excellent today. Always discuss with your healthcare practitioner if you wish to make changes to your regular regime, and seek personalized guidance from a qualified holistic practitioner to manage your medical needs.

### 10. Aligning with Universally Sound Beliefs

Belief change is what this book and the healing system are all about. Without belief realignment, it is very difficult—if not impossible—to make lasting changes to our wellbeing. We hold many beliefs about ourselves, our lives, and others, which influence our behaviours, thoughts, and emotions. Some beliefs help us to grow, stay safe, explore, innovate, and relate; others keep us stuck and unable to move forward. We must notice our inner critic and locate unhelpful beliefs if we wish to change them. We tell ourselves all kinds of stories of inadequacy, fear, unworthiness, and lack. What might it be like to be a cheerleader for yourself, believing in yourself, your gifts, skills, and sincerity? What might it be like to love and support yourself as you might your friend, partner, or child? Kindness counts, and putting yourself first is both okay and important. Belief change is the catalyst for a new vibration and a new reality.

## 11. Finding Connection with Our Soul's Desires and Life Path

We birth into life and spend many years behaving in ways we believe we should in order to be loved, successful, or accepted. We meet (or not) the expectations of our parents, our siblings, our teachers, and our employers. I frequently see clients wondering, "How did I get here?"—not knowing who they are, what they like, what their gifts are, what their passion or interests are. The need for acceptance and belonging can drive us in a particular direction, one that may actually be far removed from our true soul's path and purpose.

In order to reconnect, we must recognize our drives, likes, and desires. We must get to know and fall in love with ourselves. At the end of the day we always have ourselves, and developing a loving relationship with oneself is the greatest gift of all. It enables us to have a loving relationship with life, others, and All That Is. When we walk our own path we gather momentum and, in my experience, the magic of life begins to flow.

## 12. Finding Connection with Our Tribe

As a consequence of the above, we gather with like-minded individuals into a collective. Tribe always was and always will be important, but we cannot find our tribe if we are not intent upon being our true selves and walking our own path. Like attracts like, so being the best you that you can be puts you in a vibrational match with others doing the same. Difference is good; we do not need to be the same in order to get on. We must be willing to be ourselves regardless of our differences and allow others to be and do the same. It is our individuality that creates the expanse, and without us each being our unique true selves, we cannot create the whole.

There is enough for everyone (remember the "and" rather than the "or"). Let us celebrate each other and find the gift in what our tribes teach us, as we teach them, too.

# PART TWO

# Understanding the Mind-Body-Spirit as a Unified Whole

I HAVE IMMERSED MYSELF in others' psychological and energetic processes for many years with the intent of helping people to grow, clear emotions and limiting beliefs, and thrive. I have learnt a great deal about the importance of working with all aspects of the whole, including the physical, mental, energetic, and spiritual, in order to help people find relief from suffering.

In this section, I give you an overview of the mind-body-spirit connection, as I see it through my therapeutic practice as a psychologist and energy healer. Whilst I describe the components of the body, mind, and spirit/soul separately, each is part of a unified whole; yet, like the liver or spleen, its function is unique, with its own distinct purpose.

I discuss why working with all aspects of our consciousness and directing our attention and intention towards wellbeing is vital for transformation. The information here is for your awareness and understanding of the processes involved when using the Healing InSight method. It is not essential in order to use the system, but it will help you to understand what is occurring and how the gains made through the system can be both substantial and transformative.

Chapter 4

# Structures of the Mind-Body-Spirit

Let's take a look at the various systems in the body and their function within the unified whole of your mind-body-spirit. Your body as a temple is glorious and magnificent indeed—really rather extraordinary.

## The Physical Body

Like all physical matter, the body appears on the surface to be dense but is, in fact, almost entirely empty space. The atoms in our cells are like tiny spinning vortices that have density as a byproduct of the energy forces inside them. Essentially, we are made up of space and energy. This energy is also the foundation for biomechanical and electrical processes that allow us to live, which can be helped or hindered by the quality of air, water, nutrients in our food, and energy fields in our environment.

Let's focus first on the autonomic nervous system, which regulates involuntary bodily processes. It is divided into the sympathetic and para-sympathetic branches. When we are engaged with managing the stresses and strains of the outside world, our sympathetic nervous system is engaged in fight-or-flight; when we are happy and relaxed, our parasympathetic nervous system is engaged in a healing "rest and digest" mode. As long as we keep the toxins down (to help the liver, spleen, and kidneys), ingest plenty of fresh fruit and vegetables, and move our bodies (to help clear the lymph system and exercise the heart and muscles), our bodies will be happy and work tirelessly for us. That is, unless our energetic circuit (the energy body) becomes blocked, weak, excessive, or stagnant. This is ancient Eastern medicine wisdom which, supported by research, is now spreading across the globe. In due course, I will discuss the role of the energy body as a key to accessing healing for our bodies.

First, let's look at the phenomenon we call stress, its processes, and its impact on the physical body, using information from Dr Bruce Lipton's best-selling book, *The Biology of Belief*. The Hypothalamus-Pituitary-Adrenal Axis (HPA Axis) is the system that protects life against external threats from the environment. When the hypothalamus gland in the brain perceives an environmental threat, it sends chemical signals to the master pituitary gland, which in turn launches the body into action.

Adrenocorticotropic hormone (ACTH) releases into the blood, signalling fight-or-flight hormones adrenaline and cortisol to be released by the adrenal glands. The autonomic nervous system stress response is switched on, and a cascade of restorative and healthy functioning pathways (the parasympathetic nervous system function) then shut down in order to prime your body for dealing with the perceived external threat. Blood flow is directed away from digestive functions, and instead pumped to the muscles, enabling us to flee from the threat, leaving digestive and excretory organs under-functioning. This is why prolonged stress impacts our stomach and bowel functions.

When this HPA response is triggered, our bodies utilize all the energy available to us rather than generating more energy to top up our reserves, eventually leaving us depleted. The blood flow is directed away from our conscious mind (the information processor, or forebrain), allowing our subconscious hindbrain (which allows for reflex behaviours) to become our primary brain function. This process that can be activated in pressure-driven, high-expectation exams, disabling students from accessing their intelligent, conscious, learnt mind. I have frequently heard my adolescent student clients say "I just couldn't think". Clients with chronic ill health or pain have similar complaints, with an inability to access their rational, logical, and intelligent forebrains. This is because they spend an awful lot of time in the stress response, perceiving life and engagement as threatening.

This has become the problem of our Western culture, as survival-oriented stress and one-upmanship have taken a long-term toll on the health of nations. More importance has been placed upon status—jobs, possessions, position in society, wealth, and social success—than on levels of happiness, fulfilment, benevolence, and connection. We are under pressure to be okay (more than okay—our greatest selves) and fearful of losing status, or being perceived to do so. As we respond to demands and attempt to meet expectations, this creates a chronic cascade of stress hormones that has a long-term impact on our physical bodies and often results in illness and disease.

Through my work as a psychologist, I consider financial fear, lack of self-worth, inadequacy, and disconnection or judgement from family, peers, and colleagues to be the primary sources of stress. These are the "tigers" in our lives that are triggering the HPA axis and causing the deterioration of our collective mental and physical health. The belief cards in the Healing

InSight method are to remind you that you are already enough; society has made you forget who you are and taught you that you need to be something else, or in some cases, that you are nobody at all. This is painful beyond measure, and addressing these beliefs will bring respite to the autonomic stress response and allow the adrenal glands to rest and the body to heal.

Our immune system does an incredible job fighting foreign invaders and restoring us to health, but it is not supported by being in a constant fight, flight, or freeze response. When it is "in overload" and not meeting the expectations we have put on ourselves, the immune system becomes compromised and the bugs, parasites, and internal invaders have an opportunity to thrive. As soon as we get the opportunity to rest, we feel exhausted because our immune system is working hard to catch up.

The physical body is a manifestation of how the emotional body and mind have engaged with and stored our experiences of life. Put simply, it is a mirror of our internal state. In order to heal, we must address our stress. This means clearing the energetic stories, belief patterns, and associated emotions and fears that cause stress and disease. This was certainly my personal experience of healing my body from its "incurable" disease, and it is what I offer my clients today.

## The Emotional Body

I am passionate about the power and expression of emotion, a form of guidance that lets you know how far you are vibrationally from your higher self or soul's desire. Although physiologically a cascade of chemical and hormonal reactions, I interpret emotion as a nebulous yet tangible vibration within the physical realm that can be seen, felt, and almost tasted.

Many of us are afraid of our emotions, having had them shunted, rejected, ignored, or denied. What is it about emotion that makes people uncomfortable? Negative emotion is essentially an indicator of discord. We must become empowered to be with and work through emotion. As I contemplate the energy and power of emotion, the poet in me stirs:

*The great ocean rolls, and the great winds roar.*
*The great fire burns, and with it comes its path of destruction,*
*Then rebirth and creation, as the cycles of life continue.*
*To be free, like an untamed child, breathing the rhythms of the*
*universe.*

*To be free to howl in pain at the grief of life,*
*The suffering of men, women, and the animal kingdom.*
*To cheer in awe at the glory of creation, of life in all its beauty,*
*To feel the strength and the binding powers of love.*
*How can we express the richness and fullness of life, of existence,*
*Without becoming tamed, disconnected, or uncivilized?*
*For emotion is the felt sense of the universe that rips open our hearts*
*And renders us both powerless and complete in its path.*

As a counselling psychologist, my focus has been on helping clients who have trapped or denied the "felt sense" of their experiences regain emotional expression, but my interest goes back even farther, to my adolescent years. As an empath, I would feel the emotions of others, and find my heart pouring out to theirs, drawn like a magnet to witness their pain and acknowledge their suffering. I would sit with compassion, unknowingly allowing whoever I was sitting with to be felt, seen, and witnessed. Pain needs to be acknowledged.

To deny emotion is to be lifeless. The female archetype desires fullness and connection, whilst the male archetype desires emptiness and freedom. We contain both masculine and feminine aspects and their corresponding expressions and drives. It is the connection and fullness, the riding of these waves of life—and the processing and witnessing of "what is" with a level of consciousness—that enables the clearing, emptiness, and freedom we so desire. Emptiness leads us back to creation, balance, and connection. This is the dance of yin and yang, as written in ancient Asian texts.

Even though emotions can have a profound effect upon our lives and bodies, they do not need to form our identity. Emotion is something we all experience; we may have certain emotions and feelings about events or people, but emotion is just a sensory feedback system. "We" are not angry or happy; "we" are not frustrated or guilty or jealous. By not owning the emotion as part of our identity, it is possible to detach slightly. Emotion is a sensation we sometimes connect with, sometimes disown, and sometimes over-identify with. It's also beneficial not to attach labels of emotions to other people's identity, as this will likely skew your perception and experience of them.

See emotion as something you are "doing", as this allows a level of consciousness and free will in how you experience the emotion. If we ride the waves and proactively "do" anger and frustration, "do" happiness and bliss, "do" guilt and shame, we awaken the conscious mind rather than passively experiencing the subconscious (or unconscious) cascade of biochemical reactions. We can then start to experience emotion more fully, more consciously, and more therapeutically, rather than just re-experiencing patterns of fired chemical responses from our past.

In her groundbreaking 1999 book *Molecules of Emotion: Why You Feel the Way You Feel*, the late neuroscientist Dr Candace Pert offered a fascinating understanding of this process through her research on psychoneuroimmunology, explaining the biochemical processes that occur on a cellular level throughout the entire body as we experience emotion. Her research revealed that emotions are indeed the link between the mind and body, and cause cells to respond in ways that can produce profound changes to the body, creating either sickness or health. Emotions are biochemical waves that flow through your body as molecules (hormones and neuropeptides) arriving at the cell receptors, in turn affecting cell biology.

Health researcher Dawson Church, author of the 2018 book *Mind to Matter*, documents copious research demonstrating the effects of brainwave states upon our cells. This research shows a clear link between our state of mind and our bodily condition, both through the biochemistry of cells in response to our emotional states and the impact of vibration—specifically different speeds of brainwave states—upon our cells.

High beta frequency waves (associated with cognition, stress, and the production of adrenal hormones) have been documented to show negative effects in the body, including cellular dysfunction, ageing, and reduced ability to grow and repair. Church shows that healing takes place when we engage in positive, mindful, and coherent states of mind. The alpha brainwave state (achieved in relaxed, meditative, daydreaming states) has been shown in research to increase our production of serotonin, the mood-enhancing neurotransmitter (Yu et al. 2011). Aerobic exercise has also been shown to connect us to a more coherent and harmonizing alpha brainwave state (Fumoto et al. 2010). Slowing brainwaves down to theta levels, the dreamy brainwave state we fall into as we drift off to sleep and which healers access when connected to healing vibrations, begins restorative functions in the body. Research has shown that at this frequency, the body can repair cartilage cells, boost antioxidant levels, and increase DNA repair functions (Tekutskaya et al. 2015).

When we step down into delta brainwaves, the slowest waves of all, observed in deep meditation or deep sleep, extraordinary things happen in our bodies. The regeneration of nerve cells is stimulated. Our growth hormone levels increase, aiding cell and neuron regeneration, and we can even reverse ageing (Cosic et al. 2015). In addition to the body's increased thriving, when we reach slower brainwave states, we feel connected to the great consciousness of All That Is. In meditation experiments, Church reports that changed brainwave patterns actually change the expression of genes. In his book, he writes about scientific studies that demonstrate the regulation of cancer genes through changing the brainwave state, including genes that both suppress tumour growth and eliminate cancerous cells. This is a strong argument for tending to emotional wellbeing.

The spiritual community is becoming increasingly interested in the gamma brainwave state (the highest frequency of all). Research still needs to understand the processes occurring in gamma, as this state surpasses the wavelength of neuronal firing. Accessed through expert-level meditation, gamma brainwave state has been found to be highly active in experiences of universal love, states of expanded consciousness, connectedness, and spiritual emergence. Researchers from Bonn University show that gamma brainwave frequency remains present in these experts, outside of meditation, enabling a different awareness of everyday reality (Fell et al. 2010). I suspect it is a frequency from which we access our multi-dimensional self.

Have you noticed that you tend to experience the same kinds of emotion over and over again? This is because we tend to create strong neural pathways for particular experiences, thoughts, emotions, and feelings. The phrase "Cells that fire together, wire together" was coined by Dr Carla Shatz in 1992 to sum up neuropsychologist Donald Hebb's 1949 work on associative learning.

Hebbs explains that when we repeat an experience—which we now understand can even be created using the rumination of the mind—the brain triggers the same neural networks and emotional chemical responses. So when we practise the same thoughts frequently, they and their associated emotional responses come to be our default point of experience. This is why we repeat the same patterns in our lives. These strong neural pathways in the brain are easily triggered by associated experiences in our environment.

Healing the mind and our beliefs about ourselves can change this chain of biochemical subconscious emotional reactions. We can loosen (even clear) old, negative associations, and through repetition, develop new neural pathways for good. The more we practise these new neural pathways of thought and good feeling states, the more we experience the neural firing of the new pattern.

Imagine a field (your brain) and you have been walking on the same pathway for 20 or so years. This pathway may represent the belief and feeling states associated with being unlovable, for example—a well-trodden pathway you automatically walk down when you are triggered. If you clear this belief, you create a new pathway in the field that represents "I am lovable", with its new feeling states. The more you walk on the new pathway and tread it down, so to speak, the more this becomes the favoured pathway and the old pathway grows over. With effective energetic belief change, the old pathway simply does not resonate anymore; it is no longer there for us to walk upon. Refocusing our attention on the new positive belief and emotion associated with it has a correspondingly positive impact on our energy field, and subsequently on the healthy function and repair of the cells in the body.

A lot of information is encoded in the emotional body and its biochemical chain of responses; it is a treasure trove of information, there for us to decode if we wish. In my opinion, the emotional body contains many keys to healing—not just from this lifetime but from the soul's deepest experiences and traumas. Many emotions, both present and old, including, of course, the ones we have practised experiencing, are present in the emotional body, triggered from memories or "echoes" in the field, something I will discuss towards the end of this chapter. Emotions can also be viscerally felt through the chakras and the energy field of the body. It is as though the aura becomes a book of the emotional stories of our past and present.

This paints a clear picture that negative emotion and stress impact our mind, body, and lives. The body becomes primed for the HPA axis to be triggered if we have been practising feeling bad, guilty, lack, inadequate, shamed, angry, helpless, anxious, depressed, or like a victim (which we know constitutes poor health and a poor life experience). The new field of epigenetics has helped us understand that genes are influenced by our mental, emotional, or physical environment and turn themselves off or on according to this environment. When we are happy, feeling well, and joyful, our genes express health. When we are stressed, upset, and angry, our genes express inflammation and disease. Our emotions and thoughts are largely governed by our beliefs (which we can thankfully change) and by how we perceive and address our experiences, giving us choice and freedom over our wellbeing.

I have the genes for lupus, but by changing the vibration of my body, I have turned off the expression of these genes. This means that I no longer express vibrationally the disease that manifested in my body from my late teens to my early thirties. I do not have lupus and am not worried that it will return because I have changed many beliefs and their associated emotions, and I continue to be mindful of my physical levels of toxicity, as well as the emotional and mental vibrations of my body and mind. Just because a particular cancer may "run in the family" does not mean that it will be expressed, as long as the familial vibrational patterns of emotion and thought that express as cancer are healed and cleared. Bruce Lipton's *The Biology of Belief* and Dawson Church's *The Genie in Our Genes* offer more insight into this fascinating and insightful field of research.

Tending to emotion and smoothing our vibrations, choosing how we engage with our past and present emotions, and opting to "do" emotion consciously until it is settled and brought into a happier more peaceful state are activities that are not only healing and empowering but also enlightening. I recently read Vishen Lakhiani's 2016 book *The Code of the Extraordinary Mind*. I deeply respect his mission and approach and perceive Vishen as an important world changer, someone who, as Gandhi said, is "the change he wishes to see in the world", leading and inspiring responsibly through his offering, Mindvalley. Lakhiani discusses 10 "unconventional laws to redefine your life and succeed on your own terms", with reference to living and being extraordinary. I wanted to share with you one that relates to the Healing InSight method.

The concept Vishen calls Blissipline relates to the daily practice and discipline of maintaining a blissful state of being. By clearing our beliefs, we aim to elevate our vibration and connect with our inner joy, truth, and happiness! Blissipline integrates the discipline of engaging in three practices: gratitude, forgiveness, and giving. These sentiments are reflected in the Healing InSight method beliefs in this book.

Evidence is plentiful that the practice of Gratitude raises our level of wellbeing and happiness. I used to struggle with practising gratitude. I realized at some point in my development that it was difficult for me to access because, as a child, I was frequently told that I was selfish or ungrateful. I am the least selfish person I know, perhaps after Rob, but I had a belief that I was selfish and ungrateful, and so couldn't resonate with the feeling of gratitude. Having cleared that belief, I can step fully into appreciating what I have; a key to abundance, which feels better than not being able to resonate with being thankful. Gratitude allows us to say "thank you" and fully receive. We can all find things to be grateful for. It does take discipline, but when I have a client who is stuck in the vibration of loss or lack, I will recommend a dose of gratitude practice, which often helps lift their mood and move things forward. Try immersing yourself in the feeling of gratitude twice a day.

The second practice is that of Forgiveness. Many people struggle with forgiveness and either don't want to forgive or just don't know how. Forgiveness is a gift to self that can free us from the lower vibrations of hurt, anger, and pain. In his time at a programme called 40 Years of Zen, Vishen and others were wired up to high-quality bio-feedback equipment to experience therapeutic processes focused upon forgiveness, with the intention of observing and raising their levels of alpha, theta, and possibly delta brainwaves.

The deep practice of transforming forgiveness into love and compassion and the understanding gained from the bigger picture of these experiences boosted their alpha brainwaves (associated with love, compassion, forgiveness, insight, and creativity) to the extent that the brainwaves could be considered reflective of someone who had spent 21–40 years practising Zen meditation.

Forgiving each of the people who had bullied or denied me in my process of healing was hugely liberating, and this experience shared by Vishen helps me to see why. I have developed a forgiveness Healing InSight protocol in the Resources worksheets in the Appendices to aid in letting go of the pains from toxic or painful past relationships. Remember that forgiveness is a gift to self, as well as a gift to the person or situation that has triggered your distress, because it frees you from the painful emotions caught up in your attachment to them. Ultimately, when we hold on, we are holding onto our pain and unresolved past stories. Our past may shape us, but it does not need to define us. Our "now" creates our future.

The third practice in the Blissipline system is Giving. Many of you reading this may give abundantly, and are perhaps tipping the scales of balance with respect to also allowing yourself to receive. Giving to yourself abundantly helps address this, and when the universe reflects the giving to others back to you, be sure to receive it with thanks. Plenty of research within the "happiness" literature and research shows that happiness increases through the act of giving. Giving adds meaning to our lives. It also reminds us of our gifts, skills, or ability to be kind and loving.

I once engaged in the practice of offering a weekly session to a client who was unable to pay for her therapy. In exchange for my kindness, I suggested she perform a number of acts of kindness to people she encountered in her daily life. The result was heart-warming. I could give freely, knowing that the ripples of kindness would make their way back to me in the universal flow, and this lady delighted in letting me know of the exchanges she had in the week, from smiles with people in the supermarket to discreet acts of generosity. It was clear to me that the statement "Happiness breeds happiness" is in fact true. To see kindness extended into the world was a beautiful gift that felt good for all of us. Being of service to others in any small way (without, of course, sacrificing ourselves and our own resources and needs) is both humbling and rewarding for all involved.

I have a sign on my wall in the hallway that reads "Happiness Is an Inside Job". It is important to recognize that we can, and do, impact our own levels of happiness from within. Suspending or projecting your happiness to somewhere over in the future on completion of a goal never brings happiness to you in the here and now. Recognize what feels good, and focus on that now.

I am not advocating pushing down or ignoring pain and suffering. Our emotions are key to giving us insight into our psyche, our soul's stories and traumas, which we may be vibrationally playing out throughout this lifetime; however, using my technique in Chapter 7 to follow emotion back to its beliefs and clear them using the Healing InSight method is the best way I know of to clear the emotional stories and perpetual discharge of the past. When not working on yourself, change your filter and focus on the good. The more you practise this, you more you begin to fire new neurons for happiness and even bliss. I like the practice of Blissipline a lot; like an exercise routine that brings health to the physical body, it is a daily practice of boosting happy hormones and creating a happy vibration for an extraordinary life.

## The Energy Body

Science is now beginning to measure the "energy body", confirming what has been previously known, shared, and recorded among healers and mystics across the globe since before Christ. Just because we cannot tangibly see energy, this does not mean that it does not exist. I read recently that gravity cannot be quantifiably measured, yet we know and understand its energetic force in the quantum field. For those who do feel and perhaps see it, to deny the existence of the energy body is to deny the essence of life itself. If I could grant one wish for humanity, it would be for each individual to have a spiritual experience and recognize the energetic life force that exists inside and outside of us; there is so much more to human beings and our reality than we can see and comprehend.

When I run my qigong classes it is a delight to see people who were perhaps unaware of their own energy begin to sense and notice it through the practice. Moving the Earth and Heaven energies through the energy channels in the body is such a gift to the self. Energy of this kind can truly help people to feel connected to themselves and the universe. I cannot recommend qigong enough as an all-round health promoter for giving energy to oneself, moving energy, stilling the mind, and harnessing the deep resource within. A deep spiritual connection to who we are, in essence our soul self, can emerge with qigong practice. I will always leave a class feeling more peaceful, more resourced, alive, grounded, and ready to engage with my day. Through the path of surrender in basic qigong teaching, you can begin to experience yourself as an energy being and feel the energy field around you and others, and in this way, begin to take care, at a fundamental level, of your own *qi*, or energy.

Healing traditions from China, Tibet, Japan, and India utilize the ancient wisdom and tradition of working with energy through the chan-nels, known as *meridians* or *nadis*, and energy vortices known as the *chakras*. Healing wisdom was passed down to students of healers and sages when they were deemed competent and worthy of such teachings. Presently, it is widely acknowledged that life is vibrational and that energy flows through these nadis, meridians, or channels in our bodies—either satisfactorily (maintaining health) or unsatisfactorily (causing ill health). The meridians feed energy to our vital organs, so you can begin to see why the healthy flow of vital life force is important for physical health. The meridian pathways are thought to receive energy from the chakra system, which is explained in more detail in the next chapter. For now, it is useful to know that the chakras are like the energy storehouses throughout our body, providing energy for different functions of our human experience.

For a deep look and insight into the meridians, I recommend Donna Eden's 2008 book *Energy Medicine*. Donna also recovered from an autoimmune disease and has developed practical ways to help bring back energy flow to the meridians and energy pathways around the body, mostly through touch. She has daily routines to help maintain or bring health to the energy body. Acupuncture also works by restoring healthy flow through the acupuncture points to meridian energy lines.

There are 12 main organ meridians, six yin and and six yang, that serve the health of the organs, plus eight superhighway meridians. Of those eight, four important ones constitute the Belt meridian, or Dai Mai, which runs like a hula hoop around the centre of the body; the Central channel, or Penetrating or Shushumna channel, through which kundalini energy will travel from the base of the spine to the crown for the opening of our upper chakras and higher awareness; the Governing channel, or Du Mai, which runs up the back and over the head to the roof of the mouth; and the Conception channel, or Ren Mai, which runs between the perineum and the roof of the mouth. It is these superhighway meridians that are worked with in qigong practice, to feed the organ meridians with the health and vitality of the body.

The first study postulating the existence of meridians was conducted in the 1960s by Dr Bong-Han Kim, a North Korean scientist. Further research by Korean researchers at Seoul National University, using high-tech CT scanning equipment and dye injections into acupuncture points, has confirmed the existence of the meridians. The system has been renamed in the literature as the primo vascular system, referring to the channels and nodes as "primo-vessels" and "primo nodes". More than 50 articles offer some explanation of what these channels are and how they conduct energy. Researches have shown that meridians generate light when observed with a camera capturing biophotons in the frequency of 200-800 nanometers (Schlebusch et al. 2005). The channels demonstrating these light waves follow the meridians as we have understood them through history.

The new sciences—quantum physics, in particular—is narrowing the gap between science and spirituality. As a result, Newtonian physics, upon which our medical model is based, is having to reconcile with spiritual traditions that are thousands of years old, a different world view. We still have some way to go, though, for there are some things that are not yet conceivable to the human mind.

For the purpose of the Healing InSight method, it is useful to know that these primary transportation systems of *qi* (energy) run into, through, and out of the body; so when we are standing in our empty and open qigong posture, ready to align with new beliefs, the body is primed for being able to move energy distortions through the energy body's chakras, meridians, and superhighway meridians.

The aura is an energetic field surrounding our bodies, a little like Earth has an atmosphere. I see the aura as a reflection of our internal world. The auras of people who are fully open and giving love to the world can be warmly felt. People who carry a lot of hurt and are very closed or depleted will often draw their aura towards them. It acts like a buffer from the energetic world around us, both giving and receiving information, inside and outside of ourselves.

If the aura is drawn in and weakened, we can feel hypersensitive to external stimuli. When our energy is strong, our aura is strong, and we feel impenetrable; when our aura is weak, we feel vulnerable to external energies. It is possible for us to draw in our aura or extend it with our intention, giving us more space or protection, should we need it. The Small Heavenly Circuit, or Microcosmic Orbit, meditation in the Qigong Practices in the Appendices helps energize and make coherent the energy body and strengthens the auric field.

Changing our thoughts and beliefs can also help the auric field to smooth and expand. An amazing number of people I have worked with suddenly describe themselves as feeling taller—and indeed, they do look visibly more open, clearer and six feet tall, just from the act of changing their beliefs and clearing the negative associated emotions; the aura suddenly expands from the previous contracted state that it was in. We can smooth other people's auras by using soothing strokes across the auric field, which helps them if they feel prickly or fragmented. By using the Infinity Harmonizing movement in the Healing InSight method, you will bring balance and harmony to your own auric field.

Wearing a happy aura is like wearing the best jacket in town—it gets noticed and makes people smile; it is an emanation from your biofield, which enables you to walk around with a warm glow, spreading love to others. Our natural state is one of joy. The most fundamental lesson to learn with energy healing is that energy wishes to move; it wishes to express itself, and given the opportunity and correct conditions, it will harmonize and balance itself optimally.

## Consciousness in Mind

The workings of the mind are quite extraordinary, and I have drawn down my awareness to share it with you here in a vision I had that I named the Inner Multiverse: a plethora of inner and outer interconnected realities that exist within human awareness and the wider universe.

The unconscious mind is often compared to the submerged part of an iceberg; more is hidden below the surface than seen above it. In my depiction, it is the earth beneath the mountain. Though invisible, it is a vital and necessary part of the whole, containing buried treasures of awareness, just as crystals and precious metals may be found in the earth. The unconscious is also the shared, or collective, consciousness that fuels our drives for survival; our individual desires, and understanding of what is needed to co-exist. This informs the subconscious mind, the main body of the mountain, with its many well-worn pathways and predictable but intricate face. It is so vast that it remains largely undiscovered territory—until, of course, we reach the top of the mountain and see where we have been and what else is possible.

The Inner Multiverse

I came to see the conscious mind as the pinnacle of the mountain, representing full awareness of all that underpins it, the paths it has trodden, and the immense foundation of the unknown (unconscious) upon which it rests. There is a feeling of freedom and clarity from this bird's-eye view; a spacious awareness of what is real "here and now". Have you noticed how being present offers you greater awareness? The conscious mind is aware, in the "now", of whatever may come to its attention. We may be softly or intently focused, but we are detached from any state of doing, habit, or control.

It is thought that we only remain conscious around 5 percent of the time and operate from our subconscious mind the rest of the time (Szegedy-Maszak 2005). It is awesome to be at the top of the mountain—and collectively, we are awakening and becoming more conscious—but the main body of the mountain, the pathways, routes, and maps of the subconscious mind start to call to us in our unconscious drive for food, shelter, recognition, warmth, healing, resolution, and so on.

The point of consciousness at the top of the mountain offers connection to a wealth of information and the superconscious, and a whole new world becomes visible and within reach. When we make contact with the mystical realms, this intangible field becomes tangible. Like coming home, we connect with our soul self, which is a part of All That Is, and enter higher states of consciousness, connection, love, wisdom, and possibility.

As you can see, this Inner Multiverse has many layers of influence, function, interaction, and awareness within the self and the wider field of All That Is. Let's take a look at the subconscious mind now, for it is here that we live out the beliefs that impact our lives, whether they serve us or not. It is here that we facilitate change with the Healing InSight method, steering us along easier paths towards the conscious and the superconscious minds.

## The Subconscious Mind

Cell biologist Bruce Lipton's 2005 book, *The Biology of Belief,* is the foundation for the whole energy psychology movement, which focuses on changing beliefs to heal body and mind. Dr. Lipton's work and passion for communicating his message have facilitated a quantum shift in healing for many people. Dr. Lipton views the subconcious mind as akin to a tape-recorder that records, stores, and plays back the decisions we have made about ourselves, others, and the world. At any one time, the subconscious mind is more than a million times more powerful at processing data than the conscious mind. Once data has been processed and understood by the conscious mind, it quickly gets stored for reuse by the subconscious mind, freeing up the conscious mind for new things.

Just like learning to tie your shoe laces, these behaviours become habitual. The subconscious mind helps us drive a car whilst our thoughts ruminate on something else. Have you ever safely driven 10 minutes down the road and been unable to recall the experience? Have you ever tried slowly writing your signature? When attempting this consciously, you may even "forget" how to write the signature you have easily written for decades! The subconscious mind largely drives our thoughts, interactions, expectations, behaviours, and life. When we experience a situation in our daily lives, we make a snap perception of that event and our brain will pattern-match this experience to those in our past, so that it can prompt us in how to respond. Dr Lipton explains that 95 percent of our behavioural responses are habitual, programmed from past experiences, decisions, and beliefs about ourselves and the world.

For example, yesterday, I told my husband to use up some leftover food, but he misunderstood which food I was talking about, so the food was wasted. This triggered in me an old subconscious pattern of thought: "I am not listened to. I am unimportant". I know from experience that, left unchecked, this can snowball into feelings of insignificance. In the past, these feelings and unconscious patterns could escalate as far as the belief "There is no point to my existence". Yesterday, I got as far as "If he can't hear me, then who is going to be interested in reading my book?" My subconscious mind was pattern-matching this experience with the beliefs developed in childhood. Clearly, I have more unwinding to do!

Mental processing is always associated with the emotional and energy body. As Dr Candace Pert noted, for each pattern of thought triggered, neurons fire, hormones and neuropeptides release throughout the body, and a whole cascade of vibrational, energetic responses are felt. It is literally a trigger: a cue in our environment that begins a chain of biochemical and energetic responses. Something happens and all of a sudden we are left feeling bad, pulled away from our higher, soul self into a usually untrue story. As you become aware of the subconscious mind and its stories, you perceive experiences more accurately. Your painful past experiences need no longer be straitjackets when you know how to rewrite the stored programmes with expansive and loving beliefs.

We know that the subconscious mind is susceptible to suggestion when we are in alpha brainwave state, that is, we are more likely to programme information if the brainwaves slow down (Dispenza 2017). As we move from beta to alpha brainwave states, we are less able to consciously analyze information—this is why we are receptive to hypnotic suggestion when relaxed. We also enter this state when emotionally aroused, when experiencing a trauma or deep hurt. When our analytical mind is disengaged, we are both reactive and suggestible. Hurtful words then imprint on our brains as truth, even if they are not true according to our higher wisdom, and become imprinted in the subconscious.

My years in practice have taught me that understanding these painful exchanges, shifting perspective, and using supportive words or affirmations are not enough to prevent these negative imprints from steering our lives. Our scars and their associated stories and beliefs must be pulled into consciousness and cleared on an energetic level; otherwise, we end up with confusing dual beliefs, such as "I am listened to"/"I am not listened to", and may still be triggered into either experience.

## The Superconscious Mind

I see the higher mind (or superconscious mind) as the higher self, the non-physical part of you that has an elevated perspective—wisdom from outside of our usual awareness. When we feel blindsided or confused, we may sense that there is a higher perspective but be unable to perceive it. Psychics and mediums are often called on to help with this, but the knowledge is within us, slightly out of reach.

As suggested by Bruce Lipton's work, our ability to receive depends on how well we are attuned to our higher selves; as with a radio, we may need to adjust our frequency to access the knowledge we are seeking. Once attuned (not an easy task at first), we gain a higher perspective and answers come easily, whereas, if others interpret for us, messages from higher wisdom may be distorted, like a game of Chinese Whispers.

The idea of "tuning in" and "receiving" information still makes it sound as though the wisdom is outside us, when, in fact, it is at the core of our being. Life as a human being causes us to collect layers of beliefs that tune out our higher knowing. Tuning back into higher knowing is a natural process; it feels like home. For some people, releasing resistant beliefs can be challenging, especially if the conditioning is deep, but the more we practise and surrender our analysis, the easier it gets.

Our higher self (or soul) is too large to be fully embodied by our physical body. It exists beyond our concepts of space and time, containing the experiences of this and other lifetimes. We are, in fact, multi-dimensional beings. Your soul essence is part of you, beautiful and loving; it loves the physical incarnation of you dearly, unconditionally. It is conscious, intelligent, and will guide and support you along your path. It is your barometer for truth and is always present, whether you can feel it or not. It is not separate, but is and always will be a part of you.

With the Inner Multiverse, as I see it, although the mountain represents the soul's current incarnation (in this lifetime), the rest of the soul is not separate. Connected to and surrounding the top of the mountain is a stairway that leads to the higher aspects of the soul's expression.

Your higher self, a spark of divine consciousness, will be present when you are working with the Healing InSight method. It is always willing you into your highest vibration and directing you towards the best outcome for yourself. It is this aspect that we acknowledge when we muscle-test the body with the permission statements before engaging in the belief change process. I never recommend that you act against the guidance of your higher self. I have noticed that when the superconscious prevents us from going ahead, simply asking why can suddenly fill us with insight. Very often, once we have this insight, the superconscious will allow us to continue with the process of change. We understand very little about what lies beyond the veil of our everyday consciousness. Somewhat mystical in nature and akin to the magical possibilities portrayed in Disney films, a great wisdom, knowing, and expanse is experienced here.

## The Unconscious Mind

The unconscious mind is the other intangible phenomenon that has interested me since I was a child. This is the realm of the psyche, defined in the Oxford Dictionary as "the human soul, mind or spirit", known to the Greeks as the essence of life, and understood by the world of psychology as the mind or self (Reber 1985). The phenomenology of the psyche takes on new meaning through Sigmund Freud's theory of the personality and its components: the unconscious id, ego, and superego (McLeod 2018). Further understanding arises when we take a look at Carl Jung's writings in *The Undiscovered Self* (1958) and his collection *On the Nature of the Psyche* (1969), where Jung describes his remarkable theory of the "collective unconscious" and his understanding of how the unconscious relates to the conscious mind and their discourse through dreams.

These scholarly theories have shaped both psychology and psychotherapy immeasurably, revealing our search for the soul (true self) through the unconscious conflicts of the id, ego, and superego. We seek to resolve these unconscious conflicts as they become expressed in the face of our relationships with others and the world around us.

All aspects of the id, ego, and superego are found in the mind, part of the inner child developed in our earlier years. The id represents the desires and instinctual drives for pleasure and existence, the ego strategizes how to satisfactorily meet these drives through behaviour whilst remaining in good favour with others, and the superego, like the parental voice on our shoulder, reminds us of the "oughts" and "shoulds" of the larger collective conscious that we live by. If we are to have any hope of discovering our individual or soul self, we must separate from these aspects of our human self or at least become conscious of the roles they play in our lives.

Psychology, particularly psychoanalysis, teaches a great deal about the unconscious, as it largely involves the study of the complex human psyche. People have sat for hours exploring the musings of the mind, and the subject of dreams is an interesting gateway between the unconscious and other aspects of consciousness. The intention in therapy is often to make conscious the unconscious conflicts so that fragments of the self can be recognized, understood, and integrated as we seek to become a unified whole.

I'd like to illustrate this point here with an example, as for me, it is a fundamental aspect of deep transformational healing.

I work with clients using various healing modalities, particularly reiki, and because I am an empath, I attach to the problem. I will feel other people's pain in a particular chakra in my body. I am blessed that I have no qualms about diving deep into other people's pain, trauma, and suffering. I have dealt with my own and know the route to clearing it is being with it, understanding it, and bringing the compassionate light of the universe to heal it.

I allow the process to unfold, and the energy guides and informs me. My job is to trust that and get my ego out of the way. When a person comes to me for healing and my intention is to heal, we do what is needed by going within, listening, allowing and taking it from there. My mind's eye shows me pictures and stories of where this energy was created. It is all stored there under the person's conscious awareness—everything we need to know in order to heal!

I experience people's pain or trauma as a moment in time, floating out in the ether, away from the connection to the heart and embodied soul. It is of course not separate, because it is present, but it feels disconnected, unresolved, and is calling out, playing through the person's life as pain/suffering/anger, together with a feeling of being lost and alone with this. When I tap into these unconscious experiences of the soul and bring them into awareness, or consciousness, the person usually experiences a huge release of emotion. There is a coming into one's truth, a knowing that was buried just under the surface of awareness that was driving their repeated experiences and seeking resolution. The soul fragment is calling to come home, to be loved, accepted, and welcomed into the being that exists here and now. This is a fundamental process of becoming whole.

The unconscious mind is the deep storage tank for all of our potential knowing of our human self, our various identities (both congruous and conflictual), and our attachments to relational or extraneous aspects of life. The archetypal attributes of the self may hide within, or be expressions of, the unconscious mind. It seems to me to be the human self in its unknown, fragmented form, working internally to discover the truth and acceptance of its own identity and expression, both harmoniously and agonizingly as it seeks to evolve into its multi-dimensional consciousness. I agree with Jung and many of today's forward thinkers: if we are to discover ourselves, we must detach from collective conditioning. We must find the courage to find and speak our truth, regardless of whether it can be validated by others, and engage in enquiry that leads us to our larger universal truth.

When you are working with the Healing InSight method to align with a new belief, it may be that early memories from your unconscious mind, painful or otherwise, will come into your inner vision. This is good. See them, and welcome this hurt, fragmented aspect of yourself with love. They need to know that the belief you are aligning with is true for them, so stay with the process and lovingly show them that they are perfection and can reside in your heart. Our fears, when faced, become our soul's growth as we seek to evolve into our true perfection and become whole. (Here, we return to the rainbow metaphor, whose multifaceted aspects together form the white light.)

## Morphic Fields

As receivers and interpreters of vibration, the human self can resonate with particular frequencies from the quantum field. You may have connected with expanded consciousness during meditation or through a mystical or spiritual experience. Many of us now have had spiritual experiences from which it is impossible to return to our previous states of questioning and doubting that something more exists. There is much that our limited minds cannot comprehend, but the veil that surrounds our usual perceptions can be lifted by slowing down our brainwaves and opening to something greater.

Scientist Rupert Sheldrake's important 2009 research on morphic fields showed that information is carried through the ether to the masses.

I remember first discovering his work at a conference, interested to hear about the phenomenon of blue tits tapping into the cardboard top of milk cartons to drink the cream from the morning delivery. At first, a few milk cartons were being invaded, then a whole town, and almost simultaneously, birds all over the country were tapping into milk carton tops to drink the cream. Blue tits as a species do not travel more than four to five miles away from their home. This information had thus become part of the collective field of consciousness (or morphic field) of the birds. So much so that some 30 years later, birds in Holland were observed behaving in exactly the same way. They could not have learnt by imitating the behaviour of their species, given milk deliveries had been suspended for nearly 10 years there and the birds' lifespan is only two to three years.

"'Morphic field' is a term that includes all kinds of fields that have an inherent memory given by morphic resonance from previous similar systems," wrote Rupert Sheldrake in the 2011 revised edition of his 1995 book *The Presence of the Past: Morphic Resonance and the Memory of Nature*, as if the echo of systems from the past become recreated in form, experience, or behaviour in the present.

The morphic field carries an imprint about the whole. Each living entity has a field, and within each field exist many others: behavioural fields, thought fields, emotional fields, and even fields for particular diseases. The body has its own morphic field, as does the liver, stomach, and spleen. It is understood that like attracts like. In a 1987 journal article listed in *Semantics Scholar*, Sheldrake notes that a segment of oak tree or earthworm, for example, can re-create the whole life form from its morphic field, almost like a memory imprint.

This has practical relevance in healing work concerned with changing the energetic imprints (or morphic fields) of thoughts, behaviours, and health in our own bodies. We know the cells in our bodies are constantly renewing, and though we are not left with an entirely new body every 10 years, our cells regenerate in accordance with the morphic field of the organs. If this theory is true, and the information for cell renewal is encoded in the morphic field, then by vibrationally influencing our fields we can create positive change for our cells, and thus our whole body.

I worked with one lady using the Healing InSight method who was delighted to tell me that her latest thyroid blood test showed no antibodies for Graves', or Hashimoto's disease, prompting her to discuss with her doctor the possibility of stopping the thyroid medication she was on.

Changing one's vibration for health makes the Healing InSight method a potentially powerful tool for healing.

It has been postulated in scientific literature that memory may exist within the field, as no evidence to date has found memory to be stored in the brain. In his research, Dr Bruce Lipton recognizes the self, all the way to the cellular level, as being a receptor, or receiver, of information in the field. There are stories told of heart transplant patients who, having received a new organ from a donor, inexplicably adopt aspects of the donor's personality and life (for example, food preferences). In one case described by Paul Pearsall in his 1998 book *The Heart's Code*, after experiencing nightmares of the donor's death, a heart recipient was able to identify the donor's murderer, who was captured as a result.

In *The Biology of Belief*, Dr Lipton offers evidence that human leuko-cytic antigens, or self-receptors, are crucial to what makes us who we are. They apparently receive information from our non-physical counterpart. Without these self-receptors, receiving our individual data from the field or stream of consciousness from All That Is, we would merely be a generic human cell. Not only do we download our soul identity from the field, which interacts with and influences the physical body, but the physical and energetic environment also affects the local and wider field. Dr Lipton's 2005 documentary *As Above—So Below: An Introduction to Fractal Evolution* explains how reconnecting with our spiritual self enables us to tap into a wealth of information about the self.

This makes sense to me as a spiritual healer. When I tune into a highly charged point in a person's auric field, it feels as if I begin to stream, or download, information from a person's past. I can open to receive information about them—both in this and other existences—in which remain the energetic, emotional imprints, unresolved traumas, and unmet needs (although note that my intention when I connect is to heal wounds). This information appears at first to be in the person's energy field, but the stream of consciousness I receive is from afar, a tangible, felt experience—usually for the person on the table, too.

We are complex beings, part of a bigger picture than we might currently comprehend. We carry vibrational, cellular information from both our maternal and paternal ancestral past, and also from the individual identity of the soul's many lifetimes and experiences (McFetridge 2004). We are affected by not only our experiences in this lifetime but also those of our ancestors and our soul's journey. Knowing this may help you to surrender to the Healing InSight method, which gives you a means of self-discovery beyond the conscious mind.

The most beautiful lesson I have learnt comes from the work of Dr. Bruce Lipton: we are all different streams of consciousness from the whole, God, or All That Is, analogous to a rainbow spectrum of light. As our souls seek to know themselves more fully and return to the light, we must be our own unique, individual colour or light. If I am "yellow", for example, but I'm trying to be more like my "blue" friend, partner, or boss, then I never get to shine my unique light, and my yellow becomes lost. Thus, we lose the potential to shine as the complete spectrum of white light. Similarly, if I am "yellow" and believe that my "blue" counterpart should be more "yellow", then I am denying them their own unique identity, and again, the white light is lost. We must unite, celebrate each other's differences, and allow ourselves to truly connect with who we are. The Healing InSight method was created with this in mind: a celebration of our individuation together with the vision of a unified whole.

## The Power of Attention and Intention

Dr Rupert Sheldrake and journalist Lynne McTaggart have both written extensively about the powerful effects of "attention and intention". In his 2004 book, *The Sense of Being Stared At,* Dr Sheldrake wrote about how our minds extend beyond the brain and how we can affect someone through space by looking at or thinking about them. I am sure that we have all had the experience of thinking about someone, only to find they then telephone you. This frequently happens to me. I will become aware that I am the focus of someone's attention and then they will telephone or send an email. Sometimes, someone can be thinking about contacting me, and they will keep coming into my attention all day. I have a few times been moved to message somebody to see how they are, and they will tell me that they have been thinking about getting in touch all day! If I am quiet, I can intuit more information—sometimes their state of mind or being. This is an example of how we are vibrationally connected. In essence: we are drawn towards each other by our focus, a kind of energetic broadcasting.

In her 2008 book, *The Intention Experiment,* Lynne McTaggart researched whether we can use our power of intention to create wellbeing, peace, and success. McTaggart defines intention as directed, focused thought, and has concluded from her research that thoughts are an actual, physical energy, capable of affecting and transforming life—from plants to complex human beings—when focused in a particular way.

For example, Dr Gary Schwartz of the University of Arizona worked with McTaggart to research intention and its effects on light emitted from leaves. Two groups of leaves were grown in the same biological conditions; one group was subject to the researchers' intention for them to be luminous, and another was not. The leaves that were given the intention to be luminous were, as measured by a special camera, indeed found to be more luminous. This experiment was repeated across the globe by thousands of participants via the Internet; this time with four different groups of seeds. Participants chose which group of seeds to send intention to without revealing their choices to researchers and sent the intention for their chosen group of seeds to grow rapidly. This experiment was repeated six times. Each time, a statistically significant result showed that the group of seeds subjected to intention did indeed grow faster than the control groups.

This exciting work demonstrates people methodologically utilizing the power of their own intention for good, but also, the magnifying power of a collective in directing their intention. In her 2015 documentary, *The Abundance Factor*, McTaggart reported all sorts of incredible healings, including subjects going from ill health to complete wellbeing with repeated group intention. The power of positive, focused thought to heal, from reversing human disease to encouraging skin growth or healing bone structure, is phenomenal. The focused thoughts of one person or a group can permanently affect the physical structure of another human body.

Importantly, the conditions for optimal intention, as described in *The Intention Experiment*, involve focusing the mind and using all five senses and a focused heart state to bring awareness to the specific intention. This means imagining the person or situation being healed in every way; to see them as healed, and to hear, feel, touch, and taste that they are.

To multiply this intention, participants unite in a group, holding hands, centring the breath with this shared, focused intention. Lynne McTaggart's 2017 book, *The Power of Eight*, explains how joining intention with eight people or more (eight being a vertical infinity symbol) brings significantly greater results to intention experiments. There is power in our shared intention for good. The ongoing work has expanded to now include experiments to bring peace to violent places in the world, with apparently great success to date. For example, in the American town of Fairfield, Connecticut, rates of violent and property crime were on the increase compared with the previous year. McTaggart conducted an experiment where the specific focus of intention for one week was to lower violent crime by 10 percent. Over the next six months, there was actually a 46 percent reduction in violent crime in Fairfield. More experiments are needed in order to substantiate the theory, but already the results are compelling: we can unite to share a positive intention that impacts the behavioural choices of others. If a shared focus can do this for other people, just imagine what our thought and focused attention does to influence our own reality!

It appears that intention as a focused, loving thought for good is the key to healing, so we must be aware of the meaning behind our intentions, as this is what determines the outcome. Words spoken without purposeful and meaningful thought are not effective in creating change; it is the intention behind our words that appears to carry the strongest vibration and is felt by another. We have all experienced this when someone is paying lip service—saying one thing but meaning another; it is the vibration, intent, and feeling that is felt as truth. We know when someone is not fully on board with what they are telling us.

Our subconscious mind can interfere with our best intentions, too, preventing a full coherent resonance with our intent. To have a clear intention in the conscious mind and heart is wonderful, but we must stop the subconscious mind from emitting its own limiting broadcast and having a hand in creating an unwanted reality. When we use intention to create change in our lives, it's essential to bring the subconscious mind on board by aligning our beliefs with the intention. This disables the subconscious mind from replaying thoughts of limitation and fear while we are not deliberately engaged in manifesting positive intentions for our health, wellbeing, and prosperity.

An interesting side effect from the peace intention experiments is the so-called "mirror effect", which is also described in the Law of Attraction as "like attracting like". All participants who sent good intentions during the experiments reported a positive change in their own personal lives. People reported that not only did they feel increased harmony but also positive shifts and reconnections occurred in their personal relationships. Focusing their intentions on peace and harmonious relationships also increased these states in their own lives. It is also worth remembering that the act of giving to others adds meaning to our lives and increases our levels of happiness and wellbeing.

## The Universal Law of Attraction

As we begin to understand ourselves as vibrational beings, sensitive to our world and having an effect upon it, we can begin to see how we attract to us the essence of what we put out. Our vibrational state of being is where we attract our experiences and is created by our beliefs, and our perception and interpretation of experiences, emotional states, and associated thoughts. We are energy beings, and our vibration attracts, like a magnet, experiences from the field that match its frequency.

If we don't change our thoughts and vibration, we simply receive more of the same experiences. What we focus upon and pay attention to becomes the essence of our reality. If we are focusing upon illness and pain, we vibrationally tune into—and thus receive—a reality where we experience more illness and pain. If we place our attention upon abundance, we attune to a reality that includes the possibility of wealth and prosperity. If we focus upon lack, we have more experiences that feel lacking. (Many of Esther and Jerry Hicks' teachings on the Law of Attraction can be found on their website—see the Resources section.)

It is important to be mindful about where we focus our attention, as this will be the essence of what is drawn to us. Abraham teachings channelled through Esther Hicks (Hicks & Hicks 2005) tell us that worrying does not serve us, as it is a focus on the thing we do not want, potentially drawing that towards us. When I work with clients I may refer to this, challenging them not to think of a pink elephant in a tutu dancing across a high wire. It is, of course, an impossible task: all of the detail is there in all of its glory. It is challenging in real life to actively put something out of our minds. This is why people have such a problem with positive thinking, as they are mostly trying not to think about being chronically ill, or to avoid being fearful of lack. Going over the details just perpetuates the current state of feeling, vibration, and ultimately the issue itself.

It is in our interest to focus on feeling good, vibrant, and healthy, rather than feeling sad or helpless about our poor health. If moving in the direction of vibrant health feels too much of a stretch, we can at least move towards feeling more peaceful. When working with belief, it is important to clearly state our intended alignment with "having [our healthy desired intention]", as opposed to desiring "*not* to have the problem any more".

Applying the principles of the law of attraction is difficult when, at the same time, our biological drives are working hard to protect us from repeating previous painful experiences and warning us about a poverty mindset or ill health. This leads our biology to repeat the biochemical pattern, firing neurons that result in us experiencing the same old emotions about the same old issues. We have to focus differently, and one way is to install new beliefs, which in turn changes our perception, our interpretation of events, and our emotional responses and thoughts.

This is how I came to publish this book. I aligned vibrationally with being a "successful, published author" using the advanced Healing InSight method. I uncovered and cleared the beliefs that were unconsciously blocking me from resonating with this belief (and reality), aligned with the truth of this belief fully, visualized it (resonated at length with the vibration of the new belief/reality), acted upon my new instincts and behaviour, and received it graciously from the universe with much excitement and gratitude!

## The Power of Belief and Visualization

*The thought manifests as the word;*
*The word manifests as the deed;*
*The deed develops into habit;*
*And habit hardens into character.*
*So watch the thought and its ways with care,*
*And let it spring from love*
*Born out of concern for all beings.*

The originator of this quote is unknown, although similar sentiments have been found in the Buddhist scripture *Dhammapada*, a Chinese proverb, and late 19th-century Christianity. A version of it is often attributed to Gandhi. Ancient spiritual wisdom teaches us that in order to experience an enriching life, we must build our character with love, honesty, and compassion, cultivating a mind free of troublesome thought, belief, and emotion.

The original reiki principles formulated by Dr Mikao Usui, who died in 1926, were translated by Japanese Reiki Master Toshitaka Mochizuki in 2000 and teach these same sentiments:

*The secret art of inviting happiness*
*The miraculous medicine of all diseases*
*Just for today, do not anger*
*Do not worry and be filled with gratitude*
*Devote yourself to your work. Be kind to people.*

*Every morning and evening, join your hands in prayer.*
*Pray these words to your heart and chant these words with your mouth.*
— **DR MIKAO USUI**, *Reiki Treatment for the Improvement of Body and Mind*

Our belief is hugely powerful, especially when it is informed by an expert in authority. This is the placebo effect, which can be seen, for example, when a group of patients participate in a study, unknowingly acting as the control group. They may be told they are receiving a treatment, but actually receive a placebo (a non-treatment; for example, a sugar pill). Participants in this group tend to experience improvements because they believed that they would, after having been told that the drug/surgery/intervention would help, even though in reality it was a fake intervention.

The placebo effect is a version of a self-fulfilling prophecy, and there are countless studies that document its efficacy. One such study by Mosely and his team in 1996 that involved two groups of people who underwent knee surgery, cites this effect. All ten participants in this trial recovered from their osteoarthritic symptoms after knee surgery. All were prepared for the surgery, had the anaesthesia, and the surgery incision; however, half of the people (the control group) were given no actual surgery to the knee. After waking, they were all told that the surgery had gone very well.

The people in the control group subsequently experienced just as much relief from the fake surgery as did those who had the actual surgery. The gains in health came from the belief that the surgery was a complete success. Astounded by these results, Mosely and his team repeated the study with 180 people in 2002. It again demonstrated the same gains in the osteoarthritic knee condition, regardless of whether the operation they had was real or fake, with recovery gains still documented two years later.

The nocebo effect is the opposite—a negative belief that produces a negative result. Six years on from the first study, subjects were told that they had been part of an experiment. The arthritic knee condition returned in all but one of the subjects, who didn't believe that it was true, believing instead that their identity must have been mixed up with someone else. When a patient is given six months to live by an oncologist, they may often live up to this expectation. In my time, I have had to unpick many a belief for my clients after the authoritative diagnosis given by an "expert" doctor.

I had a young client called Grace, 20 years of age and full of potential. She had suffered with anxiety and depression since her childhood and was told at 14 by her psychiatrist that she would have "generalized anxiety disorder" and depression for the rest of her life, which she would need to take medication for. Grace had seen several counsellors before she came to see me, declaring me her last hope.

A highly sensitive young woman, she was open to energy psychology and healing methods. She worked through anxiety-inducing events from her past and addressed many unhelpful and limiting beliefs, including the specific belief taught by the psychiatrist that she would have this diagnosis for life and would always need medication. By the end of her sessions, Grace was transformed. Her beauty radiates, and she no longer considers herself a victim. She is off all medication and mostly free from anxiety feelings. When it does show up, she can cope; she addresses her feelings and thoughts and the experience is short lived, no longer impeding her life.

Teachers have a lot of power in influencing how children perceive themselves and their capabilities. If, as a child, our teacher believes in us, we also believe in ourselves and will often do well. If a teacher tells us we're a waste of time, we can often internalize this belief, wasting our time and, as a result, not doing so well. We may find ourselves living out what our authority figures have told us is true. When we are hurt, it imprints.

Those recovering from ill health and "incurable" disease must abandon the belief that they are to live with disease until they die. Many reports, studies, and books have been written about the total recovery of people from serious disease. My lupus specialist called my recovery a "spontaneous remission". Believe me, there was nothing spontaneous about it! It would be wonderful if doctors could give temporary diagnoses. Perhaps then, people may choose to opt in for self-healing and recovery.

Remission is actually a common occurrence. I have read reports of cancerous tumours disappearing within a matter of weeks or months after a significant healing, change of perspective, and use of visualization. In 1993, researchers from the Institute of Noetic Science found over 3,000 cases of medical reports of spontaneous remission from cancer in the medical literature (O'Regan et al. 1993). David Seidler, the actor who won an Oscar for best original screenplay for *The King's Speech*, reported a spontaneous remission through visualizing his bladder cancer away. He worked on his mental state, actively practising visualizing during the two weeks prior to having the surgery that was supposed to remove it. When David had the operation, there was no sign of the tumour! (Edition CNN 2011)

Visualization, as a method of guided, focused meditation, is a powerful tool for changing our reality. The Healing InSight method uses a type of visualization at the end of each belief realignment process to help you to create your new reality. If we look at observations from experts in the field, we can appreciate that the benefits of visualization make it worth taking time to practise.

In his 2008 book *How Your Mind Can Heal Your Body*, former pharmaceutical scientist Dr David R Hamilton cites many cases where people have healed health conditions (including cancer and autoimmune disease) by visualizing themselves well. One technique, the "mind movie", envisions one's future in an imaginary videography process. It was conceived by Australians Natalie and Glen Ledwell and became a huge success—exactly in line with the visions they had created for the release of the method. Leading mind-body researcher Dr. Joe Dispenza uses this process in his workshops.

It helps to be specific about one's goals. Settling into an observing rather than analytical place also helps, as the subconscious mind is more suggestible and open. My experience of using visualization with clients also tells me that visualizing using your own imagination is preferable and more effective than following suggestions from others. In allowing our unconscious wisdom to surface, our minds will often show a vision that is helpful and meaningful to us.

I worked with one lady who was addressing the healing of a long-standing cancer naturally who, in a meditation, visualized her white blood cells as wolves who would mop up the cancer. She returned one week later to tell me that the wolves were full of apathy, which represented her feelings. In visualization, she was able to commune with the wolves, understand their plight, and allow her vision to give insight into her white blood cells. Without forcing things, but observing the image, she was able to tune into the damaged white cells that had been subject to chemotherapy and to see them renewing. As she acknowledged the tiredness of her immune system, new sprightly wolves appeared in her mind's eye, so she agreed with the old wolf that he could step down and allow the new, more dynamic wolves to take over the search and destruction of the cancer cells in her body.

It can be difficult to imagine something that is inconceivable to us, so in order to use visualization effectively, we have to bring our whole self into the experience. Our spiritual nature, the part of us that knows that all is possible, can offer its guidance when we intend to step into a better or healthier future. Observing our intuition as part of the visualization by accessing the heart connection in a meditative state allows all aspects of the whole to be present. This is not searching outside of ourselves but observing what comes to mind by tuning into the body with respect to the issue.

Meditation is a skill that can be learnt—a little like flexing a muscle, but with more benefits to the body, mind, and spirit than one could dream of. A good meditation is like plugging into the grid, being focused outside time and space. It is both a journey and a destination that can leave you with a sense of connection, peace, and wellbeing for the rest of the day. See the Healing InSight website for my guide to meditation.

The joy of the Healing InSight method is that standing in the Wuji pose, the "empty" standing posture in qigong practice, also plugs you into this grid, so during the visualization stage we can more easily perceive the new belief's resonance in the body and its vibrational possibilities.

Frequently, without trying to create one, a vision representing the new vibration comes to mind, reflecting the shift in consciousness that has occurred. Your job is to allow and be curious about the vision, perhaps expanding it, but not attempting to manipulate it for the best outcome. Your higher self will work with you, offering you visions that mean something to you. However abstract they may be to others, they often represent the new you, together with your new possibilities. This makes it easy to embody the visualization and feel it in every cell and pore of your body, creating a huge broadcast to the universe that this is the reality you are choosing to align with and receive!

The Healing InSight method is unique in that it clears other layers of beliefs that vibrationally oppose your desired belief or goal. This makes visualization a lot easier, removing the doubts that can be found when we attempt to draw an energy towards us that is different to our subconscious programming.

The manifestation process in the method brings the head, heart, and gut into alignment with the belief, so that all aspects of the body are congruent. This enables a coherent visualization and therefore, the opportunity to manifest this new broadcast more easily. Visualizing something outside a congruent field is difficult and lacks coherence. Align first and then use visualization to focus and amplify the newly aligned belief.

A positive vibration is much stronger than a mixed one. Be mindful in your everyday life not to fall into imagining bad things that could happen; steer your thoughts away before they gain momentum. You may use the phrase "stop" or "cancel that" to help you escape the train of thought. Find your positive shoes again, and be your own therapist or your own best friend. Cheerlead and envision yourself all the way to your heart's desires!

Practical steps that are needed are:

1. A body-mind-heart connection. Breathe into your body, settle, and then focus on your heart and centre.
2. A quiet, focused mind by practising meditation.
3. A connection to the awareness of All That Is. Notice the space around, below, and above you. Feel your feet connected and grounded to the floor. (Some may say that we do not need this higher connection in order to visualize. I say "try it and see".)
4. With closed eyes, letting your awareness "sit" in the back of your brain, observe through all of your felt senses and third-eye perceptions the pictures, visions, feelings, sounds, smells, even tastes of what you are choosing to create. Be creative and allow your heart's desire to unfold in your imagination.
5. Continue in this state of positive emotions for at least a minute. Abraham (as channelled by Esther Hicks) says that 68 seconds of pure thought can build a momentum of energy strong enough to change your point of attraction.

Making a vision board (collecting images and written words) to focus your attention on what it is that you want to create is a worthwhile activity. Take the time to visualize what you want, especially as you fall asleep and move into alpha and possibly theta brainwaves; this an effective way to turn your dreams into destiny.

Some of us struggle to see what we want in our mind's eye. If this is the case, be guided by your other senses—you may be kinaesthetic and feel the new vibration, or you may hear new words and statements in your head. All methods of communication with your inner self are fine. I would suggest taking the time to use each of your senses as there may be information there for you. The more you open to it, the more your inner-tuition grows!

# Chapter 5

# Understanding the Whole Self
# through the Chakra System

The Chakra System has been central to the development of this healing system, as it is like a map, signposting and navigating the different expressions of the human psyche.

Each chakra governs a group of nerves, or plexus, and an endocrine gland of the endocrine system, influencing the corresponding health of their associated organs within the body. The seven main chakras are often described as energy wheels or vortices, spinning at certain locations in the body. A wealth of information is available on the chakra system, but for our purposes in using the Healing InSight method, I will just give sufficient information to allow you to get a feel for the subtle and not-so-subtle energies of each chakra. I explain how the chakras relate to our personal growth and development as we journey through life, and how each chakra governs particular aspects of human consciousness.

During a healing session, I place my hand over a client's body and intuitively pick up information, such as feelings, memories, or pictures, which I perceive are originating from the chakras or energy body. Simply put, our chakras are encoded with a map of our life story, and I often find that a person's challenges—perhaps subconscious and often unresolved—cause a disruption to the flow of energy in this system. I personally sense energy blockages as false or unhelpful thoughts and beliefs that perpetuate stuckness and prevent the associated memories from being processed to a peaceful resolution. We may never make sense of or come to terms with certain events in our lives, such as the loss of a child or another major trauma, and these are imprinted in our energy field. However, I find that working energetically with belief and emotion in the energy body consistently offers release and relief, restoring flow to otherwise disrupted chakras.

As well as seeing and feeling, I often "hear" a client's troublesome thoughts or beliefs, which may be anchoring a negative experience in their energy system. It is like a loop of feeling–thoughts–feeling, which cannot be shifted until the story that is being told changes, or is told from a different perspective. With the Healing InSight method, when people realign themselves with a helpful belief, they sometimes see a snapshot of a memory in their mind that helps them understand how they first developed the limiting belief.

Whilst beliefs may correspond typically to the consciousness of a certain chakra, all sorts of stories can be found in each of the chakras. Please know that we are complex and do not experience feelings, thoughts, and life in isolation. Our subconscious mind is always busy pattern-matching whilst our energy bodies are responding to and interacting with our environment.

## The Chakras

The table gives a brief snapshot of each chakra's colour, element, sound, and the endocrine gland it governs:

| Chakra Name | Colour | Element | Sound | Endocrine Gland |
|---|---|---|---|---|
| **Root** | Red | Earth | Lam | Adrenal |
| **Sacral** | Orange | Water | Vam | Testes and ovaries |
| **Solar Plexus** | Yellow | Fire | Ram | Pancreas |
| **Heart** | Green | Air | Yam | Thymus |
| **Throat** | Blue | Ether | Ham | Thyroid |
| **Third Eye** | Indigo | Light | Om | Pineal |
| **Crown** | Violet | Consciousness | Beyond sound | Pituitary |

The following pages give a brief synopsis of the chakra system. Some of the information is from my own learning, some through exploration with clients, and some has been channelled for the chakra belief affirmations.

## Root Chakra – Muladhara

The root chakra is situated at the perineum, the seat of our physical being; it governs the legs and feet and, in turn, our earthly and physical connection to matter. It is represented by the colour red and expresses as the element Earth. The skeletal system, hips, legs, spine, immune system, and sciatic nerve are all largely affected by the root chakra's disrupted energy flow. Long-term disruption here significantly affects the adrenal glands, which are working hard to keep you safe from the stressors in your life. From a developmental and psychological perspective, this chakra is largely concerned with issues of safety, stability, and physicality. When we are fearful and anxious, our root chakra will feel "un-earthed". Without this grounding, it is difficult to relax, let go, and trust. Our energy body is unanchored, and we can feel pushed and pulled about by forces outside of ourselves. It is not unusual for us then to go into a fight, flight, or freeze stress response, particularly if we were not parented reliably in early childhood.

From birth to six years old, we are very small and largely helpless, dependent upon adults to protect, provide, nourish, and guide. Few of us have had conscious parenting, which actively taught us that the world is a safe place, we are loved unconditionally, and we can trust ourselves and others. Old patterns of fear and the need to protect ourselves can create division and separation from our fellow human beings. We learn that we are unsafe and that other people are not trustworthy.

So how do we walk firmly upon this earth if we feel unsafe? When I am working with people who have a degree of fear or anxiety, and also when working with those wanting to spiritually evolve, establishing good ground roots is so important. I describe it as the springboard from which we take the leap into living out our potential. Qigong can be enormously helpful, as it enables us to find our feet, to root down, let go, or surrender and connect with the earth. Working with beliefs about safety, such as "It is safe for me to surrender and let go, to be in and nurture my physical body", enables us to connect with the energetic vibration of safety found in a healthy root chakra.

We can then begin to take responsibility for our impact on the earth, recognize the cycles of life and appreciate our earthly abundance in the nature around us, rather than striving only for material wealth. When our root chakra is healthy and happy, we feel connected to and supported by life, by the earth, and by others. Of all the chakras, working on addressing these safety issues will bring the greatest reward and a different kind of engagement with life. If you want to reach for the stars, you need a healthy and happy root chakra.

## Sacral Chakra – Svadhishthana

The sacral chakra is positioned midway between the perineum and navel and governs the sexual and reproductive organs, the bladder, bowel, large intestine, prostate in men, and reproductive glands. It is usually depicted as orange in colour and is a rich and delicate chakra concerned with issues of sexuality and creativity. The sacral is described as the "seat of the self", and if we think about our desires and individual creativity—indeed our sexual expression—these are birthed here in the sacral chakra. Our deepest desires connect us to our soul's path and purpose. They are driven by our gut instincts and innate drives to fully experience our human reality. Whilst incarnate on Earth, we can have the privilege of experiencing all of our senses; what it is to taste, smell, see, feel, and to orgasm at the fullness of life in this physical body.

Our cultural experiences have seen women oppressed for generations, often with regard to sexuality. Both women and men have suffered as a result of the masculine trait of dominance or having "power over" another and dysfunctional sexual expression. Many women (and men) suffer sacral chakra trauma and constriction after feeling unsafe during sexual experiences. Yet, when hearts are open and love is flowing, it is the most beautiful divine expression for two people to come together with love, respect, gentleness, and passion.

The 2018 "Me Too" movement involved a social media campaign against sexual harassment and assault—yet another example of women reclaiming their bodies and sexuality, as hidden stories of abusive sexual encounters were aired publicly in order to be witnessed and healed. Women are being called to "find their inner goddess" by feeling intrinsically beautiful and empowered by their goddess sexual energy. The essence of what it is to be male or female, and our expression and balancing of these opposing qualities within us, is centred in the sacral chakra. A healthy sacral chakra leads to a greater fullness of life.

The sacral chakra is associated with the element of water, and many emotions can be felt here in our instinctual gut. A healthy sacral chakra reflects emotional balance. A lack of emotional regulation can affect the energy flow of the sacral chakra so that it may resemble a stagnant pool of water or conversely a wild and roaring ocean. If we don't tend to our emotions, we may suffer an inability to connect with our deepest desires and creative or sexual selves.

If the sacral chakra is out of balance, we can also lose touch with our instincts, making bad decisions or simply not listening to ourselves. This is why it is okay to have desires, as they can give us direction and purpose. Any issues with the sexual and reproductive organs or the bladder and prostate gland can benefit from addressing beliefs about having the freedom and safety to create, to be sensual and sexual, to trust in ourselves and others, and to feel safe having powerful emotions. A healthy expression of the sacral chakra results in a deep connection to one's unique self and allows us to step into our personal power.

## Solar Plexus Chakra – Manipura

The solar plexus chakra is situated between the heart and the navel. It governs the stomach, pancreas, spleen, liver, and gallbladder and is associated with yellow, the colour of the golden sun. Digestive and food-related issues are affected by injuries held in the solar plexus chakra. This chakra is typically associated with our sense of personal power, our "I am" presence, which when balanced and healthy, resonates with ease, grace, and confidence.

In my experience, this chakra is almost always affected by hurt. We close up and constrict the solar plexus after being around those who have in some way threatened our sense of self. Typically, solar plexus injuries occur when we perceive someone or something to have power over us and this triggers us into old patterns of powerlessness, fear, and helplessness. The threat may only be small, but if it is a repeated experience from childhood on, we typically suffer from a freeze, or perhaps another stress response, as the energy flow in the solar plexus chakra is constricted.

Chakra theory states that we journey in seven-year cycles, beginning with the root chakra and working upwards, exploring each chakra's field of consciousness every seven years (Ellis 2002). Each year of these seven-year cycles has a secondary expression, beginning at the root chakra. At the time of writing, my youngest son is two years old and is energetically exploring his root–solar plexus and developing his sense of self. During this time (often referred to as the "terrible twos"), he is finding his "no", expressing his independence, and exercising his sense of personal power. It is difficult to parent consciously and allow him his personal power when he refuses to wear certain clothes or eat certain foods. Already, he seems to know exactly how he wants to spend his time and, if I suggest otherwise, he has no qualms in expressing loudly his upset and disagreement. It is interesting that the element expressed through the solar plexus is Fire!

We also see this in teenagers of 14–20 years old, as they develop their sense of self as individuals and start to reject the doctrines of society or their parents' rules and ideas about life. They choose friendship groups who share similar values, hobbies, and interests, where they can feel safe and accepted, and with whom they can begin to express their authentic self-identity.

So often in the world there is judgement and rejection of each other, which breeds hurt, resentment, and anger. Children, especially adolescents, can be cruel to one another, rejecting personal identities that are different from theirs or threaten their sense of self. They have witnessed and experienced the huge levels of judgement that exist around them and are often unsure at this age about who they are. Even as adults, we can all too often feel justified in responding to anger by projecting hurt and anger back and forth between each other. When we are aligned and content within ourselves, we are non-judgemental and can come to empathically sense other people's struggles and ego drives.

When all of the chakras are aligned and the solar plexus chakra is happy, we are able to stand our ground in difficult interactions, without fighting, fleeing, or contracting. This is especially true when the root and the upper chakras are healthy; we have connected with self-love and acceptance and have come to trust the universe and our belonging in the universal flow. In essence, we do not perceive the situation as a threat and can be with or rise above it.

Many of us are fearful or rejecting of our individual selves and authentic personal power, due to negative associations we have made with the idea of power. It is very clear from the beliefs that were channelled to me for this healing system that it is time for us to rise up and empower ourselves with love and compassion, both for the self and for the greater good.

In her 1992 book, *Our Deepest Fear*, author Marianne Williamson writes of our need to find our own unique creativity and self-expression. It is a delight to be reminded of its sentiment, one I wish I had heard in my twenties, when my own solar plexus chakra was injured. When we each allow our inner light to shine brightly, celebrating also the light of others, we move from "I can't" to "I can", from "I won't" to "I will", and from "I'm not" to "I am".

## Heart Chakra – Anahata

Situated in the centre of the chest, at the heart, this chakra is the point of balance between the upper three and lower three chakras—the meeting place of the physical and spiritual bodies—and is a place of great consciousness, power, and presence. It governs the heart and circulatory system, the lungs, diaphragm, thymus gland, immune system, and the breasts and is associated with the colour green. The chakra's symbol is a six-pointed Star of David, a triangle representing the earth pointing to the heavens, intersecting with a triangle representing the heavens pointing to the earth. Without either our spirit or our body, our human self would cease to exist.

The alchemy that the physical and spiritual realms create is "that which is greater than the sum of its parts"—as depicted in the Mandorla, or Vesica Piscis symbol. A form of sacred geometry, this symbol is the shape within which Jesus and the Mother Mary are frequently depicted, as representations of the creation of spirit and matter.

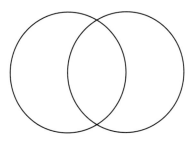

Mandorla or Vesica Piscis

Looking like two overlapping circles, this shape signifies the very point of creation as we separate from the oneness into our dualistic, physical reality. In sacred geometry, the Vesica Piscis can continue dividing to expand into the Flower of Life symbol, illustrating the unity of life that is found across many religions and in both science and mystical spirituality.

If we think about the heart in terms of its colour—bright emerald green—this reflects the balance we can find in nature. When conditions are right, life flourishes and the green of plant foliage is all around us. It is interesting to think of life-giving trees releasing oxygen for us to breathe whilst being reminded that the heart chakra is governed by the Air element and provides energy to the heart and lungs. Just as in nature, if we see our environment to be harsh, with too much sun or too little rain, we also close up and protect ourselves from adversity. When energy flows freely through our heart chakra, we can remain open, giving and receiving in equal measure.

There is nothing more beautiful than an open, loving heart. Anahata, the Sanskrit name for the heart chakra, means "unhurt, unstuck, and unbeaten". When the heart is filled with love, there is no room for fear or separation. It sings with the most beautiful tones and loves unconditionally, sees with love, feels love, and is wholly glorious.

It is my intention that this healing system allows more people to resonate with and express more love in the world. The Advanced Method in this system, in particular, can help to heal old hurts and unhelpful beliefs that keep love separate from us. I have seen lonely clients open up to true love as a result of using this system. Love is our natural birthright. We are all worthy and deserving of love; self-love, and love shared with someone who assists your growth, is your equal, and recognizes the good in you. The one thing (amongst many) I love about my husband is that he allows and supports my own self-love, my love for God or Great Spirit, and the love I have for my work, clients, friends, and family. When you practise reiki and energy healing work, you come to know that everyone is loved, lovable, and worthy of love, and there is an abundant flow for each of us.

The heart seeks peace, balance, and harmony. It is important for empaths and sensitives to create a gentle environment for the soul. The solar plexus and heart will close up when we feel bombarded with too much noise or negative vibrations from anger, disrespect, and hostility. It takes a well-practised heart to be able to stand in love with an open heart in a negative energetic space. This is why many energy practitioners speak about protecting and clearing the energy body, using practices such as shielding, wearing an invisible cloak of protection, or using aura sprays to keep your energy clear. I have different ideas about this, as fear is the pervading factor in attracting negative energy. Having said this, however, depending on my energy levels, I will protect and support myself in certain situations.

The heart carries a huge field of resonance. In triune brain theory (MacLean 1990), the heart, though concerned primarily with relationship, is described as a sensing, perceiving organ. HeartMath Institute is doing inspiring work on the intelligence and intuition of the heart, helping us understand its function in more depth. Rigorous experiments have shown that the heart responds to our environment energetically and biochemically, sending signals to important parts of the brain, both before the event actually occurs and the brain has had time to perceive and comprehend the environment itself (McCraty et al. 2004). The heart is very sensitive to the environment, and if we can allow our awareness to drop into the heart more often, rather than being led more frequently by the gut or head, we may find that life begins to evolve according to our soul's calling.

As a side note, I believe that the heart chakra is affected by strong electromagnetic fields (EMFs), such as those emitted by WiFi devices and cellular (mobile) phones. I always turn off my WiFi router at night, as a good energy and self-love practice, and a restless sleep will remind me that I have forgotten to do so. My phone is protected by a radiation shield, and I do not carry it on my person. The electrical circuits in my house are harmonized with a device that also protects my family from external sources of EMFs, such as mobile phone masts, our neighbours' WiFi, or smart meters.

Over the years, I have seen several clients with severe electromagnetic sensitivity, and many others who share some of the symptoms. Some people are unable to buffer or ground these external energy fields, which leaves the whole chakra system (in particular the upper four chakras) misaligned. Although it is impossible to avoid all EMFs, do educate and empower yourself on this complex subject by consulting resources such as *What the Doctors Don't Tell You* or the ElectricSense website. It is better not to step into a place of fear and powerlessness but to arm yourself with information and strategies to clean up your own and our global energetic environment, especially given the proposed roll-out of 5G technology. My intuition is that the heart, as our biggest receiver of sensory electrical input, will be grateful for this.

The lungs transport the life force from the air around us into our cells. They can also constrict when we struggle to take in life-giving breath, perhaps as a result of us sensing physical or emotional toxicity and choosing to subconsciously restrict how much of our environment we "inhale". I have had asthmatic clients who have improved their health by working with the belief that it is safe for them to take up their space or that there is room for them to breathe. We may be full of grief and hurt and unable to experience love or expand our lives whilst we are holding onto pain in our heart and lungs. Heart chakra beliefs in the belief chart (pp. 202/203) can support the health of the lungs and heart by helping us to open up to the possibility of bringing more love, harmony, and balance to our life. The practice of meditation and forgiveness are also wonderful for a healthy heart chakra. In fact, the Buddhist meditation of metta, or loving kindness, is a great tool for assisting in a peaceful, balanced, and loving heart. (This, plus more chakra and qigong meditation recordings and downloads, can be found on my website.)

## Throat Chakra – Vishuddha

The throat chakra, which governs the thyroid gland, is the narrowed vertical funnel through which passes the energy of the other chakras. It is very sensitive to subtle energies in the body's energetic field and is mostly concerned with verbal and non-verbal communication and expression. When we can find quietness of being, we are more aware of subtle energies and can even pick up communication in thought form, from one mind to another. Interestingly, as has been shown repeatedly in Dr Rupert Sheldrake's research on morphic fields (see Chapter 4), we need not be physically with another person in order to sense their thoughts or intention.

From the age of 14, when I was bullied at school, I began to shut down and lose my voice, becoming overly concerned with how I was being perceived or how I was impacting others. I feared being seen, heard, or rejected until I was actually in my 29th year—a year in which, developmentally speaking (28–34 years of age), we are exploring the throat chakra (throat-sacral). I was studying for my Counselling Psychology Post MSc, and was having therapy to help me deal with the very angry man that was now bullying me at work. I will never forget the day when I could no longer withstand abuse from him and shouted at him to "shut the f*** up!" For a girl who had grown up uncomfortable to use this language, it made its mark on both me and him. Although I wasn't quite sure what to do with the captive audience at the time, it was the breaking of the silence.

I continued to find my voice through the written word, facing my fears and difficult conversations, and several months later, I was able to fully embody my strength. On this occasion, he had, perhaps unknowingly, closed the door behind him and it slammed in my face. I instinctively grabbed hold of the door handle and yanked it open. For the first time, I felt my own strength, as did this work colleague. Since then, I have used my voice to communicate my disapproval to anyone actively disrespecting me and, in fact, I stopped attracting disrespect and bullies into my life.

It has taken me a long time to fully express who I am, and writing a book like this is personally challenging for me. Yet it is the perfect way for me to share all that I have learnt about personal growth and transformation, and it is my throat chakra that is allowing my heartfelt desires, instincts, and insights to pour out onto paper. I have even surprised myself by enjoying making the YouTube and Facebook videos that demonstrate the Healing InSight method.

Physically, most blocks in the throat chakra are reflected in thyroid, sinus, ear, nose, and throat issues. The element Space governs the chakra. Typically, when the sinuses suffer, we have become congested! As an empath, I find myself constantly yawning as I work with clients in order to release and clear energy around this chakra. Singing, chanting, and toning are perfect exercises for the throat chakra. Clearing old emotions and beliefs that prevent you from speaking your truth are also vital. If you are a teeth grinder, chances are that you have things to say that are not getting expressed. Write, write, write—until you discover what you are chewing over has been resolved.

The colour of the throat chakra is blue—some say the blue of a lagoon or the sky. I suggest choosing whichever blue that you like best to support this chakra. I fondly remember a work colleague saying I never wore this colour and suggesting that I wear more blue when I was going through the bullying experience. I remember getting a light-blue v-neck jumper and wearing it until it fell apart. Maybe it helped! My wardrobe throughout my thirties was largely blue, and there are some days even now when I need a little extra help to "show up" and put on a blue jumper. Blue lace agate is also a wonderful crystal for throat chakra support.

If creative ideas are conceived in the sacral chakra, then they are birthed and expressed through the throat chakra. Painting, music, dance, and the spoken word are wonderful ways to bring balance to this chakra and our thyroid function. It can take courage to speak our minds without altering our truth to make it "acceptable" to others, but practise saying what is on your mind. Speak your truth.

When channelling the beliefs in this healing system, I sank into my higher consciousness, called in my guides, and recorded what was coming into my awareness. Apart from the spoken words, I also saw visions and felt particular feelings or vibrations. As soon as I put words to the vibration I was feeling, I was placing my own interpretation on this awareness. This is where we can unknowingly veer away from truth. The first lesson from the *Tao Te Ching* by Lao Tsu (Vintage Books 1972 translation) reminds us that everything can get lost in translation:

*The Tao that can be told is not the eternal Tao.*
*The name that can be named is not the eternal name.*
*The nameless is the beginning of heaven and earth.*
*The named is the mother of ten thousand things.*
*Ever desireless, one can see the mystery.*
*Ever desiring, one sees the manifestations.*
*These two spring from the same source but differ in name;*
  *this appears as darkness.*
*Darkness within darkness.*
*The gate to all mystery.*

A clear, healthy throat chakra helps us hold true to the expression of our perceived truth. Mindfulness with conscious communication is truly a blessing for each of us. Stop and listen to what is being said before responding to those you love or engage with, and this will enable a much more mindful and conscious exchange of energy. Note that having a healthy throat chakra makes one a very good listener.

## Third Eye Chakra – Ajna

The third eye or brow chakra is situated just above the eyes, in the centre of the forehead, and governs the pineal gland, representing the element of light. This chakra is largely associated with our ability to see both that which is visible and that which is seen or sensed through our psychic awareness. The third eye is represented by two lotus petals and draws our attention to the subtle nature of duality, of the manifest and non-manifest.

The pineal gland is a small pinecone-shaped endocrine gland that is located in the centre of the brain. Just as the throat chakra perceives thought forms and sound waves, the third eye chakra perceives higher frequency light and colour vibrations. Light is responsible for many important functions in the body, just as it is for plants and animals, notably for our daily sleep cycle (Liberman 1991). The pineal gland determines our production of melatonin, a vital neurotransmitter. It receives light information from the sympathetic nervous system, transforming the messages into hormonal signals in the body. Melatonin plays an important role in the regulation of our 24-hour circadian pattern, production of important sex hormones, our mood, and immune function (Liberman 1991). Research has shown the numerous health-giving benefits of melatonin. It may hold healing potential for fibrocystic breast disease, breast and colon cancers, and aspects of Alzheimer's disease and reduce the effects of ageing (Malhotra 2004). This study also shows that melatonin lowers corticoid levels, serving perhaps as a buffer for stress, thereby improving immune function. It has been shown to inhibit inflammatory effects in multiple sclerosis (Farez 2015), and research is ongoing to reach conclusions about its role in other autoimmune diseases.

Research is also demonstrating the effects of vision-enhancing drugs such as LSD on melatonin production. We do, however, yet have to understand the full role of the pineal gland in relation to these psychedelics. A 2018 online article by Suzannah Weiss discusses how people are now self-medicating with low doses of LSD, magic mushrooms, MDMA, and ketamine to improve their mood and enhance creativity. Scientists are beginning to research the use of microdosing these psychedelic drugs to treat post-traumatic stress disorder (PTSD), depression, anxiety, and migraines. In fact the FDA in the US is currently supporting trials for the use of MDMA for the treatment of PTSD after research by MAPS (Multidisciplinary Association for Psychedelic Studies, a non-profit research organization) showed great promise (Burge 2017).

People are also turning again to ceremonies using the traditional spirit medicine ayahuasca, typically led by shamans from the indigenous peoples of the Amazon basin. I find it interesting that after a focus on reason and intellect during a long period of human growth led to the atrophy of the pineal gland, we are now seeking a more expanded and spiritual consciousness. Removing fluoride from our water source and toothpastes also helps stop its calcifying effects on the gland.

Descartes placed the home of the soul at the pineal gland, and it could be argued that it is the gateway to the light transmissions of our soul. With so much potential benefit from an aligned and open third eye chakra and pineal gland, regular spiritual practice is certainly worth exploring. My personal practice allows me to connect to my higher self's light and fills my entire body with a sense of peace and wellbeing.

A 1995 study by researchers at the University of Massachusetts Stress Reduction and Relaxation Program showed that regular meditation increases the production of melatonin, which along with many benefits is implicated in the prevention of breast and prostate cancer (Massion et al. 1995). Deep, spiritually expansive meditation certainly induces theta brainwaves, which are found in both healing and sleep cycles. Have you ever meditated and found it hard to stay awake? Perhaps this has something to do with the melatonin production when entering theta brainwave state. If you wish to develop your third eye, begin by paying attention to your inner world. There are many online meditations that assist specifically with the opening and balancing of the pineal gland to help expand our consciousness and improve our ability to perceive psychic information.

Qigong practices that focus on the flow of qi through the spine are also helpful; they bring energy into the pituitary and pineal gland for vitality and expanded consciousness. The pineal gland is actually bathed in cerebrospinal fluid, which is made in and circulates around the brain and spinal chord and is the perfect conductor for sensory and energetic information to travel at lightning speed. We can explore the connection of the spine to the pineal gland in a meditation later (see Resources). This is my favourite way of plugging in and balancing myself if I am busy and don't have time to sink into a deep, quiet meditation.

When all of the chakras—upper and lower—are aligned, we can connect with All That is Possible and hold a clear vision in its pure vibration. Once limitations and blocks to our desires have been cleared energetically using the Healing InSight method, we actualize the new belief using visualization. For example, many people told me that I should write a book and share my wisdom with the world, but I would not have done so "and secured an international publishing deal" without actually using the system myself. I had too many beliefs that said I was inadequate, unable to express myself, or that it was unsafe for me to express myself. Yet here I am following my desires and my powerful intention to help manifest healing for all. The system helped me to be in *ajna* (which in Sanskrit means "command") of my soul's chosen desire.

I remember sitting having lunch outside my place of work in London, reflecting upon recent life events, when 22 ravens flew in and encircled me just long enough for me to count them. Perhaps I needed to know that there were 22, the master builder number in the field of numerology. To me, this was a profound and beautiful message that I was not alone, that I was on the right path, and that Spirit was working with me, encouraging me to build something magical. When the third eye opens, we see all sorts of messages from Spirit and other realms to help guide us along our true path. There is nothing scary about channelling from the light and opening up to higher realms of guidance and wisdom. It is always loving and always for our highest and best good. I have repeatedly seen with clients how content and blessed they feel when they begin to trust their intuition and connect to their light.

A balanced third eye allows us to clearly see how we have created our reality through our past thoughts, expressions, and behaviours. It is like a torch, illuminating our subconscious patterns and unconscious drives of the past. When the third eye is open, active, and healthy, fed by the grounded and aligned lower chakras, we can perceive the higher truth of our own divine light, without imposing judgement upon ourselves as we might do when we are misaligned. This clear vision, with an open heart, steers us to bring compassion and empowerment to ourselves, directing the course of our reality back to our highest expression.

Meditation, yoga, and qigong are all helpful practices to enable the quietening of the mind and the strengthening of the third eye. Qigong sees this chakra as one of the three treasures or, *dan tians*, where *shen* (spiritual energy) is converted into *wuji* (the infinite space or void). Specific yoga practices also focus upon the opening of the third eye.

I once had an insightful third eye opening while channelling Archangel Michael. At one point I was invited to see through his eyes and, as if embodied, I saw colours in the light spectrum that I was not used to seeing in this three-dimensional reality. Everything—the grass, the trees, the sky—was seen through what I would describe as an "energy lens" of the brightest colours, appearing to me as pure energy, as if I could put my hand through the landscape. This was a mind-bending reality shift for me, for which I was most grateful!

## Crown Chakra – Sahasrara

The crown chakra is concerned with consciousness, not only our human consciousness but the divine consciousness of All That Is. It is situated just above the top of the head, governing the master pituitary gland that controls the release of hormones from the other endocrine glands. Together with signals from the hypothalamus, the pituitary gland's anterior (frontal) lobe releases adrenocorticotropic hormone (ACTH), stimulating the adrenal gland to release adrenal hormones. Follicle-stimulating hormone (FSH) and luteinizing hormone (LH), are released by the anterior lobe, which work together to ensure the normal function of the ovaries and testes. Growth hormone (GH) is released for ongoing cell regrowth and vitality and prolactin for breast milk production as well as the all-important thyroid stimulating hormone (TSH) to help the thyroid gland perform all of its many regulating functions. The posterior pituitary lobe releases anti-diuretic hormone (ADH), which prompts the kidneys to release water into the bloodstream, and finally, it manages oxytocin, the love hormone, which assists in mother–child bonding when breastfeeding and bonding in other intimate relationships.

When in recovery from lupus, I read many stories of people adopting spiritual practices and prayer and healing themselves from chronic ill health. Understanding the power of this little gland to regulate the glandular system, and seeing its associations with the crown chakra and potential to open to the higher spiritual realms, one can see the connection between spirituality and physical recovery from disease.

I cannot emphasize enough the importance of developing the lower chakras and embodying the lower and heart chakras in order to fully experience the crown chakra. I have met spiritually gifted people who are connecting outside of themselves and perceiving accurate messages from Spirit, but who in fact are causing hurt and pain to others in their everyday lives. They had not done their own inner work and instead demonstrated a sense of superiority or lack of compassion for other people's suffering. Transcendence away from our human selves will not change nor raise the vibration of this planet if we cannot first ground and make real the divinity within each and every one of us.

To heal is not to neglect or move away from suffering but to be present with it and bring consciousness and light into the darkness so that the suffering is transformed, not buried. The greatest healers I have known have gone through periods of suffering but have transformed their stories and expressed their pain. They are "real", true, and humble. They know that they are both perfect *and* imperfect, and do not judge or create separation or believe that they have all the answers to life's mysteries. When the crown chakra has truly opened and one has experienced the infinite, there is awe and a recognition that divine consciousness is far greater than we are able to perceive or comprehend. We transcend, becoming a humble servant; a mere speck in the cosmos.

In her 1987 book, *The Wheels of Life*, Anodea Judith gives beautiful and informative definitions of the seven chakras. She describes the dance of transcendence and immanence as currents of consciousness running through the crown chakra. When we transcend, we see beyond the ordinary veils of life into an expanse where unity—as opposed to duality—exists, where we experience no separation from self or other and no sense of time or space. Transcendence in its simplest, perhaps crudest translation, could be viewed as "rising above" the ordinary way of seeing or experiencing the everyday. Immanence is the recognition of the divine within us, when we surrender the self and allow the divine to radiate and express through us. We recognize ourselves as divine consciousness, or even as God. We could describe its simplest form as the embodiment of God; we are God. This is the essence: we are a divine soul, part of the infinite, which has a physical body for a time, through which to create.

When the crown chakra is open and healthy, we are at one with ourselves and the world around us. This is the entry-point into pure consciousness, perhaps union with God. We can recognize everything as divine, including our brothers and sisters on planet Earth. We disconnect from the desire to be divisive, losing the need to compete we have come to know and experience through our human drive for survival. The crown connects us to a higher sense of knowing, a universal consciousness, and we can begin to practise the common language of love, compassion, and peace. We start to recognize ourselves in others and feel connected in strange, inconceivable ways to other people who are reflecting the divine consciousness within themselves. No war was ever born from divine consciousness. The focus becomes "we" rather than "I", and service becomes important to us.

As described earlier, I was blessed to experience a full opening of the crown, which occurred by going deeply inward to connect with my suffering. This journey led me to a knowing, without doubt, of something so beautiful, blissful, expansive, and loving that I would never again question the divine nature of all existence and my place in it as a servant and expression of the divine.

In my work, I have seen many people with a closed or misaligned crown chakra suffering needlessly from depression. These may be people who are deeply tender beings who have not spiritually awoken to nor recognized the divinity in themselves or the world around them. Sometimes we can get stuck in a place of suffering and perpetuate more of the same in our outer reality. I myself spent a few years moving in and out of depression before I realized that there was much more to life and existence than what I had been told or perceived. It is important to find the meaning and connection to our deeper spiritual self. Helpful ways of opening to and connecting with the crown chakra include helping others; connecting with deities, the Buddha, Ascended Masters, or angels; and looking deeper within, using the practice of meditation. My recommendation is to always ground and expand the heart chakra before opening and sensing the space around the crown. Every lighthouse needs firm foundations.

The Healing InSight method enables us to realign with a different set of beliefs, so that in the Age of Aquarius, we can transition into a more spiritually connected life experience. It is important for us now to remember who we are and, like the eagle looking down from above, see the bigger picture of our human existence. A well-aligned crown chakra helps us to love each other, to accept and find understanding and compassion for each other, to unite. We can then begin to build Heaven on Earth.

# Chapter 6

# Understanding Belief Change Energetically

The Healing InSight method helps us to navigate release and realignment gracefully; cutting through the energetic imprints of the unconscious mind by releasing the negative programmes of the subconscious mind that would otherwise prevent full resonance with the newly aligned belief.

As explained in previous chapters, as a result of our attention and intention, our words, thoughts, and visions carry vibrational information, which is expressed through the ether, or universal field. When using the Healing InSight method to bring ourselves into alignment with a positive belief that opposes our subconscious patterns (that is, our current understanding of reality), we can become challenged.

Resistance to aligning with the new belief may be subtle or dramatic. Our physical bodies may "erupt" with an almost volcano-like response. Most of the time, resistance is present in sensation but is subtle. Although you have made a choice to align with the new belief, there may be reasons to hold onto the old, unhelpful beliefs, and you might struggle to let them go. This is usually felt, to some degree, through bodily sensation of fear, emotion, or heaviness. The following case study is an example of the transformation I see regularly in my work.

Mary was belittled throughout her childhood, verbally put down, ridiculed, and even hit for being visible, weak, or just in the wrong place at the wrong time. She had learnt that "the world is a dangerous place", "it is unsafe for me to be seen or heard", and "I am inadequate, unimportant and weak". She lived her life in fear of ridicule, sensitive to criticism and rejection, and still attracting these responses in her family as an adult.

When aligning with the beliefs "It is safe for me to be visible, seen, and heard; I am adequate and just as important and powerful as anyone else in my family," Mary began to have a fear reaction. Stepping into her power in her home had always resulted in her power being taken away, rendering her hurt and helpless. Energetically, whilst aligning with the new belief, I was able to give support to her in the form of reassurance, allowing, and acknowledgement, and I offer it to you now if you are using the system for your own self-healing. It takes courage to work through our limiting patterns, but be reassured that the system will help you, feelings are okay, and you can expect a positive outcome.

Resistance may surface in the form of fear, upset, anger, or hurt, which are the old emotions or issues that are surfacing to be cleared in order to resonate with the new belief. The process can be like sifting through subconscious programmes and unconscious memories, allowing an awareness and acknowledgement of them, in order to release them and make way for the new. I refer to this as realignment.

For Mary, as with many other clients working through their painful inner beliefs, a lot of emotion rose up. However, when encouraged to settle into and work through the resistance, to allow and simply observe it, the feelings passed and she felt a release. Mary then had the experience of elation as she began to "try on" the new belief as a possible reality; a new and higher truth. Of course, she *was* adequate and just as important and powerful as anyone else in her family!

When clients align with a new truth, they usually feel great relief. The Healing InSight method expands on this feeling by moving you into a visualization of what it is to live out the new, now more accessible story around a new belief. Mary was able to imagine standing with her father— the trigger for many an upsetting and disempowered feeling—and be in her power, feeling strong, equal to him, important, and visible. Mary was able to fully resonate with this new vibration, and that is what we are looking for. This resonance informs us with a sense of knowing that we have shifted and realigned to a new belief.

I worked through this belief with Mary just before Christmas and was so delighted to hear that she was successfully able to show up as herself, feeling comfortable, with none of her usual feelings or experiences of fear or disempowerment. Although not easy to process, her genuine willingness to be present with her vibration of fear and powerlessness, coupled with her intention to feel better and stronger, enabled this issue to clear, giving her a truly transformational healing.

The resonance you achieve through this process becomes your energetic broadcast, attracting new experiences to you in accordance with the new belief. Even though every experience is unique and personal, I have highlighted here in more detail what you can generally expect to experience with the Healing InSight belief change process. These are the "Four Rs of an Energetic Belief Realignment".

## Resistance

It is normal to experience a level of resistance, especially if you are undoing problematic patterns. Most of the participants in my workshops or clients in my practice experience low-level resistance. It may show up in the form of a stress response, such as fight, flight, or freeze, or as emotion, muscle tension, or avoidance. Very often when we start resisting energy flow, the body tightens up and we control or constrict our breath. Patterns of resistance may occur as soon as we identify a deeply rooted belief, manifesting as avoiding doing the work in the first place or becoming distracted, angry, or apathetic during an actual change process. Sometimes, physical sensations show up, such as a heaviness or numbness in the legs or a headache in a specific part of the head. People may feel anxious or even feel as if they have a wound in their heart or solar plexus.

Feelings are just a series of energetic expressions that will clear if the resistance to feeling or "real-izing" them is released. Energy wants to move and wants to express itself. We need not know where it has risen from, or what we may be tuning into; the more we allow and do not jump into our analytical mind, the more we become aware of. Many of us have learnt to minimize our emotions, but it is helpful to allow our feelings and sensations to naturally surface during the process. They are usually short-lived. The system itself will safeguard you to a large extent. The process, just like that of giving birth (for those of you that have), will take longer if you tighten up and resist it. Uncomfortable sensations can lead people to feel tense or out of control, which in turn creates resistance to experiencing the sensations that they ultimately intend to release. If too much uncomfortable energy builds, you can ground it by placing your hands, palms facing down, at the side of the hips to the earth, until you feel able to relax back into the sensation. If pictures, memories, or painful emotions surface, do not try to change or manipulate them or will them to pass by imagining them cleared. This would have the effect of resisting the core energetic vibration that is surfacing to be cleared. Just stay with the feelings until they clear, and you feel or see a more harmonious picture.

When you relax into fully experiencing and observing these sensations, the resistance clears and allows for a new state of being. Using Geneline Therapy, I once experienced feeling like I had fallen into a black hole; that

I was nothing, alone, almost as if I ceased to exist and was floating in the universe. It felt frightening and took courage to stay with the process but, supported by a practitioner, I did. I was spinning around, out of body, fearful, helpless, and lost. This was probably one of the scariest energetic experiences of processing a soul trauma I have had.

The practitioner suggested that I allowed myself to spin, to feel it, and accept the feelings. As I did, they began to clear, and the vision and sensation changed until I emerged, grounded and fully in my body, which I had previously disowned due to its dysfunction and pain. If I had resisted this process, as I see with clients sometimes, the issue would have remained unresolved and the difficult sensations would have remained for a while. For the best results, I recommend that you stay with the difficult feelings until they are gone.

The Healing InSight method is usually straightforward and simple, but if you are searching for deep transformation—if the space is set, and this is what you are intending—please remember that you are working energetically with the mind, body, and spirit and anything from your past that is blocking your desired goal may be thrown up. You must take responsibility for your own process.

The important point to remember here is that if something is coming up to be cleared, you are ready, and it is probably time to release it. So, be courageous, stay grounded and soft, and allow the process. Your body's energy system knows how to heal and will take any opportunity to clear if it feels safe enough and is allowed to do so. When feelings from the past or difficult memories come up, see them as rising into your consciousness to be released. Your job is to soften any resistance that is operating from a state of fear and preventing you from connecting with the vibrations that are surfacing. This will enable the process of healing and transformation. Be curious, observe, and allow.

Another form of resistance to clearing old vibrations is intellectualizing the process. When we get into our head, we move away from experiencing the feeling and begin interpreting and analyzing what we may be feeling or seeing in our minds, or we may talk about it with others who are present. This is less likely to happen if you are using the system on your own, but if you are working with a Healing InSight practitioner or helping a friend or family member, please resist analyzing what is happening, as it will detract from your connection to the energy you are intending to release. Talking or naming a sensation is fine and will not interfere, but overanalyzing the process will steer you away from being with what-is.

I believe that it helps to see resistance as your friend. Don't fight it. Resistance begins as an attempt to protect you and keep you safe. Remember that it is only there because you are not yet aligned with the new positive belief, and what you are asking of your subconscious mind goes against what it currently believes to be true. On one level we are invested in our old beliefs, and in some ways they do serve an aspect of us, but they rarely serve the whole self. This phenomenon is called a "hidden gain". It may not be obvious to us why we would want to hold onto particular beliefs when they seem to be hindering us, but on some level they often serve an unconscious need or desire.

For example, someone with chronic illness may be invested in being sick because they have an underlying belief that "being sick is the only way of being cared for". They may intellectually understand the importance of shifting this belief and choosing to align with a more supportive one, such as "I am cared for and loved when I am healthy and well, just as much as I am cared for when I am sick and tired", but they may experience rising panic and resistance when they try to change this belief. Perhaps, as a child, when they were sick, their mother would take time off work to care for them, but the rest of the time, they were looked after in nursery school or by a grumpy nanny, so they became programmed to believe that sickness was a pathway to their mother's love. When denied the hidden gain of love, time, and attention associated with illness, they now become fearful, because in the past, "being okay" meant that their mother would be absent, bringing with it a feeling of being alone. The adult child may need to learn (or programme) the new belief that they are worthy and deserving of love, perhaps, specifically, their mother's love.

Sadly, most of our beliefs are programmed in our first six years of life, when we are largely egocentric, not yet having developed much empathy or understanding of another's perspective. The child may have perceived or interpreted the mother's absence as "work was more important to Mother than me". They may have noticed their mother's absence from the home and decided that they are unlovable or unimportant and have an emotional reaction to that.

In this example, even though the mother may love the child endlessly and take any opportunity to be with them when they are sick, she may also have been torn by her need to bring in money or honour prior commitments. The child's beliefs are based upon their perception of events, and will subsequently inform their feelings, perceptions, thought patterns, and behaviours in adult life, including manifesting as sickness in order to gain love and attention from loved ones.

Most behavioural patterns after the age of seven years old is directed by subconscious patterning, and knowing this helps us to unpick beliefs that do not serve our children. Communicating with them about how you may be feeling, using a reassuring manner, helps the child to see things from a different perspective so that they do not feel responsible for family difficulties.

In yourself, when you notice resistance to changing a belief, perhaps in the form of a growing sensation or emotion—or a distraction of the mind—simply notice it, thank it for trying to protect you, breathe, and relax into the sensation and release it. Remind yourself that you are okay, and that this shift is to enable you to live and feel well. It is important that you suspend judgements about yourself and your previous experiences or reactions; they will interfere with the process. Love yourself compassionately throughout, and feel loving support from others as you face your fears and limitations, replacing them with top-grade, unconditionally loving, supportive, and uniting beliefs. Our reality may have been a long-running programme, but this does not mean that we cannot change it, upgrade it, and download ourselves an improved version of life on Earth.

### Release

Release occurs in many ways but usually involves working with the breath. Resistance can show up as a tightness or restriction in the breath, but the breath can also be the vehicle that allows us to settle into the "now" and our being. We can use it to connect into and release energy. When we feel stuck and enter a "holding" place, breathing enables energy to flow and for us to move through difficulties. Allow yawns or big breaths to come forth and release—it is the easiest and most effective way to allow an old energy to clear. I am constantly yawning whilst I am doing energy work with clients and can sometimes literally feel energy drawing up through my crown to be released as I do so.

Allow the body to move as it wishes. Some people, including myself and my reiki teacher Richard ("King of the Spasms"), will jolt or spasm occasionally; this is perfectly normal and a healthy way of releasing. Moving or shaking may provide enough movement to enable energy to be released, if needed, as does brushing or sweeping the body with the hands, or even tapping on the points of tension or wherever you are drawn to. The Healing

InSight method uses a powerful movement form in the shape of the lemniscate, a figure-of-eight drawn with the hands that follow the shape of the infinity symbol. This is a balancing and harmonizing movement in itself, designed to help energy to move through the body, ready for its release. I refer to this in the system as the Infinity Harmonizing Movement.

If you find yourself crying, allow it. Your tears will likely be brief, as the flowing movement allows releases to occur quickly. If your aim is to clear resistance and encourage a release, simply allow yourself to soften. Soften the muscles, keep breathing, and bring compassion, self-love, and the sense of a higher consciousness, or even God's love, into your being. This will help you to trust in the process and know that you are exactly where you are meant to be and that all is perfect, just as it is.

Both hemispheres of the brain are activated using this technique, and with it often comes a sense of release, which may register as clarity, relief, or heaviness lifting from the body or mind. Sensations can be either subtle or intense, and are often unique to the person and issue being processed. Sensations are your signposts, and you will come to read them more accurately the more you practise the system. I have used it with energy healers and laypersons alike, and have found that every person I have introduced to the system has witnessed shifts. The best way to know if you have released is to bring your awareness inward to see if you feel better. Chances are that you will feel clearer, happier, more positive, and engaged.

## Realign

Realignment means changing our identification with an old, unhelpful belief to identifying with a new, positive one. When we are aligned with something, we are "on board" with it, working with it, broadcasting its vibration out into the world, and receiving a reality of like experience.

When realigning a belief, you may initially experience a lack of congruence with the new belief, as though you are trying to convince yourself of the new alignment, and this may feel awkward. You may think, "But this is not true" or "I don't believe this". If this occurs, try not to add too much weight to that thought. If we dive into thinking "This is not true", we may infer that the system is not working for us and encounter a wall of resistance. When you first start working with the system and activating the hemispheres of the brain, the new belief will not feel like your truth; however, even though you are currently not aligned, this does not mean that things will not change shortly.

You must enter a process of allowing and suspending your judgements. You are going through this process of change because you are currently not aligned with the positive reality you want to experience, so try to become curious and hold a space for the new idea and for your full self to step into this new truth. It may be that, just before you are about to align, you are stopped by noticing the feeling of discord you currently hold about the desired belief. The answer is to be patient and observe.

When you begin to align with the new belief, noticeable momentum starts to build—the arms performing the infinity harmonizing movement often begin to move more freely, a feeling of lightness may come over the entire body, and the new belief may start to feel like a possible truth, which continues to build into a sense of coherence—"Yes, this feels true".

## Resonance

When a belief has realigned, we may be aware that there has been a shift, and we might feel different: lighter, happier, relieved, or stronger. However, we have not engaged fully with the new belief until we allow our whole selves to resonate with the new belief's vibration. In order to acquire the "felt sense" and meaning of the new belief, one must immerse fully in its vibratory field. If the subconscious mind is on board, we are mostly there, but we may not yet resonate with the new belief and get hold of what this realignment means for us in terms of our potential new reality.

Using the visualization process contained in the healing system allows us to fully engage with the new belief and envision how it might shape our reality. We can begin to see ourselves with this new belief and notice what is new and different. We may hear a different stream of self-talk to what has been usual for us, but most frequently, we *feel* what it is like to fully align with (or resonate with) the whole-body awareness that accompanies this new belief.

Resonance is what allows you to feel complete and able to imagine the new energetic alignment and its good vibe. When we allow ourselves the space to visualize, all sorts of pictures and visions can be gifted to us to allow us to "see", beyond ordinary sight, what this healing actually means for us. Sometimes, symbols or pictures will "speak", either metaphorically or symbolically; sometimes, old connections are made and new understandings formed. Changing beliefs allows us to hold a different, usually higher, perspective from which to interpret our experience. When we resonate with a new belief, we can access different behavioural and thought fields. For example, if we have previously felt inadequate or unintelligent, and have shifted that to "adequate and intelligent", we may now comfortably see ourselves in situations where we are sharing our opinion, whereas, previously, we wouldn't have behaved in such a manner.

What we see and feel in the visualization are often experiences we will draw to us in the new reality we have tuned in to. Once aligned with the belief that we are adequate and intelligent, we will be much more likely now to take up a class or new interest. If we add in "capable, interesting, unique, safe, worthy, and deserving", the world becomes our oyster and this can be seen in the visualization.

Mary, from the example earlier, saw herself standing in front of her father, feeling strong and confident in herself—a totally new imagining, yet she was subsequently able to do this in reality over her Christmas break. When we resonate with healthy, expansive beliefs, using the Healing InSight method, our lives are enriched, our horizon expands, and truly, all becomes possible!

# PART THREE

# The Healing InSight
# Self-Help System

THE HEALING INSIGHT METHOD was created from guidance, intuition, knowledge, and experience gained from working with hundreds of clients in thousands of therapy hours. As my practice became full and my reputation spread, I found it increasingly difficult to turn people down when they asked for help. It is not easy to refer people because I have not found many qualified counsellors, psychotherapists, or psychologists who practise energy healing or belief work.

Not to take away from the invaluable counselling psychology training I did but, in my therapy practice, when we stumble upon an insight, problem, trauma, or block, I now always, with success, turn to energy healing or energy psychology to change it. This may involve a combination of emotional clearing (using EFT, Geneline Therapy, or reiki) and belief change (using Psych-K or Theta Healing) or the Healing InSight method. The Healing InSight method is a comprehensive energy psychology and healing system that clears emotion *and* unhelpful beliefs, realigning the user with positive beliefs and vibration.

Chapter 7

# Developing the Necessary Tools

There is nothing more important than connecting with our own authentic power, being the deliberate creator of our own reality and knowing how to harness the power of our mind for good. We all need support but are capable of helping ourselves. When we do, the universe truly supports us. It is time for each and every one of us to begin taking personal responsibility for our lives. We can stop being victims of our past and circumstance, blaming governments, the banking industry, the education system, our parents, our partners, our bodies...

Maybe we have experienced corruption, dishonesty, fraud, and betrayal in our own and others' lives, but the only way up is to take responsibility for our individual reality. This requires being personally empowered enough to realign and ask, "What can I do?" When we change our own lives, we start to inspire change within others. Gandhi's message has often been interpreted as "Be the change you want to see in the world". In an article in the *New York Times* dated 29 August 2011, Brian Morton verified Gandhi's original remark to be:

*If we could change ourselves, the tendencies in the world would also change.*
*As a man changes his own nature, so does the attitude of the world change towards him ... We need not wait to see what others do.*

Earth needs us to awaken and take responsibility more than ever for what we are focusing upon and creating. Humanity benefits as each person becomes an example of living their best, most meaningful life. In tending to our deepest needs, raising our vibration, and living from our hearts, we can be that example and share our gifts with each other. It is universal that, at a soul level, we desire to uplift, bring love, nurturing, and positivity into our world. This healing system has the potential to change your life and the lives of others as you start to explore and align with the possibilities available to you in our universe of infinite potential.

There is enough love, support, and wealth for all of us, although we sometimes believe this to be untrue and block ourselves from receiving it. Rather than living out our conditioned patterns, we can create a new energetic broadcast and experience a blessed and happy life. We are all part of life, not apart from it; part of All That Is, unique, worthy of love, and important.

If you believe you have done wrong to yourself and others, please forgive yourself and start again. God does not punish or judge; the healing flow of reiki from Source does not discriminate as to whether people are worthy or not. Our past is just experience, and we are all learning about ourselves and life, all of the time.

Using awareness and the Healing InSight method, we can stop telling our negative stories (and reliving them over and over), being empowered to choose something different—especially when we change our subconscious programming and clear our lower-vibrational emotions.

It does take commitment. We do need to become more aware of our inner and outer selves. We may need to make different choices and behave and express ourselves differently. However, it is possible—and that means for you, too! In fact, once you have changed your beliefs using the system, you will likely find that your behaviours and choices change. I have had several clients who, after using the system, told me they felt and behaved very differently in situations. The system works on universal principles and thus, it is accessible to all; you are no exception.

Here's how it works: The system is simply a protocol to follow, with directions given for how to use it best. You will need to learn some skills and ideas first, which follow in this chapter. When you reach the system itself, you'll be primed and ready to use it!

## What Drives Your Negative Beliefs

It is unusual to have a quiet mind unless well practised through meditation, mindfulness, and a lot of inner work. For many of us, the mental chatter in our minds can prevent stillness and peace, however much we seek it. We often fail to notice these intrusive thoughts, which appear in our minds like a radio broadcasting in the background. Our subconscious mind is talking to us, making sense of our limited perceptions of the world, without a consciously participating audience.

This is the "tape player" I was talking about earlier. It is constantly interpreting your reality as it receives stimulus from the environment around you. An adept pattern matcher, the subconscious mind provides your awareness with a narrative based on your past conditioning. We can have many a conversation in our mind with partners, work colleagues, children, friends, and parents, ruminating on old stories without being fully conscious of them. The internal dialogue would play out differently if we consciously viewed a situation from a higher perspective. Our subconscious mind is directing our thoughts and behaviours most of the time.

How many times have you called people names in your head? Or dismissed and judged people without understanding, compassion, or even being aware of the reasons behind their behaviour? Very often our first reaction to another can be prejudiced, as we are collectively primed and conditioned (reinforced by the daily deluge of negative and controversial news) to mistrust, perceiving others to be a hindrance or threat, so we judge, blame, and wish them out of our field of awareness. This internal dialogue can improve when we change our beliefs about others and the world. What would it be like if we changed that conditioning to find the gift and joy in each relationship and new experience?

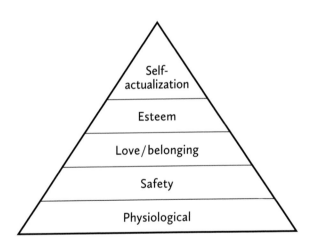

Maslow's Hierarchy of Needs

I have already talked about conditioning, about how and why that happens, so let us look at why the body is primed for threat. If we are to identify our negative self-talk, we have to be more in touch with our motivations and drives. We are physical beings and, as Maslow's Hierarchy of Needs describes, we have difficulty tending to issues of self-actualization until our basic physical needs (food, shelter, and warmth) have been met. Above these are our need for safety, followed by our relational need (not only for love but acceptance and belonging). Often, when realational needs are threatened, so too are our more basic needs, as disconnection from the tribe is associated with a lack of safety, food, and shelter; it can be a source of great fear.

For many of us in the Western world, the most basic needs for food and shelter are met. More often our unmet needs are higher up; on the levels of love, belonging, self-esteem, and even self-actualization. Unmet needs trigger us into states of emotional arousal: fear, inadequacy, and separation. As the number of people who encounter mental health problems continues to rise, the biggest epidemic in our world today is an injury of the crown chakra caused by fear, judgement, and disconnection—from ourselves, our path, and others—and this separates us from our larger, benevolent purpose.

So many of us live unconsciously, playing out stories from our subconscious mind and adopting the roles we think we should in order to be loved, accepted, and successful. This in turn puts us in a permanent state of disconnection with ourselves.

It is evident that we have collectively come to underestimate the value that happiness and joy has in our lives and believe that meeting other people's needs and expectations will somehow serve or fulfil us. There are so many people that have so much, in terms of material possessions, security, and family but are still not happy. We may have learnt that a good job, marriage, and possessions will mean success and therefore happiness, but it rarely plays out that way if we are disconnected from our true selves, or if our subconscious is still running programmes of lack and separation. There is so much to learn from our emotional body and the expressions of our subconscious mind, but our lives have become "noisy" and we have stopped listening to our "inner-tuition".

Our innate wisdom can show us how to live unlimited lives, yet we also must consider the ancestral conditioning encoded in our genes and cells, which helps inform and direct our lives unconsciously. Trauma experienced by our ancestors and their coping mechanisms are passed down to future generations. Often these ancestral threats are no longer relevant to our lives today, but they keep us vigilant, activate the HPA axis, and are a threat to our own health.

These are the prime negative or limiting beliefs to identify: ones that restrict us and keep us separate, in fear of each other or danger.

## A Closer Look at Triune Brain Theory

In his 1990 book, *The Triune Brain in Evolution*, neuroscientist Paul D. MacLean described humans as having not just one brain but three separate brains, which he believed evolved over time. Whilst the field of neurology has largely rejected the evolutionary aspect of his theory, the existence of three levels of brain function is not widely disputed.

MacLean wrote of three centres of intelligence, or "brains", which we can perceive in different areas of the body due to the associated cell and nerve receptors there, or neurons. These receptors receive information from the neuropeptides and hormones that circulate in the body in response to a trigger perceived in the environment.

The most basic is our reptilian complex, which we feel in our gut. Concerned with issues of survival, its purpose is to keep us safe. This aspect of self is on alert to protect us from previous experiences, and is particularly attuned to ancestral patterns of threat or trauma. When we feel unsafe or threatened, we often feel it in our gut. The problem is that what might previously have triggered a stress response in history has been replaced by something very different; the tiger on the horizon is now our boss if we are running late, an angry neighbour who threatens our territory, or a pan that has burnt dry, becoming a cost to our time and pocket. Our subconscious mind may be triggered by cues in our environment that may indeed have been a threat to our ancestors, many of whom have lived through war and civil unrest. But this fear may no longer be relevant to modern lives, and if we consciously calm ourselves, we may be able to rationalize that the "tiger" we are facing is no more threatening in reality than a domestic cat.

Anyone struggling with anxiety or gut-function issues likely has an overactive alert system in the body. If so, working to connect more with the limbic brain (heart) and neocortex (head) will help you master your fears.

The limbic system, or mammalian brain, is centred in our hearts. This feedback system is concerned with relationships, love, and acceptance. Fear is triggered in the limbic system when we perceive that our connection to self or others is threatened. Emotional injuries to the heart are carried in our cells, as described by Candace Pert in her 1999 book *Molecules of Emotion*. These cellular memories can create attachment issues, addictions, dependencies, avoidance of feelings, and again, undue stress.

Emotions are a helpful and valuable feedback tool and a direct pathway to our negative beliefs. The main problem when the limbic system is triggered is that we can overidentify with painful feelings and thoughts telling us negative stories of rejection or dismissal. The more we do this, the more hormones and neuropeptides are released to express this perceived reality and the worse we feel. In response, we might withdraw even more, finding ourselves stuck in a limbic brain negative feedback loop. This is very much a story of "I am not okay", which doesn't make us feel any better, whilst our minds pattern-match our environment to find any evidence that supports this limiting belief.

Many of the emotions you feel, carry, and express may not have originated with you. You have been born into an ancestral lineage, with ancestral patterning and a morphic field, and when you realize this, you can begin to heal these ancestral patterns. When you allow yourself to explore, you may find that a feeling you have been experiencing all your life may, for example, originate with your grandmother, or even several generations back. Once recognized, the feeling is released.

Heart wisdom is what helps us access higher awareness, as it serves as an interface for our spirit or higher self. It has understood our environment before our minds have had chance to perceive it. For those living in their head, to breathe into the heart and raise awareness of its bounty is a valuable practice. When we heal past hurts, forgive ourselves and others, and allow ourselves to give and receive, we help the heart—indeed, the whole body—to function optimally. When we tend to our limbic brain emotions consciously and do not allow ourselves to get submerged by them, the heart's wisdom is both nourishing and insightful.

The neocortex, the third element of the triune brain, is responsible for human intelligence. Our neocortex is our "higher brain", the seat of logic and reason and our capacity for independent thought. It has also been described by Buddhists as the "monkey mind", as through its conditioned learning and expression of unconscious "oughts" and "shoulds", it can steer us away from our enlightened path. The neocortex helps us identify negative thoughts and works best when we are consciously paying attention to what is before us, rather than living the stories of what was.

In the Manifestation process of the Healing Insight system, you will learn to check in with the gut, heart, and head for their concerns and alignment. We work at an optimum level when the gut, heart, and head are congruent, working together to achieve the best possible outcome. This is what we achieve in relation to a newly aligned belief. No one of these centres of intelligence should override another; all are important, and when in communication and congruence, inner conflicts surrounding issues in our lives fall away.

As we can see, several feedback systems influence our lives, in addition to the emotions we experience or repress on a daily basis. When you begin to pay attention to these sometimes conflicting and competing aspects of the self, you can access the stories and self-talk that have been affecting you and, likely, your ancestors for generations!

## Identifying Your Limiting Beliefs

Listen. Begin to pay attention to your self-talk. Your thoughts all have power, causing a series of biochemical changes in the body, creating vibration within and extending out of your body. Your thought vibrations affect your interaction with others. Just as other people might carry bad vibes, we may unknowingly do the same. Here's how we can clean up our internal emotional environments by changing our beliefs and inner self-talk.

First we must pay attention to our thoughts. I once had a client who had just started therapy sessions with me and was interested in belief change. I advised her to begin by simply paying attention to her own self-talk. She went off and focused on this and was surprised by what she discovered. In session she said, "I can't believe, when I allowed myself to notice the negative self-talk, just how much was there."

The reality is that it is there all the time, just outside our awareness. So we have to really listen to what it is we are telling ourselves. It is true that focusing on negative thoughts causes them to escalate; however, to empower yourself to change, you have to first know what it is you are actually telling yourself. So give yourself permission to pay attention, and write down the thoughts as you notice them. Do not judge yourself; let them go until you find the space to change them.

Our thoughts stem from beliefs about ourselves, others, and the world. Once we identify the thoughts, we can dig a little deeper to find these underlying beliefs. If you simply want to bring yourself into alignment with a positive thought, that is certainly possible and beneficial, but dig a bit deeper. I will talk you through that now.

Observing myself now, as I write, I notice the thought, "This doesn't make sense." We can use this as an example to demonstrate how to dig down to our limiting beliefs. First, I explore the thought further and as I do so, it becomes, "I can't write with the clarity that is needed to help people understand what I am trying to say", and notice that accompanying the thought is an anxious feeling. Digging deeper, I observe that having recently secured a publisher, I now have to deliver the manuscript, and my fear is that it might not be good enough or I might let down the editorial director who believed in me. Delving and listening more deeply, asking why that might be the case, the voice in my head decides that "I am a fake, a fraud, and a liar". Wow! This surprises me because I never lie and value integrity highly.

My rational mind tries to help: "As a non-scientist, explaining some of these principles may be daunting to me, but I am not pretending to be one; I am, however, equipped by my training and experience to explain my learning and understanding." Still, I don't feel better, so I muscle-test the belief that "I am a fake, a fraud, and a liar". I am amazed to discover the muscle test shows that I believe this to be true. I know the statement itself is not true, because I have always upheld the highest of standards of integrity, and that is key to my identity, as in fact I fear being misjudged or misinterpreted.

Nevertheless, somehow my subconscious mind believes it to be true. It causes me self-doubt as I write, accompanied by stress and negative emotion. So, I have some work to do to clear my limiting belief and the resulting vibration that is held in my body. I'll do this now.

> It is possible to distinguish whether your negative beliefs are "soul-level", ancestral, or from this lifetime simply by stating, "This is a soul-level belief" and muscle-testing, then stating, "This is an ancestral belief" and muscle-testing, then stating, "This is a core lifetime belief" and muscle-testing, until you get a "yes" to one of them. If you remain curious about where your belief originated, you will find out.

It turned out that it was an ancestral belief, and I was able to clear it by aligning with the positive overriding statement "I am honest, I have integrity, and I am the real deal". I did already energetically believe this to be true, but I also had a dual belief that I was "a fake, a fraud, and a liar", so I retained an "I am a fraud" emotional story and conditioning. In seeking to balance this, I remembered an old family life story from three generations ago, when a lady did live a lie, kept a family secret, and likely, felt the feelings I was now experiencing. I had been primed for that feeling and its associated beliefs and, in hindsight, have spent most of my life doing my utmost to be a "good girl" and act with integrity. Thankfully, now the belief has fallen away, I feel better, more whole and congruent, and can continue to write more freely.

This work is truly fascinating and really does start to make sense when we pay attention, ask for healing, and realign with a different reality.

The steps to follow to identify your limiting beliefs are:

1. Pay attention to your self-talk.
2. Write down any negative or limiting self-talk.
3. Expand upon that by writing it out more fully and freely.
4. Find the general statement(s) that is (are) less specific to a particular scenario but familiar to you. These are the beliefs we have generalized across conditions or situations.
5. Ask "Why do I believe that to be true?" You might find a deeper, underlying belief that is maintaining the one you have discovered.
6. Release your thoughts about this until you have time to change your beliefs.

NOTE: you may find that you also believe the positive counterpart of a negative statement, as I did. This is called a dual belief. Nevertheless, we will work with the positive statement in order to collapse the negative one you have identified. The Healing InSight method removes all it can from the path of your chosen energetic alignment.

## Following Your Emotions to Find Your Beliefs

We are vibrational beings; in fact, everything is based on energy and vibration. Vibrations, feelings, and thoughts do not occur in isolation. When we repress our emotions, our thought patterns—and hence our vibrations—are affected adversely. English people are particularly practised at this, as we can be rather stoic and reserved as a nation, especially when compared with the Italian culture, for example, where expression of emotion is acceptable. In many societies, our children are taught to suppress emotions when a parent attempts to comfort or for their own peace of mind says, "It's only a scratch", "You'll feel better soon", "Be brave", "Boys don't cry", or "I don't want to hear that." As children, we may feel that our perspective is dismissed when we are told, "It will be fine", and hold onto the wound, feeling invalidated. If you have children, practise expressing empathy towards them. When your child is hurting, acknowledge that it *is* difficult, tricky, or painful. Validate their feelings—once witnessed, feelings clear energetically. Empathy rocks!

We often feel much better having expressed and acknowledged our feelings, and this is what we now need to do with ourselves. Although this may take a bit of unwinding, begin to see your emotions as useful feedback tools, letting you know that something is wrong and causing stress or upset. Once you have received, deeply understood, and accepted the information from the emotion, it usually clears.

You can use the following technique to help clear a negative emotion, but before we proceed, I would like to talk a little about fear. Fear is a difficult, sometimes disabling emotion that tends to cause us to fight, flee, or freeze. In practice, this looks like closing down, feeling stuck, and unable to move, talk or think and deal with the issue creating the fear. This feeling may also come with very difficult sensations, such as lightness, dizziness, shaking, a racing heart, rapid breath, weak legs, a sickness in our stomach, and a disconnect from our rational logical selves.

I understand that people wish to avoid facing their fears. Fear is pretty much at the root of everything that is difficult for us. I will say that if we can begin to see it as just a feeling—"just fear"—we can begin to acknowledge that we can survive with fear (often, the underlying fear is death); that the fear will not kill or disable us if we address it.

Your soul will call you towards your fears, which may mean moving through a short and temporary period of crisis. When you can stand, however challenging, with yourself and your feelings, with love and the intent for healing, magical transformation can occur by calling home the lost and fragmented soul part of you that experienced this intense fear. We may only have two to three of these experiences in a lifetime—we may have none or many more depending on the soul's desire for evolution—but when it is upon you, so too is transformational growth.

The Healing InSight system was designed to make healing easy and usually, it is. I want you to be equipped and understand the process—that we move through fear and pain as part of our soul's evolution to become whole—so that you are ready to stand in the face of your fear, should it show itself to you. For the purpose of both unlocking feelings (of fear and otherwise) and for use of the system, we will notice that, with every feeling, there is an associated thought and belief.

So these are the steps to follow when a negative feeling shows up:

1. Allow the feeling, and become an observer of it in your body.
2. Name the feeling(s); write down what emotion(s) you are feeling.
3. Where in your body do you feel this feeling? Write this down.
4. Begin to see the emotion as energy, or a series of hormones and neuropeptides engaged in an energetic reaction.

5.  As an observer of the emotional energy, what does it look like? It may show up to you as a picture if you are particularly visual (a dagger, a ball, a tyre, for example). What shape does it have? What colour is it?

6.  How does the energy want to move and/or express itself?

7.  If you gave it permission to make a sound or speak, what would it say? This is key. What language is associated with the emotional energy? Again, write this down.

8.  Ask: Why do I feel this way? Is there an old story running in the subconscious mind that is perpetuating this emotion and pattern-matching the circumstances from your environment that trigger it? We are bringing into awareness the thoughts and beliefs that limit us, causing us to contract or play small.

    If you wish to continue working with the emotion, drift back in your mind to the earliest point in time you remember having this feeling. Bear witness to what rises into consciousness. Observe, acknowledge, and allow it to be.

9.  Once you have captured your negative thoughts, stories, beliefs, and their associated emotions, acknowledge and accept them, and let them go until you can clear the beliefs using the Healing InSight method.

Every time you find a limiting belief, resist the urge to judge it. Believing it does not mean that it is true, it just says that your subconscious mind decided it is true. This is part of your conditioned learning and, true or not, this belief does not need to keep directing your emotional responses and behaviours. Clearing each belief elevates your vibration and brings healing into your life.

Remember that your emotions are your feedback system. They are also the things that we most resist exploring or being curious about. You will get the greatest energetic shifts from the Healing InSight method if you immediately clear from your body the lower vibrations your feelings are showing you. Whenever you feel an uncomfortable feeling, explore it; find the belief, and change the way you feel! I'm cheering you on. Always harness your strength, and find your innate power and potential to transform! It is only resistance and belief that keep us stuck, and both of these we have the power to observe and release.

## Developing a Healthy Belief Statement

Occasionally, our negative self-talk rises and expresses all that is wrong, bad, or dangerous about ourselves. In Gestalt therapy theory, this voice is described as the "introjected parent". As children, we swallow the negative attributions of parents or others as if they are truths, and these then constitute our oughts and shoulds, judgements, and beliefs. We swallow beliefs such as "You have to work hard to get what you want" or "You have to achieve in order to be loved and accepted". We might hear "Your brother is the creative one" and internally reject our own creativity as a result, thereby limiting our potential.

As impressionable children, we may hear a negative judgement of us from our parents or teachers, and internalize it as absolute truth, whether it is true or not.

We can change these introjections. For the purpose of clearing these, I invite you to listen to your inner critic or negative self-talk—just as my workshop participants do, tuning into this voice a few days before the workshop. Often they are amazed by how discouraging their inner dialogue can be. The joy of identifying this limiting self-talk is that we can start to unpick it, and this is how:

1. **Flip the limiting statement into an affirming one**. For example, in place of the negative belief "I have to work hard to get what I want", substitute its opposite, "What I want comes to me easily".

Come up with the statement that feels right to you. You may want to add "My work is easy and uplifting", if you are telling yourself the story that work is hard, boring, or draining. By addressing these beliefs, you may find that your reality changes and your actual work (or your perception of it) may shift. You may realign with a new job, or even start to notice the things you like about your job rather than what brings you down.

Another example is, "I have to achieve in order to be accepted and loved" can become "I love and accept myself *un*conditionally". This leads us to point number two:

2. **Always make beliefs about the self first**. Keep your beliefs in the first person; use "I" statements.

We can change ourselves, but not others. Using the above example, if we brought ourselves into alignment with "I am loved and accepted unconditionally", we may feel better in relation to others and strive less to be perfect for them. However, if we do not love and accept *ourselves* without condition, we will likely be unable to conceive *how* others could wholly love and accept us, for how can they love us unconditionally if we cannot love our whole selves unconditionally?

This is a goal that most of us hope to achieve in our lifetimes, and changing the belief is a key step in starting to resonate with that; in being able to imagine what it would look like and how that will feel. If you did align with the belief "I am loved and accepted unconditionally", you may notice more love and acceptance from others and remove yourself from those who are not loving. However, you must change the "I" statement first. Often when we change the statement about ourselves, the belief about others (in relation to us) aligns without us needing to change it. The universe is a mirror, after all!

3. **Keep the statement in the positive**. Avoid the use of negatives, such as "do not" or "is not".

The subconscious mind does not do well with negatives. (Remember the "pink elephant on the high wire with the tutu" and the instruction not to think of this?) I had a lady in my workshop want to move away from the belief "I am alone". Her positive statement was "I am not alone". This is not affirming enough, and as the subconscious mind thinks largely in pictures, it is really programming aloneness. A better statement would be "I am connected" or "I am an important part of All That Is".

Here is another example.

When my client Stacey was growing up, the belief in her family was that her brother was the creative one. Although she loved to paint and draw, she always felt dissatisfied. Her feelings, when explored, were that she frequently "felt second best"; this translated into the work place as well. She muscle-tested the negative belief using the statement "I am uncreative" and then brought herself into alignment with the affirming statements "I am creative", and rather than "I am not unequal to my brother" she framed the belief positively, "I am, and have always been, equal to my brother". She also added the belief "I am free to create".

4. **Keep the present tense**. The statement is happening in the "now". If we want to bring ourselves into alignment with our desire to acquire some thing or feeling, we must use a belief statement that exists in the now, bringing the object or situation to us here, as if we already have it.

For example, we would align with the statement "I am healthy and well" rather than "I want to be healthy and well" or "I will be healthy and well". Another example relating to wealth is "I am abundant" rather than "I have lots of money and love coming to me". The future is always somewhere "over there" so we must make statements as if we *have* it now. A lovely example of this is from a client I worked with who was up for a second interview for a great job. She was nervous, so we explored this, and through the simple Healing InSight method, the lady aligned with the belief "I now have a wonderful new job" with the intention to clear anything that would be in the way of acquiring this wonderful new job. At first this felt uncomfortable, and the client had a desire to use the statement "I will have …", as it felt presumptuous to assume having the new job. When working through her beliefs, fear of being disappointed came up as the resistance.

The client was able to understand that this fear of disappointment was, in fact, the energy that would affect her interview and potentially create disappointment. The client released the resistance and envisioning the job she had applied for, aligned with now having a wonderful new job. As with everything, there is our plan and there is a divine plan, so we left the session with an acknowledgement that she could have "this job, *or something better*". Lo and behold, she got the wonderful new job.

It is our work to clear the limits and blocks to what we want to achieve, take action, then surrender. This work is not about manipulation or control; it is about becoming empty so that we can make good choices for our whole selves, physical and spiritual. I see it as clearing the pathway to our desire, enabling us to resonate with it, so we can manifest it in this physical existence.

5. **Try to keep your belief statement short and specific**. Of all of the belief change methods known to me, the Healing InSight method, with use of the Advanced Method and life issue protocol, is both forgiving and accommodating when our beliefs are cumbersome. Our intention and attention are working with us throughout the process.

It is helpful to keep beliefs short enough that they are clear, so that we can process and understand them adequately. It is beneficial to address both global and specific beliefs about ourselves, others, and the world, but it is important to address the specifics. For example, if we are wanting love in our lives and have brought ourselves into balance with "I love and accept myself", it is important to delve further into our loving (or lack of loving) relationships; we may discover that we feel uncomfortable receiving love. Underneath this statement may lurk a belief that we are unworthy of love. When we home in with focus and curiosity, we create the ability to see more of what is stopping this coming to us.

We may then want to align specifically with "I am, and always have been, worthy of love", and perhaps then address the specifics, "I give and receive love freely" or "Love is safe", as it is no use feeling worthy of love if we also believe that "Love is dangerous" and that we are safer if we keep it away. Again as a reminder, the advanced process will guide you to where you may have blind spots but in order to empower yourself and get the greatest benefit, following the emotion and self-talk as suggested earlier will help you to reach the specific beliefs that need realigning.

6. **Think big**. You are an aspect of the divine. You may not have had an easy time or even been the best human being to date, but it is done, and you have largely been expressing your own ancestral and cultural pain unconsciously. Forgive, understand, and free yourself. You are entitled to think big, be great, and choose safety, love, peace, connection, and abundance. You have free will and the possibility of changing your reality. To do this you must change your beliefs and practise new vibrations. What do you want to create? If all were possible, what is the reality you would like to align with?

I have seen miracles with this work, with people who were stuck for years starting to unwind, becoming conscious, and making good choices for themselves. There is much suffering in the world, but stand in it with an intention to bring consciousness into the dark spaces and transform them. Believe in possibility, knowing that love is the driving force of life that we ultimately seek. You travelled far to be here; you have a right to exist, and you are now invited on a journey to be the best version of yourself you can be. Welcome lightness into your heart as you discover your true essence. You are no greater or lesser than any other; you are a beautiful, magnificent creation.

## Considerations for a Comprehensive Belief Statement

### 1. Address beliefs about safety.

Begin statements with "It is safe for me to…", when necessary. I have had clients challenge me when I have suggested that we align with "The world is a safe place". This is particularly useful for clients who have anxiety and live with the fear of threat happening. People have questioned that the world is a safe place, and yes, undeniably bad things do happen, this is a universe of infinite possibility, and whilst danger is a possible alignment, so is safety.

If we are on the lookout for danger and have associated fears, the law of attraction suggests that we will attract a like resonance. Conversely, if we align ourselves with the belief and feeling of safety, we are more likely to find ourselves attracted to safe situations. A way to do this is to notice when you are actually safe, and enjoy that feeling rather than fearing being unsafe and putting energy behind those feelings. Referring back to Maslow's Hierarchy of Needs, we need to feel safe in order to expand, explore, and take our adventure to new levels. My recommendation is to align with and create a reality where safety prevails.

### 2. Address beliefs about possibility and capability.

Try to begin your statements with words like "It is possible for me to…" or "I can… and I do". For example, we may align with the belief "I am worthy of love", but we may not believe that it is possible for us to have love, so we would first need to align with the belief "It is possible for me to have a loving relationship in my life". With the above safety statement in place, we may wish to add "and I do", as a way of making the statement a present-tense action statement; for example, "It is safe and possible for me to speak my truth, and I do".

We may feel that we are worthy and capable of attracting love but incapable of sustaining long-term relationships. Ask the following questions of yourself, and align with statements that include these attributes:

• Do I feel capable?
• Is this possible?
• Is it safe?

## Muscle-Testing

You are made of energy, and your energy field can be strengthened or weakened. An image or thought that supports you and feels good will usually strengthen you, but your system will be weakened by a thought or image that threatens or inhibits you, which often can be felt as a disruption in the body's energy system. It is this strength, or energy disruption, that we discover in the muscle test.

There are a few ways to muscle-test. I will describe three, but I recommend teaching your body the sway test first. If you are able-bodied, this test works well with the Healing InSight method, as we will already be in the qigong standing posture for the belief alignment method.

As you begin to muscle-test, keep in mind that you are testing your subconscious mind to discover what it *believes* to be true, whether it is a limiting belief or an affirming one. Our subconscious truth will be reflected as a strengthening "yes", whilst "no" is expressed as a weakness in our energy system.

For example, I may muscle-test "yes" for the belief that "I am inadequate", and though the belief doesn't serve me, I feel physical strength because it is a truth in my subconscious mind. This belief may keep me safe from hurt or rejection, perhaps by my not trying too hard in case I fail. In the world of the subconscious, I may test "no" for "I am adequate" or "I am good enough", and if I have been running the story of inadequacy for years, this will feel safe and familiar; it may not serve me, even make me feel bad, but it has been an anchoring belief. Conversely, using the affirming statement "I am and always have been adequate" may cause me to feel weak and sad, recognizing its absence—and I would feel that in my body as a "no".

The single most important trick to muscle-testing is to release any investment in the outcome of the muscle test. Try not to anticipate the result, instead remain curious throughout. Muscle testing does work—not for discovering what is true, but what the subconscious mind has been programmed to believe is true.

If the muscle test is not already easy, it will become easy—you teach your body how to muscle-test, and it will want to engage in this process, so be patient. Your muscle test will be clearer when you are well hydrated and it can be easier to practise without shoes. Once you have learnt the qigong Wuji standing posture, and let go of some tension, the muscle test will become clearer still.

## The Sway Test

The sway test is where we invite our bodies to work rather like a pendulum. You can anticipate that your body will fall forwards or backwards once you have made a statement and come into observing the response. Practise this now:

1. Make a true statement to begin with, such as "My name is_____ (insert your name)". Stand tall, relax your body, wait, and observe. Just like magic, you will feel a push or pull, either backwards or forwards. The truth will usually push you forwards. For the purposes of the Healing InSight technique, it does not matter whether you fall forwards or backwards; you just need to know which way you fall when you are strengthened: this direction is your "yes".

2. Now make an untrue statement, such as "My name is_____ (insert a name that is not yours" and again, stand tall, become relaxed, and observe the direction of push or pull: backwards or forwards; this is your "no".

3. Say "Yes, yes, yes", and observe the direction of sway. Wait, be curious, and allow it to occur. The direction your body sways should be the same as with the truth statement in step 1, regarding your name.

4. Say "No, no, no", and observe the sway—again, wait, be curious, and allow. This sway should be in the same direction as the untrue statement about your name in step 2.

Sway Test

Once you have discovered your direction of sway for each response, you are now ready to muscle-test for the presence or absence of a belief in your subconscious mind. For example, you can make the statement "I am, and always have been, worthy of love" and observe the direction of sway. If you get your "yes" response, then your subconscious mind does believe this statement to be true. If you observe a "no" response, your subconscious mind does not believe this to be true, and you have found a belief to come into alignment with.

Hopefully you now have your "yes" and "no". See the troubleshooting section at the end of the book if there are any difficulties here.

NOTE: You may doubt yourself, or try to get in your own way. You do not have to be invested in any particular outcome. If you find that you are aligned with negative beliefs, you have the possibility of changing them, thus improving your life.

## The Finger Lock

With your non-dominant hand (e.g. left, if you are right-handed), place the finger and thumb together with reasonable pressure. With this we are creating a lock in the fingers with an energy circuit that runs through them. Our "yes", which is our subconscious truth, strengthens this lock. Our "no", which is our subconscious untruth, causes a weakness or disruption to this energy pathway.

Make your truth statement ("My name is … [insert your name]"). With your dominant hand, place the index finger inside, and try to push it sideways through the connected fingers. If the statement you are testing is subconsciously true, that is, a "yes" response, your fingers will remain locked. With a "no" response, the disruption will allow you to break through the finger lock.

Make your untrue statement ("My name is … [insert a false name]"). Again, take the index finger and try to push it through the connected fingers. If this is untrue, that is, a "no", you should be able to push your finger through the connected fingers, breaking the lock.

Make your "yes, yes, yes" statement to confirm this is your "yes".

Make your "no, no, no" statement to confirm this is your "no".

You are now ready to muscle-test for the presence or absence of a belief in your subconscious mind. The accuracy of this muscle test is dependent upon the amount of pressure that is applied by the connected fingers and the index finger against them. I tend to see the most accurate results from this muscle test when a reasonable amount of pressure is used. Because this can vary, I recommend getting to grips with the sway test, as it is easier to observe the test result rather than engaging with it. That said, some people are comfortable with this test, so if that is you, of course do what works best for you.

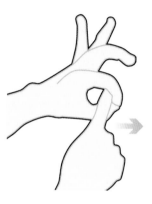

Finger Lock

## Using a Pendulum

Using a pendulum can be helpful for someone struggling with low energy and fatigue. It is important to distinguish between muscle testing for our subconscious truth and discovering our "higher" truth, that is, what our higher self knows at the soul level. This can be accessed by a pendulum, which acts as an extension of the energy system, with its vibration passing through the chain to the crystal or weight at the bottom.

Hold the pendulum chain so that it can hang over your index finger. To find out your subconscious truth, ask for the pendulum to show you your "yes". Say or think "Show me my 'yes'". The pendulum may swing forwards and backwards, or from side to side. It may circle in a clockwise direction or an anticlockwise direction. Observe and then repeat, "My name is ...[insert your name]". It should give the same response as your "yes".

Now ask the pendulum to show you your "no". Repeat "Show me my 'no'". Observe to see whether the pendulum swings or circles in one direction. This is your "no". Repeat "My name is ... [insert a false name]", and observe the direction of the pendulum. This should be the same as your "no".

Make a "yes, yes, yes" statement, and test to confirm this is your "yes". Make a "no, no, no" statement, and test to confirm this is your "no".

You are then ready to muscle-test for the presence or absence of a belief in your subconscious mind.

## Summary

Muscle testing is used throughout the Healing InSight method. The key is to be curious and let go of thought and intention. Take your time to do each muscle test, and do not rush it. We are working with the body's subtle energy systems which are affected by thought, intention, and vibration from our environment. Create a sacred space by going inward, holding the intention to develop this intuitive ability to communicate with your subtle energy body. I do have some clients who need to know how everything works and spend much time in their heads figuring it all out, which can sometimes get in the way of a muscle test. I remind them that the system wants to support them, and that their confusion or lack of clarity in the muscle-testing process is a form of resistance to letting go and becoming an observer.

To help achieve clarity in the muscle-testing process, I find that qigong practice is a wonderful way of helping people to experience emptiness, get in touch with the body, and come out of the analytical mind. Working with beliefs such as "It is safe for me to let go of control" are helpful. You can even bring yourself into alignment by saying "Muscle testing is always easy and accurate for me". Working through any blocks to muscle testing is important because it gives us new insights about our beliefs. So, take the time to set up quiet conditions to do your practice and, if in doubt, work with a practitioner until you are comfortable with the muscle test.

Please do not muscle-test your energy body to ask questions about the now or the future. This can lead to all sorts of confusion and is not an accurate way for psychically determining our future. When we muscle-test we make statements that resonate with us as truth or as untruths, statements that weaken or strengthen us. This gives us the direction and guidance we need in order to follow the protocol. It may be that, over time, you begin to tune into the subtle body and start to intuit what your response will be. That is fine, but continue to observe and confirm using your muscle test. I have intuited responses in myself and others that are different from what the muscle test shows. The mind can get in the way, but your body will delight in telling you how it is if you simply allow it the space to do so.

If your "yes" and "no" are giving you the same response, or you are struggling with this, see the questions and answers in the Resources section for further guidance. Occasionally, the body becomes stressed and the energy system gets scrambled, interfering with an accurate result. Be assured, there are ways to rebalance your system and engage with the process.

## Qigong

Qigong has helped me understand and connect with myself as an energy being. Different forms of qigong emphasize different qualities, from meditative and healing to medical and martial arts; some incorporate branches of philosophy, such as Confucianism, Taoism, and Buddhism. If you wish to understand this further, I highly recommend Kenneth Cohen's 1997 book, *The Way of Qigong*, for further enquiry, guidance, and technique. This book became a bible for me during my training, and I was honoured to eventually be able to meet and train with Kenneth. The book will provide you with deep insight, inspiration, and tools to engage with the work. In my opinion, a great teacher is one who facilitates the foundations for the qigong itself to be the teacher. This deep, experiential training was gifted to me by my dear teacher and friend Clara Apollo, who I endorse as an expert in this field in the UK. Ultimately, finding a class and teacher who facilitates your own exploration with the qi in your body will awaken you to its health-giving properties.

There are hundreds of studies that document the huge health benefits of this energy medicine, from healing diabetes and autoimmune disease to overcoming sleep disorders and balance issues. Qigong brings substantial health to the body's biofield, energy meridian flow, breath and nervous system, immune system, endocrine function, and mind. It is a practice of engaging the mind and body wholeheartedly, using gentle distinct movements and standing, walking, and seated meditations to allow ourselves to empty, observe, and move energy for health, relaxation, and vitality. This can feel challenging for beginners of qigong, who may be used to the mind's drive to be in action or to manipulate reality rather than observe. We are largely *doers* rather than *beings*, and are conditioned through cause and effect, exemplified by the common belief "We must work hard in order to achieve".

When you first experience qigong, you may find discomfort as you begin to notice where your stresses and tensions are. Chances are that you already have some awareness, but this can be amplified when the rest of the body begins to relax. Qigong can truly be an antidote to stresses, enabling them to unwind and be cleared from the body's energy field and mind, thus releasing tension patterns built up in the physical body.

Qigong movements that help to cultivate energy and bring healing to the body have been found in Taoyin illustrations dating back to 168BC. The practice is largely influenced by Taoism, the early Chinese spiritual philosophy that teaches simplicity, our innate connection to the cosmos, and principles for living that enable this connection to both radiate into and reflect the inner worlds of our mind, body, and spirit. With deep qigong practice, we are one with the cosmos, as it is one with us. The Tao Te Ching, written by the legendary spiritual teacher Lao Tzu, is classic literature that speaks of the wisdom beyond the knowing mind. Qigong practice reflects the philosophy depicted in that time. The principle movements in the Healing InSight method will help you to connect with yourself, the earth, and the heavens, and move into a realignment process.

It is a sacred art and practice where, with dedication, we can have the opportunity to nurture our being towards its fullest potential. Ultimately, this is through a practice of surrender and engagement, of emptying and activating, and of harmonizing the aspects of duality in our consciousness. Qigong is a gift in itself, which connects us to our internal treasures, from which life begins to shape itself. It helps direct our higher truth and knowing towards a righteous path, a coming back to ourselves, and a harnessing of our qi in the soul's journey. No wonder it was shown to me to be part of the magic in the Healing InSight method! There are more exercises for you to play with in the Resources section, but the following information covers all you need to experience in order to use the method.

## Wuji – Empty Energy

Wuji is the standing posture that we do the majority of movement from in qigong. It is a standing posture that represents limitlessness, whereby the physical body becomes a conduit for the opposing forces of heaven and earth, bringing these forces into balance, thereby resolving and transcending issues of duality. In Wuji, the body is relaxed yet active, is balanced and rooted. Standing in Wuji is highly beneficial, both to release body tension and to raise awareness of your whole self. This is a practice of mindfulness, as we become observers of our whole being. If you are unable to stand, practise this posture seated in a chair that is of a height where you can place your feet on the ground and sit without leaning on the back of the chair. Wear flat shoes to help your posture or bare feet, as we are going to connect with the earth energies and activate our kidney meridian.

1. Place your feet parallel, shoulder width apart. Allow your feet to spread and imagine them rooting down. Settle your body weight down through the centre of the balls of the feet (known as the bubbling spring or kidney point) into the earth.

2. Soften your knees and ankles so that they are slightly bent and unlocked, to help this sense of rooting down and to allow the energy to flow.

3. Begin to relax the muscles in the legs, trusting the skeletal structure to support you. Allow the joints to soften, with the muscles active enough to hold you up but still relaxed.

4. Relax your hip joints and the area where the tops of the legs meet the trunk of the body, and start to unwind and correct the posture of the pelvis (known as the *kua*). Allow the pelvis to drop, imagining it open and spacious, like a cradle or hanging basket, and position it so that it hangs neutrally. This will open up the *kua*, the *ming men* (back door to the *dan tian*), and help release the hips.

5. Maintain this sense of downward connection in the legs through the feet and into the earth by surrendering to gravity; in doing so, the Yin energy of the earth will come to meet you, and rise through the "bubbling spring" points in balls of the feet. From the coccyx up, bring your awareness up along the length of your spine, through all of its natural curves. Create a sense of space through each vertebra as the energy rises through the neck to the top of the crown. Visualize the muscles of the neck and back opening and lengthening.

6. Allow your head to feel like it is suspended by an imaginary golden thread from above the crown, then as you sense the space above your head, align this so that the back of your neck is lengthened. Allow your jaw to release, which may bring the chin slightly closer to the chest. Take some time to do this, allowing tensions to unwind, until the head becomes free, as if suspended and balanced on the top of the spine.

7. Place the tip of the tongue on the roof of the mouth in order to connect the energetic pathway of the small heavenly circuit. This is a superhighway meridian, which runs up the spine, along the top of the head, drops down the front of the body, and connects under the perineum, forming a circuit.

8. Relax your shoulders, creating a little space underneath the armpits to aid energy flow. Allow this relaxation to spread down through the arms and slightly extended fingers until they are actively relaxed. Much energy travels down through the arms and hands in qigong, and holding the arms lightly enables a clearer energy flow.

9. Relax your stomach muscles. This enables the diaphragm to engage, and breathing can become easier. The breath will self-regulate when you give it the conditions to do so. Now bring in the intention for your breath to slow down. Without changing your breath in any way, just have the intention (tell it) to slow down.

10. Calm your mind. Again, have the intention for your mind to calm. As you connect with the vital forces of heaven through the crown of the head and the earth through the feet and begin to sense and observe your body through a different lens, your mind will quieten. Begin to observe your internal world and experience. The internal critic may show up, and if it does, welcome it in to receive and witness the qi flow; it will soon be grateful to surrender!

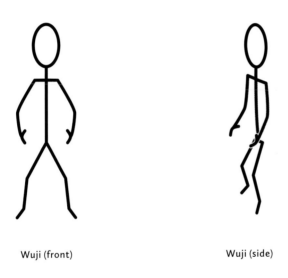

Wuji (front)                    Wuji (side)

When you take the time to connect deeply with yourself, with the intention of bringing about positive change, you will gain internal knowledge and healing that are, in my opinion, your greatest gift to yourself. This is an honouring of you, of your own alchemical process, and a practice of self-love. The world will wait and will surely benefit from you engaging in your own process of self-healing and discovery.

## The Bubbling Spring

The bubbling spring is the point to be aware of when you come into your Wuji stance. It is located in the centre of the balls of the feet, at the acupuncture point "kidney 1", through which the water element of the body connects with the rising energy of Gaia, our living, breathing, beautiful, resourceful Earth. As you enter Wuji, setting up this energy pathway with intention in your mind, it is like plugging your phone in to charge its battery. Everything below you is made of molecules and peptides, energy that is connected all the way to the earth. You, of course, will get a beautiful connection by simply standing on the earth's surface, but activating the bubbling spring point and intending this connection is enough for the energy pathways to open and flow.

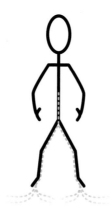

"Kidney 1" acupuncture point

The Bubbling Spring

## Introducing the Lower Dan Tian

The lower *dan tian* (of Chinese origin) is sometimes referred to as the *hara* (Japanese origin) in other energy healing modalities. It is a large energy centre, or field, situated just below your navel and a few inches inside the body. Its energy field, when strong, will resonate all the way around you and be palpable as a sphere in front of your body. By bringing your hands out in front of the lower *dan tian*, with your palms facing it, you will begin to gather and increase energy flow here. When standing in Wuji and relaxing the belly by allowing it to relax and hang, we can begin "belly breathing", which brings energy into the lower *dan tian*. This enables the body to be resourced and replenished with the life force we refer to as qi.

The *dan tian* is often described as an ocean of energy, your deepest resource. It is no surprise to me that this is the point that new life inhabits, for it is where the foetus grows, receiving qi and nourishment from the umbilical cord of a mother. When the lower *dan tian* is replenished, energy flow rises to the middle *dan tian* at the heart and then the upper *dan tian* at the third eye. These are referred to as the three treasures. For the purpose of the Healing InSight method, we work with and observe the lower *dan tian*. If energy wishes to travel up, it will do so as long as we remain relaxed.

## Grounding Posture

From our Wuji position, we can bring our palms to face the earth to the sides of our legs, roughly level with the groin. In this way, we connect with the downward flow of the gallbladder meridian and can use this pathway to ground and earth us. It brings our focus downward, and can settle any disruptive or uncomfortable energy sensations as you are working through the method. This posture is stabilizing and reassuring.

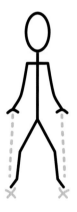

Grounding posture

We will use this pose to ground and plant the new belief and vibration once aligned with in the method, beneath your feet in the Earth star chakra. As you practise this, you may notice your legs becoming heavier, more "planted", and your awareness and energy will sink, as if providing you with a strong foundation from which to step forward.

## The Infinity Harmonizing Movement

When I had my full list of channelled beliefs, and was considering how the therapy system would harness the belief change, I had a flash of insight that appeared in the form of an infinity symbol. I have known and loved using this symbol in my qigong practice to bring balance and harmony to my body and mind, so I paid attention for what was to follow. I very quickly saw the qigong movement, the rod of light passing through my central channel from heaven to earth and earth to heaven, and saw that we would need to activate both hemispheres of the brain whilst repeating a belief.

I anchored into the earth through my imaginary energy roots, sunk into the Wuji pose, and performed the infinity harmonizing movement. I repeated a belief that I knew was not true, "I am a millionaire," and paid attention to my right hand whilst repeating this belief. When I did this, I felt energy starting to move through my body and, sure enough, the right hemisphere of my brain began to have sensations: it became active in relation to this belief. I then did the same with the left hand, and activated the left hemisphere. When playing with this technique with my husband, a few friends, and some willing long-term clients, the rest of the technique became evident, in terms of what was needed for lasting change. The Advanced Method, utilizing all the beliefs in a process of clearing the layers of the subconscious onion, as it were, then became visible to me.

The magic of the system lies in this ancient and powerful symbol. Otherwise known as the lemniscate, the infinity symbol has been used throughout time and across cultures, seen on the headbands of ancient Egyptian pharaohs, in the staff of Hermes, and representing kundalini energy in the Indian culture (Heider-Rauter 2018). It weaves its way up the caduceus medical symbol, which was once used to represent the two entwined cobras of the healer Goddess Isis. The shape of this symbol is found in the structure of our genes, our cells, and our DNA. Our body knows this pattern. I have found myself drawing it out with my hands, repeatedly, in healing sessions with clients over an area of the body that feels a little stuck. It represents the "immeasurable and the boundless", bringing balance to opposing forces, finding the centrepoint of harmony between the Yin and Yang.

It enables the transcendence of opposing forces: the initial energy of creation being more powerful than the dance of the opposites. It seems to bring movement and harmony into something that has previously been stuck or stagnant, as if the "dance-off" of opposites begins to find a mutually beneficial song that both forces can dance to in unison. I'm reminded again that our bodies know how to heal, when we allow for movement, one of the conditions necessary for healing.

I find it interesting that this symbol, when upright, constitutes the number eight. This is a powerful number in its own right. As Barbara Heider-Rauter describes in her 2018 book, *The Power of the Infinity Symbol*, eight is the number of the initiate. In spiritual terms, this is the number of those who have transcended the seven stages of awakening. Eight is the number of people required for small groups to perform miracles, according to intention expert Lynn McTaggart in her 2017 book, *The Power of Eight*. This is also the number associated with both Thoth and Isis, the deities present on the Healing InSight crown chakra card. Thoth being the bridge between worlds and the harmonizer of opposing good and bad forces; the keeper of harmony, justice, and balance; able to stand in the centrepoint of unity and oneness with God and with All That Is. I had not realized the association of the infinity symbol and the number "8" with Thoth until now, and see it as fitting that he, together with Isis, the magician and healing medicine woman of birth and creation, should govern the chakra card deck. May both they and the lemniscate bring healing, balance, and harmony to all who use it.

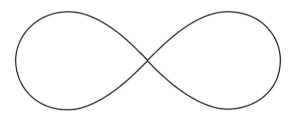

The Lemniscate

The Yin–Yang symbol

The infinity harmonizing movement is beneficial for bringing balance to the body. As with the Yin-Yang symbol, it reflects a dance of opposites in perfect balance. As well as having both masculine and feminine aspects within ourselves, we also have our physical earthly bodies and our spiritual soul selves.

This movement enables us to connect with all aspects of the self, bringing balance and harmony to these different parts of our whole. The infinity harmonizing movement, as used in the method, seems to allow us to harmonize both the subconscious and conscious mind with our chosen new belief (which means also clearing away the opposing vibration that prevents this harmonizing from occurring).

Our higher self knows that we are perfect, worthy, and deserving, and will not support you in aligning with anything that is not for your highest good (more on this later). Let us now learn the movement that will be performed throughout the aligning process. You can follow the steps in the illustrations on the next page:

1. Standing in Wuji, bring your hands in front of the lower *dan tian* with your palms facing each other.
2. Following the shape of the infinity symbol, or sidewards figure of eight, turn both palms up to face the heavens, connecting with the Yang *qi*.
3. Drop the palms down and out along the diagonal line, with palms still facing up.
4. Lift the hands slightly, and moving outward, turn the palms to face each other again, this time on the outward periphery of the infinity symbol.
5. Raise the hands further, moving them inwards and turning the palms to face the earth, connecting with the Yin *qi*.
6. Drop the palms down and inward along the diagonal line, palms still facing down.
7. Move inward further and slightly upward, as you turn the palms to face each other, as you did at the beginning.
8. Continue this movement, following the shape and flow of the infinity symbol, palms facing the heavens as you move outwards and palms facing the earth as you move inwards.

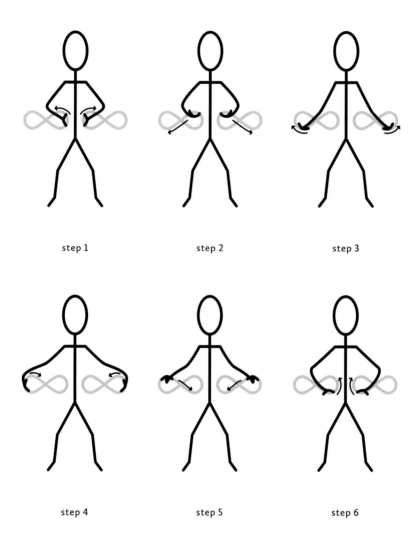

step 1          step 2          step 3

step 4          step 5          step 6

The Infinity Harmonizing Movement

This may seem complicated at first, but it is a movement your body knows innately. Take your time to feel into it. The more you practise, the more this can become muscle memory, enabling you to focus on the beliefs you intend to align with in the Healing InSight method. If you struggle with this movement, practise it with me in the videos on my website and refer to the Q&A in the Resources section.

## Becoming Whole-Brained

The two hemispheres of the brain operate with different functions. The left hemisphere is concerned largely with logic and reason; it connects us to space and time and is responsible for detail and order. The right hemisphere governs our creative and expansive self, operating outside of space and time. It is visual rather than linguistic and is concerned with the whole, the group, our ability to empathize rather than focus on our ego and self.

Neuroscientist Jill Bolte Taylor suffered a stroke in the left hemisphere of her brain in 2007, which allowed her to experience nirvana, or bliss, and gave the scientific community insight into the functions of the mind and brain. Her TED Talk is an interesting watch.

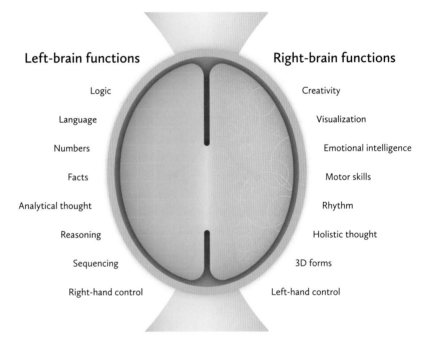

Brain hemisphere functions

The Healing InSight method utilizes whole-brain activation. When we achieve a whole-brain state, the two hemispheres of the brain are communicating, the *corpus callosum*—the band of nerve fibres joining the hemispheres, dubbed the "brain-bridge"—allows the speedy transfer of information between the left and right hemisphere and more efficient brain function, achieving a symmetrical bilateral brainwave pattern (Fannin et al. 2012).

Emotion and stress affect brain function. When we experience stress, brainwave patterns change, the amygdala fires unhelpful signals of fear and worry, and it is hard to access our logical brains and think rationally. Generally, neuroscience suggests that the right hemisphere of the brain perceives negative emotions and the left hemisphere of the brain rationalizes them. Research shows that the left hemisphere of the brain does respond to emotional stimulus, perhaps processing positive emotions (Killgore et al. 2007). We don't know enough about what happens in the brain when we experience belief change. It would make for a very interesting scientific study to observe the brainwave activity of belief change with the Healing InSight method! We do know, however, that in order to become fully congruent with the belief, the whole brain—both the left and the right hemispheres—need to be communicating; in flow and coherence with each other in relation to the belief statement you are writing into the subconscious mind. From this whole-brain state, all functions of the left and right hemispheres are able to support alignment with the new belief statement, which is felt throughout the body as sensory feedback.

As noted, the Healing InSight method uses ancient qigong techniques and healer insight to activate and align each hemisphere of the brain with the new desired belief, creating coherence within the whole body-mind, literally writing over the opposing limiting belief.

My work with clients seeking to install new beliefs using the Healing Insight method suggests a correlation between disruptions or distortions in each hemisphere of the brain in relation to limiting subconscious beliefs and their associated emotional experiences. No matter where the distortion lies, in practice there is resistance, followed by a releasing and a realignment process that occurs with respect to both hemispheres of the brain as they are activating in accordance with the new belief. Resonance with the new belief seems to build at the moment when both hemispheres of the brain are activated and a coherent whole-brain state in relation to this belief is achieved.

Some people may be one-hemisphere dominant and need help activating the other hemisphere of the brain. Please see the Q&A section in the Resources section for help if this is happening for you. It may be that you are always led by your emotions (right-brain dominant), or always turn to your head to figure things out and avoid emotions at all cost (left-brain dominant). Balance is always the best way forward. Daily qigong activities and an awareness of your process—and willingness to challenge or change it—will help you to find balance here. Aligning with the belief "I have balance in my brain and life" may help with this!

In order to activate each hemisphere of the brain in accordance with the belief, we perform the infinity harmonizing movement and focus upon each hand in turn—whilst repeating the desired affirming belief statement—until the hemisphere of the brain starts to experience sensation. This may be heaviness, tingling, or light—in essence, energy moving. The combination of Wuji, intention, movement, and focus on the hand whilst repeating the belief enables this activation process.

NOTE: It is not necessary to look at the hand in question—merely become aware of it in your mind.

Whole Brain Activation and Congruence

You are now ready to learn the Healing InSight Simple Belief Realignment method, and I am delighted to share this with you!

Chapter 8

# The Simple Belief
# Realignment Method

In the preceding chapter, we learnt how to identify our negative beliefs, giving us an opportunity to shift our vibration and realign with healthier, happier, more supportive beliefs. This positively impacts our emotions, behavioural choices, and lives in general. We have taught our body how to muscle-test, and are aware of what our "yes" and "no" look like. We practised the Wuji standing posture, grounding us and setting us up as an empty vessel between heaven and earth, ready for energy realignment. We have also learnt the infinity harmonizing movement which brings balance and harmony to our energy body and, thereafter, our physical body.

Now it is time to learn the simple belief realignment method. There are seven main steps to the protocol, which are as follows:

1. Permission Statements
2. Which Hemisphere to Activate First
3. The Movement
4. Left and Right Brain Activation & Congruence
5. Belief Embodiment Visualization
6. Grounding It and Planting the New Belief
7. Test It.

An easy-to-follow table at the end of this chapter recaps the steps once you have learnt the protocol.

## STEP 1: Permission Statements

This step is really about getting every part of you on board with making this shift; that is, getting the conscious self, including the protective ego, working together with your higher self and your subconscious mind.

Once you have acknowledged that your whole self is ready to make this belief change, you will use the muscle test that you learnt earlier to check that what you are about to change is indeed for your highest and best good.

NOTE: If it is not for your highest good that the belief statement you have selected changes, it means that either you need a little more conscious awareness about your resistance or it is not the right time or the right belief to do the protocol. Perhaps you need to change your belief statement from, for example, "I am worthy of a loving relationship" to "It is safe for me to have a loving relationship".

Issues involving fear and safety can play a large part in keeping us stuck, so you may need to rethink your belief statement to support your fears around change and letting go of beliefs that limit but protect you. The Advanced Method and Healing InSight belief pages can help you navigate through this resistance, and you will learn more about this in the next chapter.

There are four parts to follow in this step.

**Test Your Beliefs**

Muscle-test your unhelpful belief (the limiting belief you would like to change), then your new affirming desired belief. Hold the intention here that the negative belief will fall away as you align with the positive. We test the unhelpful belief and then the desired belief so that the mind-body-spirit knows what we intend to do.

For example, if I want to align with the belief that I am worthy of love, I first make the opposite statement, "I am unworthy of love", and muscle-test my subconscious mind to discover the absence or presence of this belief. The answer will reveal whether or not I currently believe this statement to be true. I also then make the statement "I am worthy of love", then test whether or not I currently believe this to be true.

We will also test the two beliefs after the process is complete for confirmation of the realignment and to also ensure that the negative belief has fallen away. We are anticipating here that you will have a "yes" muscle-test response to the unhelpful belief and a "no" to the desired belief. Remember: This does not mean that it is true but that the subconscious mind *believes* it to be true.

Should you believe both the positive and negative statements to be true, your mental program has both running and you can go ahead and align with the desired belief, knowing that this process is about clearing away the unhelpful belief and its associated vibration.

### Permission for Highest and Best Good

STATE: "It is for my highest and best good to align with this belief now", then muscle-test. If the test result is "yes", continue to the next step.

### Permission to Align on All Levels

STATE: "I give my full permission to align on all levels with this belief now", then muscle-test.

NOTE: We include the words "on all levels" to allow the inclusion of beliefs from our lifetime, our ancestors, and from the soul level.

If you get "no" to either of your permission statements, explore why. Is there any reason to hold onto this belief? For example, are there hidden gains? This is often something that just needs to be brought into consciousness. Once you are aware of it, muscle-test for permission again. If you get a repeat "no", rethink your belief statement.

### Discover Which Method to Use

STATE: "It is for my highest and best good to use the Simple Method", then muscle-test. If "yes", continue the steps here to align using the Simple Method. If "no", state, "It is for my highest and best good to use the Advanced Method" and test. If you then get a "yes", skip forward to use the Advanced Method, which is laid out in the next chapter. If this is required at your first attempt at the process, familiarize yourself with the Simple Method first, anyway, as it is used in the Advanced Method. We are going to look at the Simple Method now.

If tests indicate that you are not ready to align with a desired belief, several things may be at play. It's important to explore these, as resistance to change is usually the result of certain ideas or beliefs, frequently concerning issues of safety. I recommend the following steps:

- Become aware of any reason you may not wish to align.
- Ask: What would the consequence of believing this be?
  Are there any other negative beliefs there that need shifting first?
- You might need to change the language of the belief by adding:
  "It is safe for me to..." or "I am able to..."

## STEP 2: Which Hemisphere to Activate First

In the following procedure, we are going to activate each hemisphere of the brain in relation to our desired belief. I have found that it is easier to muscle-test which hemisphere we need to activate first as there is often more resistance to the belief in one hemisphere than the other. Ask and see what your energy system requires to make the process easier.

**Muscle-Test Which Hemisphere to Activate First**

STATE: "I need to activate the left hemisphere first", and muscle-test. If "yes", remember that you will need to perform the movements in step 4 with your left side first, and then your right side. If "no", remember that you will need to perform the movements in step 4 with your right side first, and then your left side.

## STEP 3: The Movement

We will use the infinity harmonizing movement throughout the entire realignment process. Practise it to develop the muscle memory, and you won't have to think about the movement after a short while.

**Stand in Wuji Posture**

Align your body using the Wuji posture. Feet apart, knees soft and open, hips neutral, shoulders relaxed, breath relaxed, you are coming into being an empty vessel between the energies of heaven and earth so that these can flow through you to assist in your energy realignment. Be sure to plant your feet on the floor/earth and rise through your spine to the crown of the head and beyond. For more information, review the previous chapter of the book.

Wuji (front)                    Wuji (side)

**The Infinity Harmonizing Movement**

Perform the infinity harmonizing movement over the lower *dan tian* (the area just below the navel). This is the sidewards figure of eight with palms turning at each end to face the heavens or the earth. (See description on p. 132 and my website for video links, if help is needed with the movement.)

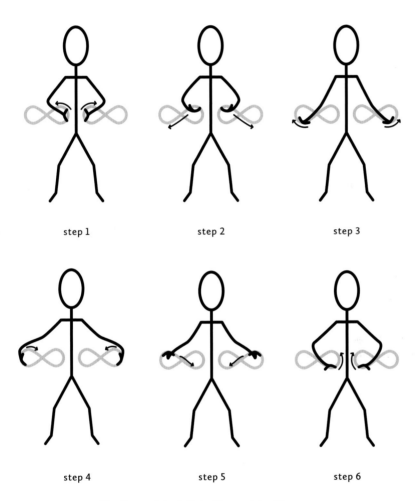

step 1       step 2       step 3

step 4       step 5       step 6

The Steps of the Infinity Harmonizing Movement

## STEP 4: Left and Right Brain Activation and Congruence

This process will activate the hemispheres of the brain in relation to the new belief you are repeating. For some people, the activation is obvious; for others, it is more subtle. It is often experienced as tingling, heat, heaviness, or lightness in the hemisphere you are working on; sometimes, it is accompanied by clarity. You will focus on one hand, and maintain an awareness of sensation in that hemisphere, too. Very occasionally, the other hemisphere will activate first. This is fine, but continue with the process, repeating your statement until the intended hemisphere activates. We then repeat this process, focusing on the other hand and hemisphere until the second hemisphere is activated. Both hemispheres will need to activate in order to achieve whole brain coherence in relation to your new belief.

**Activate the First Hemisphere**

Bring your awareness and attention to the energy in your left hand (or whichever hand should be first, as discovered in step 2). Perform the movement, and repeat your belief, until the same (left or right) hemisphere of the brain feels activated.

**Activate the Second Hemisphere**

Bring your awareness and attention to the energy in your right hand (or whichever hand is not first). Perform the movement, and repeat your belief, until the same (left or right) hemisphere of the brain feels activated.

**Whole-Brain and Whole-Body Awareness**

Hold both hemispheres of the brain in whole-body awareness, simply as an observer, softening, continuing to repeat the belief, as you witness the sensation of release and/or belief alignment. Wait until you are sure that the hemisphere has activated.

Whole-Brain Activation and Congruence

## STEP 5: Belief Embodiment Visualization

Once you are aware of the hemispheric activation and alignment, you can then use mental imagery to connect with this belief. Visualizing in this way will help you to develop a resonance with the new belief. In this process, we are allowing and observing, rather than creating intentionally with our minds.

Of course, our minds do create, but let the vision come to you, and as you do this, allow the feeling to expand and be felt in your body. The more you practise this, the more your intuition will work with and speak to you, showing you what the belief means for you, going forward. You may see a useful vision that you wish to remember to help attune you to this new vibration when desired.

### Bring Your Hands Towards Your Body

When the hemispheres are activated and the belief alignment feels congruent, bring the hands towards the body, wherever they wish to land (the heart and the gut may be helpful and feel supportive), and close your eyes.

### Visualize and Feel the Vibration of the New Belief

Take as long as you need, or what you sense to be just over a minute (the magic law of attraction timeframe is 68 seconds) to connect with what your belief now feels like in your body. Allow a vision to come to mind that represents you with this new belief and its associated possibilities in your life.

Belief Embodiment Visualization

Let your imagination run with it! This process gives you an opportunity to start to resonate with a new vibration, so if it is heading that way, make it as big, bright, and shiny as you can. Your mental imagery may evolve as the energy moves and changes. Stay with it, and be curious, accepting, and observing. It is the perfect place for your higher awareness to communicate with you. It is true that if you can imagine it, it is possible; so take your time to work with the law of attraction, basking and resonating in the vibration you would like to experience more of in your life. Give yourself permission to be brilliant and magnificent, safe and loved, free and connected, and whole.

If you find this process tricky, simply follow whatever thought, picture, or feeling comes into your awareness, and you will find that this should resonate well with the new belief. If it does not feel good, then try going back to repeating the belief and activating the hemispheres more fully. In my experience, when we align with a positive belief we can access that good feeling. If you still can't connect to a good feeling, observe what you are being shown; you may be steered towards a "yes, but. . .", showing that there is another belief that needs to be cleared. Follow your intuition and just make note of your observations for now. You may need to go on to do the manifestation process, which will then enable a full resonance.

Follow the steps, and if need be, you can come back to the "yes, but" once this process is complete. You are wise and you do know what you need, just listen and honour your own process.

## STEP 6: Grounding and Planting the New Belief

Once you have the new vibration, ground it. Plant the belief underneath your feet (into the Earth Star Portal chakra) as if you were planting a seed ready to blossom and grow. You will get a sense of energy "landing" and sinking to the earth. Your feet and perhaps legs will start to feel connected to the earth, feeling more solid, ready to step forward into the rest of your day. Without doing this we can be left feeling a little top-heavy and unbalanced, so take your time completing this important step.

### Send the Belief to the Earth

Place your hands at the sides of your hips, palms facing the earth, soften your knees and send the belief (plus any excess energy) down the legs, planting it into the earth beneath your feet.

**Remain Until the Belief and Energy Are Grounded**

Remain until you sense that the belief has landed and you feel grounded, ready to get on with your day.

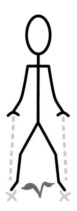

Grounding and Planting

NOTE: At any time during the procedure, if you feel discomfort or excess uncomfortable energy, you can stop and use the aforementioned grounding posture to settle yourself and clear excess energy before continuing. I have witnessed clients clearing quite traumatic memories, or noticing heaviness and the feeling of fear in them surface to be cleared. Trust the process and your fundamental wellbeing. Go at your own pace, taking breaks if you want to ground at any stage of the process. You do not have to "push through"; commit yourself to seeing it through, and let it be easy.

## STEP 7: Test It

**Confirm the Presence of Your Desired Belief**

Make your desired belief statement, and muscle-test to confirm its presence.

**Confirm (If Present) the Absence of the Unhelpful Belief**

Make your unhelpful belief statement, and muscle-test to confirm the absence of the unhelpful belief. If both are "yes", it is so. Well done! Allow yourself the relief and joy of a new possibility. This is the most likely outcome. In a moment we will muscle-test to confirm whether you need to do the manifestation process for this belief (found in Chapter 10). It is not always necessary—your muscle test will inform you if it needs to be done. The manifestation process allows for whole-body coherence with the new belief.

In the unlikely event that the belief has not aligned, ask whether you need to do the process again by stating: "I need to realign with this belief now", and muscle-test. If "yes", repeat the process.

If "no", make the statement: "There is another belief to align with", and muscle-test that. This may be a belief that you became aware of earlier (your "yes, but…"), or a belief from the Healing InSight belief pages (read Chapter 9 for help with this). Once you are aware of this, go ahead and work through the protocol again. Your original belief should then have aligned.

### The Manifestation Process for Whole-Body Coherence

Finally, occasionally our three centres of intelligence—the head, heart, and gut—need a little help in order to integrate change. If required, the following process will allow you to establish whole-body coherence with the new belief, helping you to manifest it in your reality.

Muscle-test the statement "I need to do the manifestation process in relation to this belief". If "yes", continue to Chapter 10. If "no", this is not necessary, and your process is complete.

This is the end of this stage of the Healing InSight method. Are you finding this exciting? Belief change and energy realignment are like opening new doors, so don't be afraid to step through them when they appear in front of you. Change is good! Joy is your natural state of being. Use the system to help you to clear your fears and limits, specific and global. Keep a note of what you have changed and, in time, you will see how this manifests in your life. It can also be helpful as a means of assessing whether any other aspects relating to this belief need addressing, such as "safe to … possible to … worthy of…".

You are now ready to move on to learn the Advanced Belief Realignment method.

# Chapter 9

# The Advanced Belief Realignment Method

The Advanced Method was created to help us delve deeper into our unconscious minds and subconscious programming. Beliefs can reinforce or support one another, layering on top of each other. Our minds and conditioning processes are indeed complex.

In the Advanced Method we will work with the belief pages and, through a process of discovery, muscle-test to discover which chakras are impeded by which beliefs (and their associated feelings). These chakra beliefs are framed in the positive, and you may find through muscle testing that you may well have an opposite (negative) belief that is getting in the way of your desired alignment. These are what I call Priority Beliefs. We will identify and change these priority beliefs, one at a time until we are completely aligned with our initial desired belief, identifying and peeling away the layers as we go.

The process itself is a little more complex, but you will get the hang of it quickly as you follow the protocol. There are plenty of video clips you can watch to help you see it in action (see the Resources section).

The key to using the Advanced Method is curiosity. Simply be curious and open to what you may discover. Our brain likes to pattern-match to make sense of what we are experiencing, so we might have our own ideas about what is at the bottom of an issue. Suspend your judgements, and engage your observer curiosity to help you move through the muscle-testing process smoothly.

During the process, it is common for people to get insights into where a particular belief came from (or how it has been played out), with visions of people, circumstances, or past experiences. You don't have to do anything with these. They are coming into your conscious awareness to be resolved and healed with the method. Once brought into awareness, notice and acknowledge the memory or insight, breathe, and stay focused on the process. You may find that the picture in your mind changes, or you may perceive the event differently or from a higher perspective, once aligned with your belief. Suspending judgement and allowing are important here, as with any energy work.

REMEMBER: resistance arises so that it can be released. Permit the breath to flow, and allow the body and muscles to soften. Release may come in the form of tears or yawning. These are usually short lived: once the resistance holding the conditioning in place is cleared, the belief and the emotion will clear. Stay focused on the movement, the hand (hemisphere activation), and—importantly—on repeating the belief.

So, are you ready to play?

Once you have established that it is for your highest and best good to use the Advanced Method (using the Simple Method Enquiry in Step 1 of the previous chapter), turn to the Advanced Method's process of discovery. You will also need the Chakra Aspect Chart and Chakra Belief Chart (see Chapter 12) or the app or card deck on hand to help with the process of discovery.

## STEP 1: The Process of Discovery

We will now discover which priority belief(s) you need to align with by first discovering which chakra the beliefs are in. Muscle-test this as follows:

### Find Which Chakra the Priority Beliefs Are In

STATE: "The priority beliefs for me to align with are in the root chakra", and muscle-test.

If "yes", go forward to the step below entitled "Find Which Aspect of This Chakra the Priority Beliefs Are In".

If "no", state: "The priority beliefs for me to align with are in the sacral chakra", and muscle-test. Keep making the statement with each chakra and until you find your "yes":

- "solar plexus chakra"
- "heart chakra"
- "throat chakra"
- "third eye chakra"
- "crown chakra".

Once you have found your "yes", do not muscle-test the other chakras, but as above, simply move on to the section below entitled "Find Which Aspect of This Chakra the Priority Beliefs Are In".

We will now discover which priority belief(s) you need to align with by discovering which aspect the beliefs are contained in.

There are seven aspects per chakra. These aspects are listed for ease in the "Chakra Aspects Chart" at the beginning of Chapter 12 (bookmark this, so that it is readily available as you work through the advanced process). The aspects are also the title headings on the Chakra Beliefs Chart(s) and on each Chakra Aspect Card, which can also be used in the discovery process (see Chapter 12, or use the Healing InSight app or card deck).

If there is more than one aspect that needs to be worked with, it will show up again later in the process. For now, we are looking for one priority aspect. You do not have to keep muscle-testing through the other aspects of the chosen chakra.

### Find Which Aspect of This Chakra the Priority Beliefs Are In

STATE: "The priority aspect for me to align with is [name aspect one]", and muscle-test. If, for example, your muscle test selected the root chakra, aspect one would be Grounding.

If "yes", this is the priority aspect you will work with now. If "no", keep muscle-testing through the seven aspects in the Chakra Aspect Chart, until you have found your "yes".

Once the aspect within the chakra has been discovered, we go on to discover which belief(s) within this aspect are the priority beliefs to align with. It may not be necessary to align with all four beliefs here, so we muscle-test to discover which beliefs to align with. The beliefs are numbered in order of their appearance in the chart or cards. (The fourth belief is the short "I" statement to the top right of the beliefs in the chart, or at the bottom of the card in the card deck.)

### Find Which of the Four Beliefs Are Priority

You may need to align with beliefs one, two, three, and/or four on that aspect, which means keep muscle-testing through numbers one to four, to ascertain which ones to include in your statement.

- STATE: "The priority beliefs for me to align with are":
- STATE: "Number one"—muscle-test.
- STATE: "Number two"—muscle-test.
- STATE: "Number three", then "Number four"—muscle-test.

Once you have identified the belief(s) to bring yourself into alignment with, follow the simple alignment method and read *all* of the identified statements you muscle-tested "yes" for in one long string, following the same change process as before.

**Continue as with the Simple Alignment Method**

Continue the process with steps 2–6 of the Simple Alignment Method (these have been laid out again here for ease). Then continue to step 7 of the Advanced Method.

## STEP 2: Which Hemisphere to Activate First Muscle-Test

STATE: "I need to activate the left hemisphere first", and muscle-test. If "yes", remember that you will need to perform the movements in step 4, with your left side first, then your right side. If "no", remember that you will need to perform the movements in step 4 with your right side first, then your left side.

## STEP 3: The Movement Stand in Wuji Posture

Ground, feet apart, knees soft and open, hips neutral, shoulders relaxed, breath relaxed. Extend up as an empty vessel, between the energies of heaven and earth.

Standing in Wuji

### The Infinity Harmonizing Movement

Perform the infinity harmonizing movement over the lower *dan tian* (the area just below the navel).

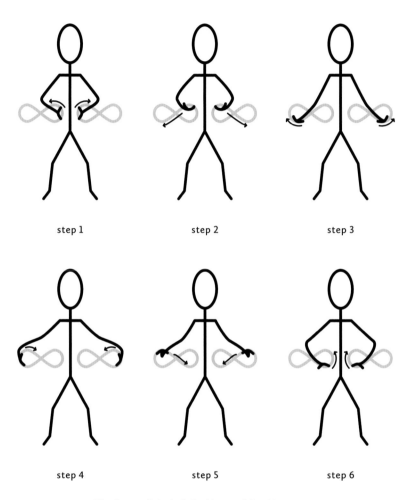

The Steps of the Infinity Harmonizing Movement

## STEP 4: Left and Right Brain Activation and Congruence

### Activate the First Hemisphere

Bring your awareness and attention to the energy in your left (or right) hand, repeating your string of priority beliefs, until the left (or right) hemisphere of the brain feels activated.

### Activate the Second Hemisphere

Bring your awareness and attention to the energy in your right (or left) hand, repeating your beliefs, until the right (or left) hemisphere of the brain feels activated.

### Whole-Brain and Whole-Body Awareness

Hold both hemispheres of the brain in whole-body awareness, simply as an observer, continuing to repeat the belief, and witnessing the release and belief alignment.

Whole-Brain and Whole-Body Awareness

## STEP 5: Belief Embodiment Visualization

### Bring Your Hands Towards Your Body

When the hemispheres are activated and the belief alignment feels congruent, bring the hands towards the body, and close your eyes.

### Visualize and Feel the Vibration of the New Belief

Take at least 68 seconds (what you sense to be just over a minute) to connect with what this now feels like. Allow a vision to come to mind that represents you with this new belief and its associated possibilities in your life.

Belief Embodiment Visualization

## STEP 6: Grounding and Planting the New Belief

### Send the Belief to the Earth

Place your hands at the sides of your hips, palms facing the earth, and imagine planting the belief (plus any excess energy) into the Earth Star Portal chakra beneath your feet.

### Remain Until the Belief and Energy are Grounded

Remain until you sense the belief has landed and you feel grounded, ready to get on with your day.

Grounding and Planting

## STEP 7: Advanced Alignment Test

You will now muscle-test your chosen belief statements in one long thread to confirm the new alignment.

### Confirm the Presence of the Desired Belief

Make your desired belief statement and muscle-test to confirm its presence. "Yes" to the affirming statement? It is so. Well done! If "no", do you need to do the process again? STATE: "I need to realign with this belief now", and muscle-test. If "yes", repeat the process.

Once you have aligned using the Simple Method, there may be several more beliefs to discover and align with. This is the layering process I talked about earlier. Discover and realign the layers in order to get to your desired outcome.

### Check to See If Another Alignment Is Needed

STATE: "There is another priority belief to align with in order to complete this process", and muscle-test. If "yes", continue the process of discovery outlined above in the steps of the Advanced Method to discover which chakra, which aspect, and which belief(s). Then align using steps 2-7 of the Simple Method until there are no more beliefs to align with in order to complete the process. When there are no more beliefs to align with, move to your final muscle test and belief embodiment visualization.

## STEP 8: Final Test and Realignment

### Confirm the Presence of the Initial Desired Belief

Speak aloud the initial desired belief, and muscle-test to confirm its presence (your "yes").

### Confirm the Absence of the Initial Unhelpful Belief

Muscle-test your unhelpful belief to confirm its absence (your "no").

### Final Belief Embodiment Visualization

It's lovely after that sometimes long process to bask in and build upon your new resonance. The belief embodiment visualization is designed to help you harness the power of the law of attraction, so take your time to create this resonance, noticing the specific things that come up, and allow the vibration to grow and become as bright and beautiful as possible.

Bring your hands towards your body to conduct the Belief Embodiment Visualization for your initial belief. Hopefully you will have enjoyed a lovely new resonance.

### Plant and Ground the Belief in the Earth

Bring your hands to your sides, turn your palms towards the earth. Imagine planting the new belief beneath your feet in the Earth Star Portal Chakra.

### The Manifestation Process for Whole-Body Coherence

Muscle-test the statement "I need to do the manifestation process in relation to this belief". If "yes", continue to Chapter 10. If "no", your process is complete. Enjoy your new resonance and new possibilities! If you are guided during the visualization towards something you might describe as incongruent with a positive vibration (for example, whilst there may be a change in perception, something has not shifted and still feels uncomfortable—a "yes, but..."), simply notice it, without judgement. Stay with the process, and your vision may change. In my experience, Spirit is working with you while you are switched on and in full awareness, leading you to an associated issue or the next place you need to go to. In essence, you may still be aligning, and energy may still be moving through you into full resonance.

This work can be a little like a Jenga game. We can pull belief after belief and sometimes need to do more than we realize for a whole life issue to collapse. Awareness is key to success, so stay with the vision until it feels complete. If the final visualization does not feel fully congruent, it is likely that there is more work to do with the body's integration of the new belief through the Manifestation Process (see Chapter 10), which enables a fully coherent gut, heart, and head resonance with the new belief.

NOTE: These processes can be stopped and picked up again at a different time. If you have become tired, write down where you are (including your next step), take a break, and come back to it another day.

Although I describe worst-case scenarios here, the process is often simple and easy. The important point to remember is that you are transforming your deepest conditioning every time you work on yourself, so honour your process. Some of us have had it harder than others, and often these belief programmes have been running for decades! If the alignments do not come easily, there may just be a little more unwinding to do. Be patient, and honour and celebrate your successes.

# Chapter 10

# The Manifestation Process

The manifestation process is designed to be used to enable a gut, heart, and head coherent resonance with the new belief/life issue. This whole-brain, whole-body coherent state is the optimum place from which to manifest your desired new alignment. The process is there for you to use whenever you would like to manifest a belief more quickly, but I would always recommend checking by performing a muscle test at the end of each alignment to see if the manifestation process is needed.

I developed this process because sometimes, even after aligning with a belief, it feels like there is more to be done to enhance the body's resonance with the belief. The system gives us an opportunity to shift, align, and release, but we can use the manifestation process to create visions and vibrations that match our sought-after experience. When we have done this work, it is easier to hold positive vibrations, anticipate good things happening, release attachment to our desires, and listen to our intuition to guide our choices and receive our gifts.

This clever process utilizes aspects of Geneline Therapy, inspired by Grant McFetridge's work from The Institute of Peak States (see Resources). When we fully resonate with a belief statement, the visions are strong and powerful, and the vibrations clear and expansive. We feel totally on board with this new energy and what it feels like/looks like. Even though we have only just aligned with it in the subconscious mind, we can tap into the field of this new vibration and receive it at a cellular level. If, after the belief is aligned and negative emotions have been released, you still feel unclear about how the new belief feels or what it looks like, it means there is part of you that still needs to catch up and fully integrate the new alignment. Using this process, we can figure out which part of you is resisting and use the manifestation protocol and bring it up to speed with the changes.

## Listen to Body Intelligence

As we discussed in the earlier sections on qigong's three treasures and MacLean's triune brain theory, the gut, the heart, and the head are powerful energy centres, each of which contains its own wisdom and intelligent function. If we place our hands on any of these centres and muscle-test the belief or life issue we have just aligned with, we can get a specific reading of whether or not that centre is on board with the change. We can tune into that field for further insight.

First listen, acknowledge, and accept whatever comes into your awareness from this part of you, then create a mental "vision board" from the centres that *are* in alignment with the change. We then communicate this to the centre(s) not in alignment, which helps them to become coherent. Full body-mind-spirit coherence will accelerate the manifestation of belief into physical experiences. Examples of the manifestation process can be found in the later case studies. These will help you to become clearer about how this looks in practice. For further insights, check out my videos, available on my website and YouTube channel (see Resources).

Remember: In order to feel positive and happy, take the time to create (allow) mental vision boards. Be with what-is, listen, observe, and don't force it. Our gut, heart, or head may need a little further processing and reassurance. It does work; just stick with it.

## The Step-By-Step Process

1. After doing a Healing InSight belief change process, muscle-test the statement: "I need to do the manifestation process to integrate this belief."
   - If "yes", go ahead and follow the protocol.
   - If "no", there is no need and you are likely to already be fully coherent.
2. Place your hands on your gut, repeat the life issue/belief you have brought yourself into alignment with, and muscle-test it.
   - If you sway forwards or test "yes", you are aligned and, after step 5, can create a gut-happy vision board.
   - If you sway backwards or test "no", your gut needs a little help. Continue to muscle-test using step 3.
3. Place your hands on your heart, repeat the life issue/belief you have brought yourself into alignment with, and muscle- or sway-test.
   - If you sway forwards, or test "yes", you are aligned and, after step 5, can create a heart-happy vision board.
   - If you sway backwards, or test "no", your heart needs a little help. Continue to muscle- or sway-test using step 4.

4. Place your hands on your head, repeat the life issue/belief you have brought yourself into alignment with, and muscle- or sway-test.
   – If you sway forwards or test "yes", you are aligned and, after step 5, can create a head-happy vision board.
   – If you sway backwards, or test "no", your head needs a little help. Continue to muscle- or sway-test using step 5.
5. For each centre—gut, head, or heart—that tested "no" (not fully on-board with the changes), place your hands on the area and ask how the gut/heart and/or head feels about the new alignment. Take a paper and pen and write it down, if need be. Ask: "A head/heart/gut, show me what you see and feel about this."
6. If two of the three are not aligned, start at the bottom, working up to discover what each of the centres *not* in alignment with the belief have to say about this. The only thing stopping us from moving forward is fear. What are the fears? Just listen, observe, acknowledge, and allow.
7. Place your hands on areas of the gut, head, or heart that *are* testing in alignment with the belief. Remind yourself of the belief, and take a few deep breaths to recalibrate in accordance with this centre, then ask this bodily treasure to show you what the new alignment looks and feels like:
   "A head/heart/gut, show me what you see and feel about this." Take some time here to create a mental vision board, observing, listening, and feeling what the belief or life issue statement means to you, once manifest. Try to involve all of your senses here; the more you see, hear, feel, taste, and touch, the more you are able to manifest a similar vibration.
8. Repeat for each of the centres that are in alignment with the belief.
9. Now turn to the centre(s) that were not in alignment. Place your hands here, take a few deep breaths, and talk it through in your mind, telling this centre what the other aligned centres have seen as possible. Bearing witness to each centre in this way allows the body to fine-tune coherence. If we disconnect from or disown our head, heart, or gut, we lack a fully coherent vibrational possibility for changing our reality and calling in that which we desire.
   – Ask this part again to show you how it feels about the new alignment now, having heard what the other parts of the team know to be possible. Listen, observe, acknowledge, and allow.

- If, after acknowledging and allowing its concerns, it hasn't come into coherence with the other centres already—which I anticipate it will have—it sometimes needs a little reassurance and reminder of what the other centres are feeling and seeing, or a question to be asked, such as, "What do you need to come into coherence?"
- The body should be fully aligned by now. If it isn't, go back to the parts that were aligned and communicate the fears of the part that is struggling to let go. They may be able to share insight and wisdom to bring this part of you fully on board. Keep the vision boards and communication going between the centres until all are in agreement.

10. Muscle-test to confirm that all centres are coherent with the belief (or life issue statement).

11. Tap on the third eye, or upper *dan tian*, to awaken the pineal master gland (20–30 times).

12. Bring home the grand manifestation.
    - Sit or stand and take a good few deep breaths.
    - Breathe light into the body, feeling your whole self expand and be aware of your heart opening and softening.
    - Place the left hand on your heart, right hand on your gut, and repeat your affirming belief statement.
    - Close your eyes and begin to imagine what this looks like and feels like. You may get a similar visualization, or it may have changed; just observe, and allow it to be as big and bright as you can. Be curious, and allow it to develop or change. Visions are interesting and unfold as you watch them.
    - Try again to include all of your senses, and allow for the best feeling you are aware of. This is not about imagining and manipulating the image! We can get into distortion and interference when we begin to create with our minds. It is about allowing what-is to prevail.
    - Be curious, and enjoy this process for as long as feels good.
    - Please thank yourself. Appreciate the work you have done and the time you have given yourself. Self-love, gratitude, and appreciation are key.

# Chapter 11

# The Life Issue Process

Often we are aware of our own life issues. The system I offer here enables you to work with current life issues that are more pervasive or abstract, as opposed to specific beliefs. This process can be useful when you are feeling stuck with a life issue and are unsure what deeper aspects or beliefs are maintaining or perpetuating your current experiences.

It works a little like the Advanced Method, in terms of the process of discovery, and can provide insight about what alignments are needed to find resolution for yourself. It is also possible to muscle-test to ascertain which aspect is the priority for you to work with as a life issue. You can follow either protocol, depending on if you are working consciously with a known life issue, or discovering one to resolve.

I have developed a questionnaire called The Life Review (see Resources section) for you to work through to help you identify your life issues. It contains sets of opposing beliefs that span every chakra and, therefore, will encompass many areas of your life. This is an invitation to assess where you are now, in terms of these beliefs and perhaps, in a year's time, compare it with where you may be then. It facilitates a process of reflection and awareness wherein you can muscle-test yourself to affirm the presence or absence of these beliefs in your subconscious mind. You will likely be surprised at what you actually believe to be true! You can then use this insight to decide which aspects of your life you wish to prioritize harmonizing with the Healing InSight method.

Many of our life issues involve sour or painful relationships from the past and present. I have included a forgiveness protocol in the Resources section for you to work through if you wish to forgive yourself or others for triggering painful patterns and feelings in you. This is the final piece of treasure within the system.

I highly recommend using this protocol to work through all of your painful relationships. It does not mean condoning behaviours and actions. It is hugely freeing for all involved and one of the greatest gifts that you can give yourself. Just think how much lower vibrational energy we hold onto from toxic or challenging relationships. It is possible to release this, and to see the circumstances from a higher, loving perspective. I have included a case study for you in the Resources to demonstrate the forgiveness protocol; further case studies are on the Healing InSight website.

## CASE STUDY: How Exploring My Fears Led Me into Processing a Life Issue

Most of us are aware when there is a gap between where we are and where we want to be. It is this gap that causes unease. Frequently, though not always, we also know what is stopping us from getting there. These kinds of explorations are commonplace in the therapy room and, whilst people can be assisted in identifying their limiting beliefs or blocks, the concern is what we then do with that insight and how we make the necessary changes.

Feeling unsafe, vulnerable, unworthy, or inadequate can trigger fear of hurt, rejection, or abandonment. Going inward and listening to our fears helps us to see which beliefs and obstacles need to be addressed in order to help with a specific life issue. The information we need is already within and speaking to us!

When I first came to write this book, I joined a writers' workshop to discover the "platform" I would need, what would be expected of me in terms of marketing, and what structure was needed in order to write an acceptable book proposal. The 300-odd workshop participants were invited to submit their book proposal, in a competition where one lucky winner would receive a publishing agreement. Committed and keen to get the Healing InSight method out to the world, I endeavoured to write my proposal, along with chapter summaries and samples. I stumbled into writer's block, so I decided to use the system itself to help me through it.

Exploring my fears and thoughts, I became aware that I feared being inadequate so I used the system to align myself with being a successful author. I chose to use the life review process to see what conditioning or beliefs were stopping me from being able to write and share the system. I intended to find my way into believing that it was safe for me to be seen and heard, and also that I was capable of being a successful author—not only did I want to write the book but I also wanted a publishing deal. I worked with these beliefs as a life issue, wrapped up in the statement "I am a successful author".

Witnessing the beliefs that came up to be healed was an extraordinary experience. I found it such a gift to be able to hand over to the wisdom of the system to provide insight into my writing blocks. I needed to both know and align with the beliefs that I was worthy, safe, capable, and that I belonged. Here are the aspects and beliefs that came up for me to align with:

### Solar Plexus Chakra—Greatness
I like, love, and accept myself. I am wonderful, talented and know that greatness resides within me. I harness my greatness and show up in the world. I allow myself to be seen and heard. I am wonderful.

### Root Chakra—Safety
I let go of the need for protection when I realize that I am safe. I trust my instincts and inner guidance to help navigate me through life's twists and turns. I am safe.

### Crown Chakra—Possibility
All is possible for me in this universe of infinite potential. I release all conditioning and limits that I have placed in my path unknowingly. All is possible.

### Root Chakra—Natural World
I belong.

Each of these beliefs spoke to me, and that's the usual feedback that I get from users of the system with the life review or advanced process. There's a sense of "aha", or knowing, as one brings their conditioning into consciousness.

I had quite an emotional release whilst aligning with the last belief: "I belong". I have always struggled to find my place. My family are very loving, I have good friends and rationally I knew that I belonged, but on a soul level, I have always felt a degree of unease and discontent, which has played out in my life through the bullying and rejection I experienced.

Healing our hurts can often transform and drive us into choosing what we do want. Interesting that my intent is to create Heaven On Mother Earth (aptly named HOME)—a spiritual and therapeutic retreat, hosting crafts, arts, and good food. I know as a spiritual being that I am not alone in wanting a more cohesive, loving, and supporting reality to exist within, where people are celebrated rather than denigrated, cherished rather than dismissed.

I wrote for many hours that day, feeling good about myself, my potential, and the system. With my blocks cleared, I knew that I had done my bit. When I handed in my proposal to the competition, I did not feel elated but in fact completely misplaced. I listened to my inner guidance, which compelled me to go to the London Book Fair at the last minute. Without a plan, I found myself inadvertently stealing 10 minutes of Findhorn Press Editorial Director Sabine Weeke's time.

Having had that 10 minutes, I knew why I had gone to the fair and that my book had found its home! I am so pleased that I listened to my instincts and inner guidance to help navigate me through this! All truly is perfect when we can get out of our own way and allow the universe to point us in the right direction.

The Life Issue Process can be used as described above, to resolve a specific issue that you are aware of—or, if you are not sure what you want to work on, you can muscle-test the chakras and the aspects (as described in the Advanced Method) to identify your priority aspect to align with. You would follow the Using the System to Discover and Resolve a Specific Life Issue protocol to bring healing to this aspect. The Life Issue Process is usually for bigger, more complex issues that have not been separated into bite-sized, discrete beliefs. The specifics can always be mopped up afterwards.

## Using the Advanced Method for Resolution of a Specific Known Life Issue

If you have a known life issue that you would like to work on and are struggling to identify a specific belief, you can hand over to the system to begin resolving this issue. (Remember: this may not be an immediate transformation, as physical reality has to catch up with the energetic shifts we create.) This process removes the energy behind whatever blocks are in the way of resolving the life issues by aligning you with the positive opposites of those limits so that your life issue can resolve itself more easily.

You should have more insight and freedom within the issue, together with a higher perspective. We know how to heal and evolve when we get out of our own way! Life issues can be anything from the resolution of a health complaint or a difficult relationship to an addictive behaviour, a desired job, or house sale. This is really about clearing any limiting beliefs that are preventing you from being in harmony with your intention and goal. Be specific with your intention and your life issue!

1. Simply state your life issue, such as "My life issue is… desiring true love", "lack of money", "wanting to feel secure in myself and avoid blushing when people talk to me", "being unable to make a decision", "my exhaustion health issue", "insomnia". Remember: the more specific you can be, the more helpful the result will be for you. Start your process by asking for permission to resolve this life issue.

2. STATE: "It is for my highest and best good to resolve this [name] life issue now", and muscle-test.

3. If "yes", state: "I give my full permission to resolve this life issue on all levels now, using the advanced Healing InSight method", and muscle-test.
   - If "yes", go ahead and align with the process of discovery, the method, and the muscle test through to the end of the Advanced Method. Repeat until there are no more priority beliefs to align with.
   - If you get a "no" to your full permission statement, explore why. Is there any reason to hold on to this issue; for example, hidden gains? This is often just something that needs to be brought into consciousness.
   - Once aware of your reasons to hold onto the life issue, muscle-test for permission again.

4. Once all alignments are complete, confirm with the muscle test that the life issue is now resolved by stating: "This [name] life issue alignment is now resolved."

5. Muscle-test to see whether you have to do the manifestation process for whole-body coherence in relation to this resolved life issue. STATE: "I need to do the manifestation process now." If you get a "yes", and do need to do the manifestation process, follow the guidance in the subsequent section.

6. Check action steps by muscle-testing: "There are action steps to take to help resolve this life issue." If "yes", there are steps to be taken. Close your eyes, and allow to come to mind what your next few steps will be. Write this down to help solidify your intention and capture your next course of action. If I had not listened to my intuition to go to the London Book Fair and actually taken action to do that, I may not have had the same opportunity to publish with Findhorn Press. We have to engage with the world in order to let the universe play in our lives.

**Using the System to Discover and Resolve a Specific Life Issue**

If you wish to work on yourself but are unsure where to start, or what issue is your priority, you can ask your subconscious mind what the priority life issue to be resolved now is. Test the following statements out loud in the process of discovery:

1. STATE: "The priority life issue for me to resolve is in the root chakra." Repeat for each chakra until you get a "yes" (sacral chakra, solar plexus, heart, throat, third eye, and crown).
2. Discover which aspect within this chakra is your priority life issue to address.
   - "The priority life issue for me to resolve within this chakra is [name aspect one]." Repeat for each aspect until you get a "yes".
3. Get permission to resolve this life issue. The aspect will hopefully speak to you and relate to some aspect of your challenges or struggles.
4. STATE: "It is for my highest and best good to resolve this [name aspect] life issue now" and muscle-test.
5. STATE: "I give my full permission to resolve this [name aspect] life issue now, on all levels, using the advanced Healing InSight method"; and muscle-test.
6. If "yes", go ahead and align with the process of discovery, the method, and the muscle test through to the end of the Advanced Method. Repeat until there are no more priority beliefs to align with.
7. Once all alignments are complete, confirm with the muscle test that the life issue is now resolved by stating: "This [name aspect] life issue alignment is now resolved."
8. Muscle-test to see whether you have to do the manifestation process in relation to this resolved life issue ("I need to do the manifestation process now"). If you do need to do the manifestation process, go ahead and follow the guidance in the subsequent section.
9. Check whether there are action steps to take by muscle-testing the statement: "There are action steps to take to help resolve this life issue." If "yes", there are steps to be taken, close your eyes and allow to come to mind what your next few steps will be. Write this down to help solidify your intention and capture your next course of action.

## Conclusion

Working with our life issues can be a powerful way to bring healing into our lives. You really can work with any issue, from nervousness about having to make a difficult call to deeper issues of jealousy, guilt, and self-worth. It can be emotional work, but the benefits far outweigh the comfort of staying stuck in familiar, unhelpful patterns.

REMEMBER: the beliefs in the Advanced Method and life issue process that are selected for you via the muscle test are not in alignment with your energy system until the procedure is worked through, which means that there is sometimes a lack of resonance during the beginning of the process. Our resistance can actively work against us, with our minds becoming very vocal about it simply not being true. Persist, persist, persist. You will realign if your muscle test has said that it's okay for you to go ahead and align, and once aligned you will build a new healthy resonance and feel so much clearer, having released the energetic resistance and old pattern. Make way for the magic, and clear, clear, clear. The more we clear, the more we align with integrity, truth, and love and find our connection to self, others, and something greater than ourselves. This is where life begins to feel meaningful, and it becomes a pleasure to both connect to and be in awe of, the wonder of being alive.

As you are moving through your process of change and awakening, remember to be positive as much as you can. Raise your conscious awareness of your self-talk.

REMEMBER: what you focus on, you draw towards you. Negative self-talk leads to negative feelings, and so on. "Stop, cancel, and delete", and find an alternative, positive, reassuring thought, or find a better feeling (see Introducing Your Chakra Animals in the next chapter). Aligning yourself with that positive thought will shift your vibration for good. This whole process is a journey of self-love, of honouring the "you", the "we", and the all.

My love to you.

Nikki.

# Chapter 12

# The Healing InSight System Beliefs

It is with great pleasure that I share these beliefs. Even if you only use them as affirmations, let them inspire you to adopt a different way of thinking. If you feel challenged, try to be open to a new perspective and mull over what the suggestions on the cards mean to you. Sometimes, when we are misaligned with a belief, we don't actually understand what it is expressing, and our monkey-mind resistance steers us away from engaging in the change process. Stay with it. You deserve to feel good about yourself and the world we live in. This is an opportunity to create a better reality—you always have a choice, and I encourage you to go for it! Find your belief, and use the system to align with it. Life is short, and now is the time to create happier, healthier realities. This is my gift to you!

# Chakra Aspects Chart

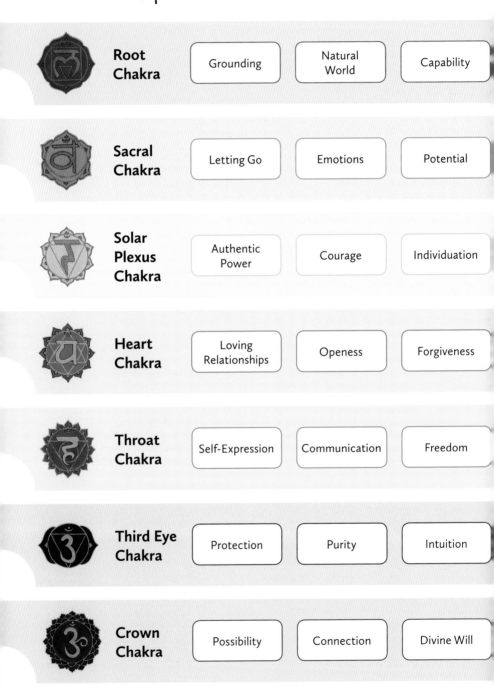

| | | | |
|---|---|---|---|
| **Root Chakra** | Grounding | Natural World | Capability |
| **Sacral Chakra** | Letting Go | Emotions | Potential |
| **Solar Plexus Chakra** | Authentic Power | Courage | Individuation |
| **Heart Chakra** | Loving Relationships | Openess | Forgiveness |
| **Throat Chakra** | Self-Expression | Communication | Freedom |
| **Third Eye Chakra** | Protection | Purity | Intuition |
| **Crown Chakra** | Possibility | Connection | Divine Will |

| | | | |
|---|---|---|---|
| Stability | Abundance | Physical Body | Safety |
| Self-Worth | Creativity | Instinct | Sensuality |
| Greatness | Boundaries | Free Will | Autonomy |
| Gratitude | Harmony | Ease & Grace | Compassion |
| Transmutation | Clarity | Truth | Space |
| Healing | Peace of Mind | Psychic Awareness | Unity |
| Integrity | Knowing | Consciousness | We |

# Root Chakra
## Aspects and Beliefs

### Grounding

*I am earthed*

I am anchored into my physical existence and resonate in perfect harmony with the physical world.

I am of the earth, as I am of heaven. I root down and yield to the world around me.

I connect with the life-giving energies of the earth and lovingly release lower vibrations to Gaia to be transformed.

### Natural World

*I belong*

I am one with nature and nature is one with me. I honour the rhythms of nature and flow with the seasons.

I walk upon this earth gently but firmly, as my ancestors have done before me.

I know when to move forward and when to retreat, when to cultivate and when to grow, when to yield and when to harvest.

### Capability

*I am strong*

I remove obstacles from my path. I can actualize what I set out to achieve.

I cultivate my strengths and capabilities with focus and determination.

I am brave, strong and capable.

## Stability

*I am supported*

I allow myself to give and receive support.

I trust in the pathway that unfolds before me, I recognize the inter-connectedness of all things.

I lovingly support myself with kind thoughts of encouragement, compassion and understanding.

## Abundance

*I have*

I gather easily and effortlessly all that I need to support, nourish and comfort me.

I focus my attention upon all that I am grateful for.

There is an abundance of nourishment, support and love for me.

## Physical Body

*I exist*

I celebrate my physical body and recognize it as the wondrous vessel through which I see, feel, hear, touch, smell, and taste.

I connect fully with my physical existence on this earthly plane.

I breathe life force into my body and nourish it with good food. I love and accept my body.

## Safety

*I am safe*

I let go of the need for protection when I realize that I am safe.

I trust my instincts and inner guidance to help navigate me through life's twists and turns.

I can cope with adversity because I am always there for myself in loving and supportive ways.

## Root Chakra Main Card

It is the nourishment from the earth that feeds our food source and grows our bodies and bones. We literally are what we eat, and that is of the earth. The root chakra card puts us in touch with our physicality. Our bodies are nourished directly from our connection to the Earth. When we see the universe and the earth as our providers, we feel safe, supported, and connected to our beautiful planet. Remember to give back as much as you take and nurture Gaia.

The root chakra is depicted here as a boy, still and centred in his physicality, kept safe by the sleeping wolf, who has no need for vigilance or alarm, as he sits on the four-petalled lotus flower representing the four directions: North, South, East, and West. The boy sits under the abundant cherry tree, whose roots are anchored into the earth, reminding you to do the same. Invest in building and connecting to your earthly roots, as they offer a strong platform from which to springboard and create. Ganesha is the elephant-headed deity, son of Shiva and Parvati, worshipped in Hindu tradition, and indeed across the world, sitting behind the boy. Ganesha is the remover of obstacles and the God of new beginnings. He is a powerhouse to call upon when we feel blocked or need help to find our way.

The gentle and wise elephant—representing power and strength—and the focused, grounded snake are the root chakra spirit animals to aid our connection to the earthly plane. Imagine being these animals to help you connect with these qualities. When the root chakra is clear we feel solid, firmly connected to our selves, safe, and nourished. We can acknowledge all that we already have. Go ahead and align. Use your body as the gift to harness your greatness.

## Grounding

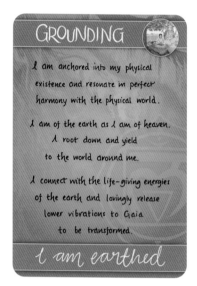

This card is calling you to ground. Perhaps life is pushing and pulling you around a little too much? Take some time to plant your feet on the floor, be still, and anchor yourself. When we are anchored, like a tree rooted in the ground, we can bend with the breeze but won't be pushed off course. It's important to feel connected to the earth, so that we may develop the possibility of being less rigid and yielding to the world around us.

Most of us now live in environments awash with man-made electrical energies, and we can sometimes be overloaded by our own (or others') emotional energies, which has a negative effect upon us. Gaia is not only the greatest mother, support, and nourishment for us but also has an ability to compost negativity, transforming it so that we may be energetically restored. Release negative energies by grounding and plugging into the Earth's resonance. Every cell of your body has developed from the nourishment of Gaia, every breath has come from the oxygen she has supplied. It is time for you to come back to the Earth and recognize with awe all she offers you.

## Natural World

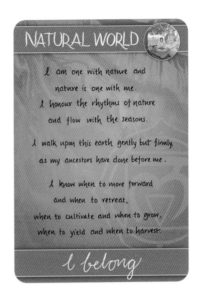

You belong. You chose to incarnate and experience the kind of life and lessons you are experiencing. There is an ebb and flow to life, a time for everything and everyone, and you are being reminded now to reconnect with the natural cycles of life. Perhaps it is time to let go of attachment to something or someone so that you may find your own rhythms and flow. Turn inward to listen to your inner guidance and knowing about whether or when to retreat, gather, let go, or move forward. The cycles of change are in motion, and this card is offering you a possibility to hold a little less tightly and go with the natural order of life.

When we disconnect from the natural world we become lost at sea. Our cells are encoded with the path of man and the way of the land. We may forget our heritage and be consumed with the ever-stimulating environment around us, but as human beings, we need to reconnect with who we are. Take time to listen to the calling of the wind, and take guidance from the elements, the sun, water, and stars. More is going on behind the scenes than you are aware of. Great spirits of the sky and land, including the animal, plant, and crystal kingdom, are speaking to and supporting you now through this process of surrender and reconnection.

## Capability

 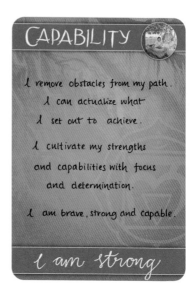

This aspect reminds us that we are capable of achieving whatever it is that we set our sights on. As sensitive beings, all too often we are made to feel or decide that we are wrong, inadequate, or weak. Is this something you have been telling yourself? You have the potential to be incredibly strong, and this aspect reminds you of this. Whenever you perceive an obstacle in your path, it is just that, a perception; a limit or block to clear and release. The universe is abundant, and all we must do is release our fears, recognize our strength and greatness, and allow ourselves to follow our passion. Aligning with this aspect allows you to be strong, focused, and determined like the elephant; cultivate your strengths, and stop telling the story that you are weak or vulnerable. Be brave, dear friend; you can actualize what you set out to achieve.

## Abundance

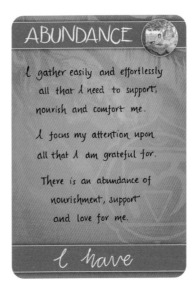

We often compare ourselves with others, recognizing the difference as lack. Stop comparing! You are wonderful and unique. Please, please stop focusing on the lack. We even practise lack by focusing on what we want when we notice the gap between what we desire and where we currently are. The universe is abundant and has no problem providing nourishment, support, and love for you—money, even, if that is what you desire (though abundance does not always flow in the form of money). Focus on what you have—past, present, and future—with gratitude, and align with the belief that it is easy and effortless for you to gather all you need. Step into the energy of "having". You are worthy and deserving of having, and this can happen without there being a cost to others. This is real abundance: knowing that there is enough—enough love, support, success, or money for you and everyone. Give and receive with thanks as you become one with the flow. The earth provides abundantly. Connect with the power of that possibility right beneath your feet.

## Stability

Sometimes we can get caught up in the storm, and it may not even be our own. It's time for you to recognize your own solid foundation and tend to your rootedness in the earth. Keep yourself in balance, particularly in relation to giving and receiving, and set boundaries around others who are asking too much from you. When we support ourselves with kind and loving thoughts, we maintain a sense of stability. Try not to allow your own thoughts and stories to pull you too far from your centre. When you steady yourself and root down into the earth, like a tree, you come to trust in the cycles of life and the bigger picture. Steady your breath, and trust your body and mind to serve you and recognize your sense of self as you bring into balance your inner and outer worlds. Receive the support that is available to you.

## Physical Body

 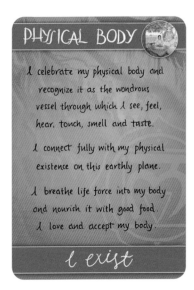

Stop! Look! Listen! Your body is speaking to you. What does it need right now? Your body is a wondrous vehicle for you to experience life from. If your body has been letting you down and you have a poor body image, it's time to address that now. It is empowering and enlightening to change your beliefs about your body and learn to love the vessel you have been given. This is a journey of self-love. Disowning and neglecting your greatest gift will not bring reward. Our bodies know how to heal and become stronger; they will do so, if we give them the right conditions, as our cells are constantly renewing. By changing the physical environment, giving our bodies fresh air, nourishing food, and clean water, and improving the emotional environment by expressing emotions and clearing their associated beliefs, we can heal and strengthen our physical bodies. Come into alignment with your physical strength. Your body is a magnificent creation.

## Safety

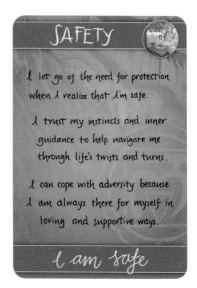

We exist in a universe of infinite possibility, and one possibility is the vibration of safety. When we align with safety, we experience more of this and are guided and steered towards safety. Being constantly on the lookout for danger is both tiring and unnecessary; it is our birthright to live within the vibration of peacefulness and safety.

In the Western world, being late for a friend or a meeting, failing to make a sale, or having a business proposal turned down can all trigger the stress response in a catastrophic thinking pattern wherein we are primed to believe that we are unsafe and may lose our home, tribe, and the safety that tribe offers. When we feel safe, we are free to explore and experiment, and life begins to expand.

For too long, we have felt unsafe in this dualistic world of fear and separation, of conflict and having "power over" each other. The new Earth paradigm we are entering requires us to let go of fear and beliefs of unsafety so that we can choose love, peace, and safety for all. Choose safety for yourself; believe in the safety of your children, your neighbourhood, and the world. Trust that you will be kept safe when you choose to align with safety.

# Sacral Chakra
## Aspects and Beliefs

### Letting Go

*I release*

I release repressed or trapped emotions and their associated beliefs with ease and grace.

Where appropriate, I let go of those people and situations that perpetuate hurt and unease.

I release my investment in staying safe and stuck. I surrender, trust and allow the light to guide me.

### Emotions

*I feel*

It is safe for me to feel emotion as I experience relationship with myself, others and the universe.

Emotion is there as a useful tool to give me information.

As I listen to and name my emotions, clarifying the messages and beliefs behind them, I liberate myself.

### Potential

*All is possible*

I am alive with potential and fertile with possibility.

I allow my dreams and desires to gestate and birth.

I am expression of the infinite potential of the universe. I nurture my potential and possibility.

## Self-Worth

*I nurture*

I am worthy.
I listen to my needs
and desires and
honour myself.

I give myself the time,
space and loving
kindness that I need
to make manifest all
that I am.

I discover my true self
by going inward and
becoming my own
best friend.

## Creativity

*I flow*

I am free to play,
free to love,
laugh and
experiment.

I am free to
experience,
to create and
to manifest.
I am free
to be myself.

I allow my creative
potential to flow
through me in all
of its glory and
magnificence.

## Instinct

*I sense*

I allow my senses to
fully experience the
physical world and
trust my instincts.

I connect to my
deepest sense
of self for
balanced guidance
and truth.

I release all fears
and listen to the
wisdom of my
ancestors through
the resonance
of my body.

## Sensuality

*I experience pleasure*

Sensuality and
pleasure are my
birthright, to be
experienced with
blissful joy.

I honour and embrace
my sexuality,
recognising the sacred
sexual connection
with myself and the
intimate partner of my
choice.

It is safe for me to be
sensual and sexual
and be respected for
this. Pleasure and
enjoyment are good,
clean and healthy.

## Sacral Chakra Main Card

The sacral chakra is our sacred-to-self chakra, the seat of our sensual and sexual desires and expression, and the birthplace of our creativity and creations. When healthy, we feel safe in our sexuality, free to explore this aspect of ourselves. All too often, the sacral chakra can contract, restricting the flow of energy and leaving us feeling unattractive and unreceptive to desire. This is a reminder that this part of us needs nourishment, too. When nourished, we connect with our deeper sense of selves, and new ideas begin to manifest. The sacral chakra contains the Yin feminine energy, like the gentle but brilliant moonlight. The creative, flowing water element of the ocean, bathed in moonlight, gives rise to Aphrodite (or Venus), goddess of love, beauty, pleasure, and procreation, who is birthing from the orange water on a pod of playful dolphins. The dolphins remind us to be playful with our creativity and sensual selves. Male or female, give yourself full permission to be beautiful. Appreciate beauty in and around you. Venus is carrying Neptune's trident, representing a unity with the masculine, a coming together of the planetary representations of earthly love with divine unconditional love, ensuring magical alchemy. The whale on the horizon reminds us to go deep inside our sacral selves in order to tune in to the soul's song and sing our desires into creation. Tap into your potential, and bathe in the moonlight. The sacred feminine lies within us all.

## Letting Go

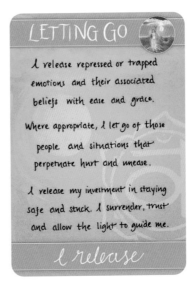

If you have chosen this aspect, it is time for you to release emotions, beliefs, or patterns of behaviour to the elements. Surrendering our limiting beliefs enables us to move into the flow of what serves us best. In qigong, our lower *dan tian*, the energy centre just below our navel, is our deepest resource. Connected with the water element, it is like a beautiful blue lagoon or ocean. We can surrender our fears and limits to the water to be cleansed, purified, and released, making way for the new. Fears for safety can make us hold onto old unhelpful patterns and relationships. It's time for you to let something go; trust that you are being supported in this process, that it can be easy and graceful as you transition to a lighter you.

## Emotions

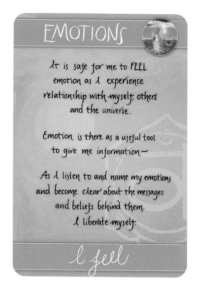

As young children we are taught not to cry; our anger is rejected, our upset belittled. So many of us resist emotional expression because we have been conditioned to do so, and because emotion builds upon emotion, we become afraid of it consuming us. It is time to build a better relationship with emotion, including your emotional self. What have you been holding on to? Acknowledging and accepting that the feeling is there is a huge start—and I mean really acknowledging and accepting it. Allow it to be there, and listen. Listen to what it is telling you, then ask yourself lovingly what it is that you need? Perhaps you have always needed this? You are your own greatest gift, so give to yourself what you need, and thank your emotion for guiding you. It's just feedback, nothing more and nothing less, but addressing it puts you back in the flow of life.

## Potential

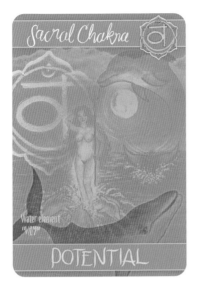
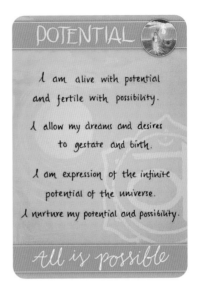

It is time for you to recognize your potential. If everything were possible, what would you be attaining right now? It is time for you to take the next steps on your path to becoming and fulfilling your potential. If you have been doubting yourself, it's time to stop this doubting, expand those self-limiting boundaries, and take that leap of faith. Align specifically with your goals, and clear your limiting beliefs in order to step into who you truly are as a unique spark of the divine. See yourself through eyes of love and compassion, and quieten the inner critic, who is communicating from a place of fear. Your ego or inner child may have introjected negative thoughts about yourself and your capabilities, and has likely developed patterns of thought and behaviour that are keeping you safe and small. You have picked this card because it is time to release those patterns now and fulfil your role, as an aspect of consciousness, which is greater than you are giving yourself credit for. All truly is possible—feel the excitement and meet your potential.

## Self-Worth

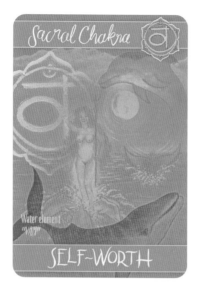

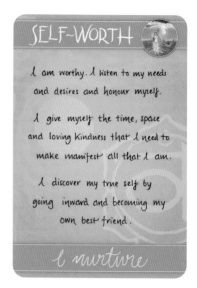

You are important. You are part of what makes the universe whole. Without you the world is a lesser place. You are—and always have been—worthy of love, kindness, attention, prosperity, and success. When you take the time to connect with yourself, you begin to recognize your inner calling, needs, and desires. Take some time to do this now. What is it that you wish to express? What are your needs? We all have them. It is not only okay to pay attention to your needs and begin to nurture yourself more, it is essential to do so. When you recognize your own worth, others recognize it, too. We do not have to prove anything to anyone nor be overly concerned with what other people think of us when we know who we are and recognize our worth. Give yourself permission to step into your worthiness; it is a gracious and easy place in which to exist.

## Creativity

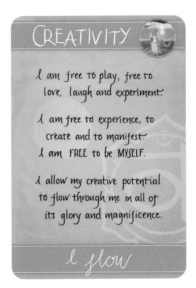

It's time for you to release your blocks to creativity. Breathe deeply, and fuel your sacral chakra's boundless creativity. The only thing in your way here is you! You have all you need, and you can play and experiment until your heart is content. Don't take life too seriously, and don't underestimate the importance of creating. The universe needs you! What is it that your heart and soul want to express? One creation leads to another, so give yourself permission to make a start. You are a beautiful creation in and of yourself. Play confidently and fluidly, just as the dolphin does in the moonlit lagoon. You really can't go wrong right now. Go create!

## Instinct

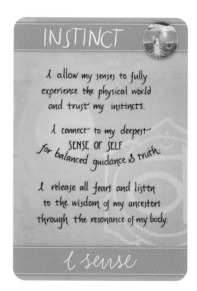

Yes, you are being told to pay attention to your instincts. Your gut is speaking, and you may not be listening. What would happen if you paid attention to this? Would it be a difficult conversation? Would it lead to a turn in the road on your journey through life? Your instincts are there for a reason, but you have to go a little deeper to ascertain whether this is just ancestral fear talking or ancestral wisdom. Place your hands on your gut, and go inward to listen to what your gut is saying. Your heart may be telling a different story, or have a different perspective, and that is okay. You always have a choice and can decide what course of action to take. You are reminded not to make decisions based upon fear but to listen to what your fears or instincts are telling you. Trust your senses, and ask your heart and your gut to work together on this issue, and watch how the magic unfolds!

## Sensuality

 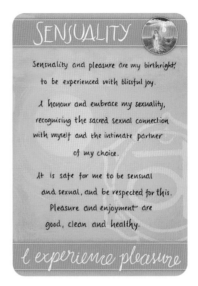

If you have picked this card, there is peace to be made with your feelings and beliefs about sensuality, pleasure, or sexuality. We have been through decades of shame surrounding sex, pleasure, and sensuality. In earlier times, women were empowered sexually, and sex was a spiritual, blissful practice—an act of divinity. It is time for you to reclaim your power and ability to have and express desire and sensuality, and be respected and respectful to others in relation to your sexual expression. If your boundaries have been loose or invaded, it is time to strengthen them and honour your body and sexual experiences, as well as those of others. It is safe for you to be sexually expressive and experience pleasure, joy, and bliss as you connect with your deepest self and your intimate other in sacred union of body, mind, and soul.

# Solar Plexus Chakra
## Aspects and Beliefs

### Authentic Power

My authentic power is achieved through self-esteem, love, truth and authenticity.

I forgive myself and others, release responsibility for others and take responsibility for my life.

### I co-create my reality

It is safe for me to be powerful. I think and speak affirming, supportive words and imagine a life that I love.

### Courage

I have the strength, courage and will-power to face my fears and see my desires, dreams and goals through to completion.

I release the need to be anything other than who I am in order to succeed.

### I am possible

I believe in myself and have the courage to fail and succeed.

### Individuation

I recognize others as different aspects of consciousness – no greater than or lesser than myself – all journeying at our own pace.

I acknowledge, accept and celebrate difference as I go inward to connect with my deepest self, my truth, desires and joy.

### I follow my own path

I am a unique spark of the divine, expressing my own unique vibration and life purpose.

## Greatness

*I am wonderful*

I like, love and accept myself.
I am wonderful and talented and know that greatness resides within me.

I harness my greatness and show up in the world.
I allow myself to be seen and heard.

I cultivate my genius and observe with love and excitement, as my greatness makes a positive difference in the world.

## Boundaries

*I stand my ground*

I stand my ground where and when I need to.

I recognize that my truth is just as valid as other people's truth and assert myself appropriately.

I trust in and expect a positive outcome and have the strength and kindness needed to enable me to stand my ground.

## Free Will

*I always have a choice*

I recognize that I always have choice and free will in any given situation.

As I face my life lessons and learn from my experiences, I realize that there is never a wrong decision.

I trust the decisions that I make and choose love, forgiveness and expansion over fear and lack, every time.

## Autonomy

*I am a limitless being*

I move beyond the limits that my ancestors, society and I have unconsciously placed upon me.
I am free.

I recognize myself as an autonomous being of infinite possibility and potential.

I am free to shine my light and strengthen my ego as I discover my potential.

## Solar Plexus Chakra Main Card

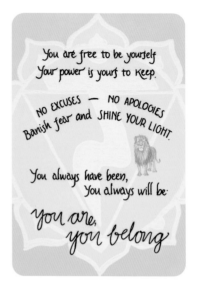

You are a unique spark of the divine, and this card is a reminder of your duty to be the best you can be. The solar plexus is our "sunshine state", our power centre; when healthy, we radiate sunshine and personal authority. The image reminds us that our power, represented by the dragon, need not fight the good fight in an unwieldy manner but can be gentle, trusted, even tamed. Quan Yin, the East Asian bodhisattva, the goddess of mercy, rides on the back of her tamed dragon and, through her love and compassion (rather than force) spreads peace and loving kindness throughout the world. We can develop a poor habit of giving our power away to others, particularly if we have a fear of others' ill treatment or judgement of us, or if we judge others to be better, wiser, kinder, and so on, than we are. Our solar plexus may contract at the prospect of being hurt or rejected, and the greatest injury may come from believing that we are separate. This is a reminder that you are here and you belong. Acknowledge your differences to others, and celebrate them; give yourself permission to be "all that you are". Harness the courage of the lion, and stand your ground like the bear. There is enough space for every one of us. Banish your fear, and shine your light as you fully embrace your individuality.

## Authentic Power

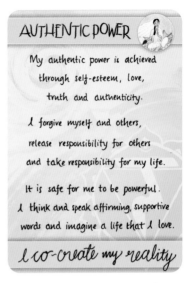

We all need help with moving away from the collective unconscious field of what it means to be powerful. Power has caused hurt, war, greed, negligence, pain, and suffering; thus, we have become fearful of having too much power, yet feel estranged from ourselves without it. You, as an autonomous individual, are absolutely powerful. The expression of authentic power does not stray far from the heart; in fact, when the heart is disengaged so too is your authentic power. Forgiveness frees you from staying stuck in powerlessness. In forgiving, you are carried into your own stream of consciousness, your truth, and are freed from being responsible for others—you can still care for them but without taking responsibility for their lives. You are, however, responsible for yourself. It is time to create your own reality, dance to the beat of your own drum, and recognize that it is safe for you to be your authentic self. Create your life with conscious, positive intent.

## Courage

Harness the power and courage of the lion that stands in its complete truth, and do whatever it takes to see your dreams and desires through to completion. Yes, you may need to change tack, or even retreat for a while to gather clarity, but face your obstacles and find a way forward. We all have courage, even the sensitive souls amongst us. Stand up tall and strong to support yourself through this, and recognize the courage you do have. You can do this. The lion doesn't take on battles unnecessarily but knows of its capability to stand in its power and see it through to the very end. Believe in your robustness and ability to do whatever it takes to achieve your goals. Have the courage to show up as "you"; it might just pay off.

## Individuation

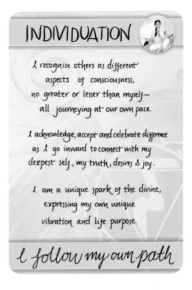

Your calling is to be fully yourself. What sets you apart from others? What are your unique gifts, skills, and talents? We spend so much of our younger lives learning how to behave in order to be successful, loved, or acceptable, then we have to unlearn all of that to discover who we actually are. It is time to become aware of the "oughts" and "shoulds" you live by that don't actually serve you. Working with this aspect involves giving yourself permission to acknowledge your differences to others (neither better nor worse) and connect with your deepest self, truth, desires, and joy. The world will be a better place when you express fully who you are, rather than who you think you should be. Follow your passion, and watch how your own beautiful expression complements the other beautiful expressions around you.

## Greatness

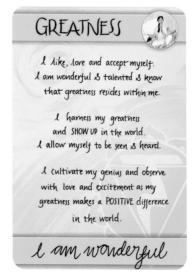

You (yes, you) are great! It's time to stop doubting yourself, and give yourself permission to be who you truly are. Greatness does not mean being perfect. You are a human being doing your best, and that doesn't mean that you have to get everything right all the time! Greatness resides within; it is yours to step into any time you choose. Playing small, deprecating or denying yourself, does not serve you or your fellow brothers and sisters. Shine your light, and allow your gifts and talents to be developed to their fullest potential. You can be an inspiration for others if only you recognize the wonders within you. True greatness does not speak of itself as supreme; it knows inside that good enough is actually good enough and allows itself to be witnessed without fear or apologies. Love, accept, and appreciate yourself, and the world will love, accept, and appreciate you right back.

## Boundaries

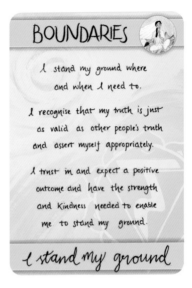

It is okay to have boundaries and assert yourself. "No" is just as valid an expression as "yes". You have a right to say yes, and you have a right to say no—not as a show of force but as a definition of your personal boundary. This card is really about standing in your truth, which means respecting and honouring yourself. The bear is a fabulous representation of what it is to stand your ground, so call upon the bear to support you in finding the strength to assert your boundaries in this situation.

Imagine what it feels like to "be the bear" in the situation you are enquiring about. When we stand our ground with grace, we need not overpower or overshadow another. Perhaps there is a lesson to be learnt here in considering the possibility of asserting yourself with loving kindness. What is truly right for you is usually right for everyone. Expect a positive outcome. How could this turn out better than you have imagined?

## Free Will

Have you been feeling trapped? Perhaps fear has been getting in the way of you making choices for yourself and moving forwards with your life? We are gifted with free will and choice. Sometimes we choose a difficult pathway to walk but the greater the challenges the greater the potential for transformation, *if* we learn from our experiences. It is time to be conscious about your process and rise aloft like the eagle in order to see the bigger picture. We can always choose to steer the ship in a different direction. Trust yourself, and try something different from what you have always expected or what has been expected of you. Let go of your fears, and make your decisions based upon a desire for love and trust, keeping faith in a higher vibration and an expansive reality. If we are to create a new Earth, we have to start making different choices for ourselves, our children, and our planet.

## Autonomy

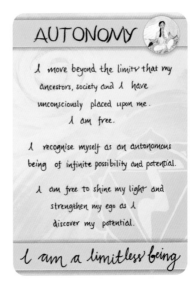

Dancing in the shadows was okay while you were experimenting and growing, but just take a look at who you truly are. You are unique, an individual who is blossoming inside a protective cloak. You are breaking free from your familial patterns and healing your ancestors. You can free yourself now. Honour your heritage and your ancestors; they will support you in shining your light. Give yourself permission to strengthen your sense of self and realize your potential. You are being helped to remove the limits that have constrained you and are being reminded of the infinite potential that exists for you and all.

As the golden dragon flies through the sky, he weaves his magic in powerful ways. Crossing limits and boundaries, the dragon meets his fullest potential tamed by the powerful, loving force of the compassionate bodhisattva Quan Yin, spreading peace, love, and light to those in need. Freedom is yours when you realize that true freedom comes from within. Liberate your heart and mind.

# Heart Chakra
## Aspects and Beliefs

## Loving Relationships

*I choose love*

I open my heart to love and joy and move gracefully through my relationships.

It is safe for me to feel love for myself, life and others.

I allow universal love to permeate every cell of my body. I am worthy of love – I am loved.

## Openness

*I give*

I am free to give generously to others, and do so with love.

I breathe love, light and nourishment into my body, mind and spirit, allowing my inner well of resource to be fully replenished.

As I weave loving kindness out into the world, I receive loving kindness from the universal web.

## Forgiveness

*I forgive*

I forgive myself for my imperfections, do my best and find contentment with that – I am good enough.

I recognize my hurts and nurture my inner child with all that she/he needs.

I forgive others for their preconceptions, judgements and behaviours, trusting we are all doing our best with our current levels of awareness and patterning.

## Gratitude

*I am grateful*

I am thankful and humble as I move through life.

I receive willingly, lovingly and graciously.

I recognize and appreciate the small things in life, the synchronicities and beauty that can be found in each and every moment.

## Harmony

*I am balanced*

My mind, body and spirit work in harmony with each other, aligned with both my will and the divine will.

I have balance in my life with room for both pleasure and purpose.

My giving and receiving of love and abundance are in perfect balance.

## Ease & Grace

*I flow gently and easily*

Love is the gentle, powerful presence that radiates through me when I quieten and deepen.

It is safe for me to be gentle and graceful. I follow my heart's desire and take the path of least resistance.

It is easy for me to be gentle and graceful when I connect to the rhythms of the earth and the universe.

## Compassion

*I am compassionate*

I see all things through 'eyes of love' in my heart.

I find compassion and understanding for those who are struggling and misaligned with themselves, their higher wisdom and purpose.

I am kind and compassionate with myself and others and forgive myself for my judgements.

## Heart Chakra Main Card

 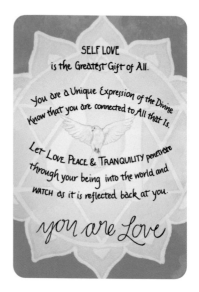

The heart chakra is depicted here by the loving and nurturing Mother Mary, holding her beautiful baby Jesus, embodying the essence of love, compassion, gentleness, and stillness. The surrounding energy welcomes in the spirit animals of the deer and the dove. The rabbits represent the innocence of the new birth and the creative abundance that emanates from the essence of love. The deer moves close, and all are safe in the presence of the loving baby Jesus and Mother Mary. In perfect harmony and balance, a finely tuned presence of Spirit surrounds all. This card is a reminder to bring yourself back to love and back into balance. You will be supported and protected when you do so.

The Star of David represents the Merkabah, a geometric crystalline energy field or container for the mind, body, and spirit. It symbolizes both the sacred geometry of the universe, the light activation of the human body and the light codes of the higher self's life purpose. Sitting here, Mother Mary and Jesus represent the unity of divinity and humanity.

As the upper triangle points to Earth, and the lower triangle to the heavens, there is a perfect meeting place that offers protection within this sacred coming together of Spirit and matter—the heart chakra—thereby creating the magical abundance of life in growth, purpose, and expansion. Fully step into your heart now.

## Loving Relationships

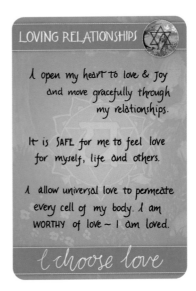

Love is real, it is generous and kind, it expands and centres our being, offering us meaning and a sense of deliverance to that place in our hearts called home. Loving relationships are part of life's greatest joy, so it is important to pay attention and give time to opening to, honouring, and developing the loving relationships in your life.

Allow yourself to give and receive love; for yourself, life, and others. A flow of universal love is there for each of us. You are worthy of love, and it is true: the more love you feel and give, the more you focus on the love you have, and the more that love is reflected back to you. Choose love in your every moment. Love yourself, love your life, and love your fellow brothers and sisters as we unite in the journey back to love.

## Openness

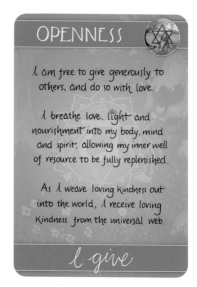

Perhaps you have protected yourself from being hurt and have built up heart walls to keep you safe. You deserve love. It's okay to begin to heal these heart walls now and take a risk on love. When we attach to love we are always at risk of loss and hurt. If someone is consistently hurtful to you, it is okay to expect better and weave a different story of loving kindness into your life, practising by loving yourself first. By allowing and feeling hurt, you create more of the same.

Be open to love now. Love the parts of yourself you have previously rejected, that are hurt and afraid. Send love into the darkest corners, and nourish yourself so that you may open to both love and to others. Give freely and generously without concern for the scales of balance, for the universe will reflect love back to you in great measure. Practise opening your arms and hands out wide to beam love into the universe, and open yourself to love.

## Forgiveness

Forgiveness is a gift to oneself. It's sad that the person who is hardest on us is often ourselves. We react unconsciously much of the time, and while we are raising our levels of consciousness, we must forgive ourselves for those times when we act without love and compassion, for we are healing the journey of many lifetimes. Most of us hold deep hurt and fear, and holding onto these will create more of the same experiences. Sadly, we are prone to reject or disown our own difficulties and project them onto those we love. There is someone or something you need to forgive now. Free yourself of anger and blame, and set others free, too. Release ideas of perfection; we need only be good enough. If we can forgive ourselves and others, we will be able to move closer to love and compassion. God, or Great Spirit, does not punish, and neither should you. Nurture your wounds, and call for healing. It will serve you to practise forgiveness at this time.

## Gratitude

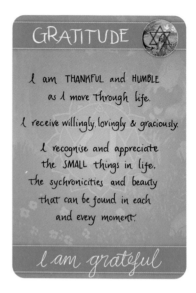

It is time to stop and smell the roses. Often they are there but we don't see them, and if we do see them, we don't take the time to stop and fully appreciate their beauty. When we look with eyes of appreciation and gratitude, we see and sense so much more than we would otherwise. You do have things in life to be grateful for, and the more you take the time to recognize them, the more your heart will sing. There is beauty, especially in nature, all around us. Sometimes it is as subtle as the way a beam of light hits an object, giving life and illumination to it. If you have shelter and food, be grateful for it; appreciate the "having". The practice of gratitude illuminates the darkest of minds, bringing peace and hope and abundance to the heart's desire. This is an important belief to align with if you have been conditioned to believe that you are selfish or ungrateful. You are not responsible for other people's realities. It is okay to release the past and come into the present, appreciating fully, here-now, what-is.

## Harmony

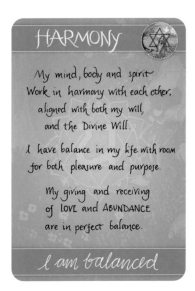

The green of nature exemplifies life flourishing in perfect balance. When we are in balance, we expand and flourish; when we fall out of balance, we have neglected an aspect of the trilogy of self: the mind, body, or spirit, or we are focusing on an aspect of duality. We need to come back to emptiness, back to our centre, in order to find the balance of Yin and Yang energy again. The heart seeks peace and harmony. Noticing your sense of balance—finding your centre, your inner harmonious point—will enable you to thrive now.

Scan through your life to discover what is out of balance, and take time to recalibrate the scales of balance. We may have to think out of the box, but we always have a choice.

REMEMBER: what we focus on grows. So if you need more fun, take time to focus on fun in your life. It is important to avoid focusing on what you *don't* have or *don't* want in your life or you may end up attracting more of the same. So empty yourself—using reiki, qigong, or walks in nature—and realign with what your body, mind, or soul needs.

## Ease & Grace

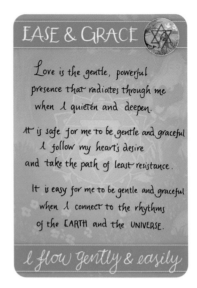

Grace and ease are beckoning you now. Don't work so hard that you override your essence of being. We can only keep driving for so long before we have to refuel, and running on empty begins to do damage to the vehicle you inhabit. Go gently, and come back to your natural flow. Allow a stream of higher consciousness to carry you down the river for a while; rest and observe. Quietening, deepening, and softening are required now. It may take practice, but as you take the time to do so, like the deer, you will become more aware of your surroundings and listen and intuit your next move. As you soften, so does your presence, and you become more receptive to help, support, and love. You are never alone and will be slipped downstream to more solid ground. It is safe for you to soften and let go of beliefs (for example, that "life is difficult") and the steering wheel for a while. When you feel the impulse to drive again, try to maintain the softening in your heart so that you may flow and welcome more ease and grace into your life.

## Compassion

The heart knows love and compassion and will seek it wherever it goes. Like Mother Mary, and Jesus himself, find compassion now, for those who are upsetting or disturbing you are taking you away from love. Whilst all may not be as you desire, there are reasons for others' emotionally driven behaviours. When conscious and aware, people generally do their best. As Gandhi taught, "Be the change you wish to see in the world". Shower yourself and others with compassion. Allow your heart to teach you about love and compassion, for it is capable of bringing you wondrous and bountiful gifts when you see through its "eyes of love".

The peacefulness of the dove also teaches us compassion. As a spirit messenger it brings from heaven a stream of white light, soothing heavy minds; enabling us to follow, with compassion for self and for all, the righteous path.

# Throat Chakra
## Aspects and Beliefs

## Self-Expression
*I speak up*

The passion felt in me cannot help but be expressed as I use my voice to put my message, wisdom and teaching out into the world.

What I have to say is important and I will say it.

I now make myself heard as my heart and soul express through my body, eyes and voice.

## Communication
*I collaborate and co-operate*

I communicate with others in healthy and meaningful ways.

My communications are constructive, honest and purposeful.

I communicate with respect, positive regard and an intention of growth for all.

## Freedom
*I heal*

I release all tears, sadness and the attachment to closing up and playing small in order to allow my throat to open fully.

I open my throat and allow myself to breathe, sing, laugh and cry.

My voice is an instrument through which I heal myself and others.

## Transmutation

*I transform*

I release the negative thoughts and expectations of myself, others and the world.

It is easy for me to transform negative beliefs and expectations into positive and supporting ones, and so I do.

I recognize the power of my thoughts and words as they vibrate through the universe, creating my future reality.

## Clarity

*I have clarity*

I know when to stay silent and when to speak. I speak with clarity, knowing what to say and how to say it.

I take enough time to go inward, listen, reflect, understand and gain clarity of thought.

I take the time to say and express exactly what I need to.

## Truth

*I express my truth*

It is safe for me to align with and express my higher truth, wisdom and knowing.

I allow others to hold a different perspective to me and know that there is enough space in the universe for all of our truths – including my own.

I am honest with myself and hear the resonance of truth in my words.

## Space

*I have space*

I have all of the space that I need to flourish, grow and express myself.

I take up my space in all areas of my life.

The space around me is clear and I continue to cleanse and make sacred my space.

## Throat Chakra Main Card

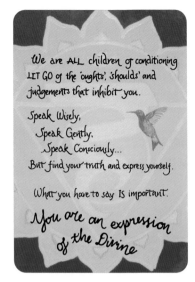

Melchizedek (sometimes thought of as an archangel), shown on the throat chakra card, is known as the king of righteousness who governs the kingdom of peace within the Universe. Melchizedek's offering is the teaching of oneness. He spoke of the birth of the son of God to the earthly Mother Mary and facilitated the path of Jesus Christ, who later followed the priesthood of Melchizedek. He is personified as the enlightened priest who supports us, with the help of the angels, and Archangel Michael, in particular, to find our true inner voice and to acknowledge and learn about the sacred forms of reality and consciousness through sacred geometry and meditation practices. An evolving force, he supports us to be pure in our intent to move closer to our one true God-like essence; to be of the light, in our hearts, giving us courage to express our light in this world.

In his hand is a hand-drawn representation of the cosmic mandala of Bhutan. This is one in a series of mandalas that depict the "spiral involution of energy into matter", as discovered by British voice teacher and Family Constellation therapist Jill Purce in her 1974 book *The Mystic Spiral: Journey of the Soul*. A triple spiral, spinning in the centre, creates the four-armed swastika, which spirals eventually into the third-dimensional materialization of 12 geometric rings, two of each representing the four directions, North, South, East, and West, plus two each representing the vertical directions, ascetics (up) and brahmins (down). This card is a reminder to look at how your energetic transmissions in the forms of thought and sound are transforming into matter and creating your reality.

The white mountains are representative of the wings of Archangel Michael, sometimes interchanged with Melchizedek. The wolf, guardian of loyalty and trust, teaches us how to howl from deep in the belly, expressing the sound vibrations of our heart and soul's song, which are then carried into the ether. If we are conscious about the power of our presence and remain pure of thought and mind, we will create a strong vibration that can influence the possibility for earthly peace. We are encouraged here to be mindful of that power and to impact in positive ways our own and others' reality in service to the highest good of all.

## Self-Expression

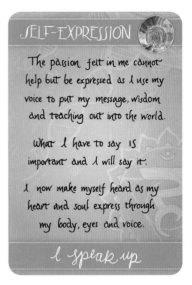

This powerful card signifies your readiness to break silence—sing, speak, write, and express with your whole being what it is you have to say. If you have ever felt shut down, dismissed, or silenced, it is now time to feel deep into your belly and allow your true self, your desires, and heart's expression to rise through you and out into the world. If you have been holding back your truth, give yourself permission to speak it. What you have to say is (and always was) important. The more you express your truth, the more wisdom comes forth. You may express through your clothes, your body language, or the written word to begin with, but finding your own voice is important. If it comes out a little clumsily at first, forgive yourself. People do not have to agree with you, nor do they have to accept your truth as their own, but like the wolf howling from deep in his belly, it's time for you to sing your own song and allow it to be heard.

## Communication

A lack of effective and meaningful communication is disrupting your energy channels and affecting your ability to find peace and clarity within your relationships. Work on your methods of communication now. Avoid passive or aggressive methods of communication. Assertively work towards appreciating others' point of view, gaining understanding, then express whatever it is that you need to communicate. Be clear in your intentions. Why do you need to communicate a certain message? Is it so that you can feel better, or is it to build bridges with an intention of growth and collaboration for all? When we communicate with positive regard, we can be constructive and maintain meaningful, healthy relationships. Good communication takes practice, so be kind to yourself and others while you work out what it is that you really need to communicate. We all need to feel understood, so practise listening as well as expressing. It is important now for you to take the time to communicate, collaborate, and co-operate.

## Freedom

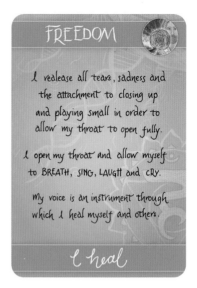

Healing of the throat chakra is called for. Recognize all of the times you have swallowed your pride, pushed down tears, and suppressed emotion. Acknowledgement and acceptance of this pattern are needed so that you can let it go. There is only so much we can "swallow" before we create energy blockages that cause suffering in the throat chakra and thyroid gland. Release your tears and emotion now, and allow your throat to open so that you may be a clear channel for the expression of your heart and soul. Renewal of this delicate space is what is being offered here. Use whatever means of healing you are drawn to, but realign your beliefs so that you have freedom to use your voice to heal both yourself and others.

## Transmutation

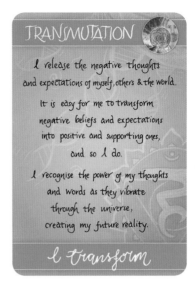

Our thoughts and words carry vibration into the world as thought forms. The message in this card is that you are being too hard on yourself or others, and there is negativity to unwind and transmute. This statement gives you permission to release negative thinking patterns and expectations, and lets you know that it can be easier than you think to simply change your beliefs. You are a powerful creator of your own reality and have the ability to transform your life. Negative energies, thoughts, and words are holding you back, so transform these into positive ones, and begin to watch your reality shift. It is time to expect the best from yourself, others, and the world around you. All is well. When you see how your thoughts affect your mood, behaviours, and ultimately, your reality, you can choose to intervene powerfully and energetically to bring positive change into existence.

## Clarity

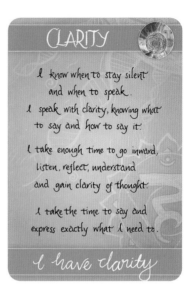

This card brings you the opportunity to fine-tune your expression. It offers you a chance to go into detail, to gain clarity of thought and mind, so that your expressed vibration may be pure and distinct. This fine tuning may require reflection and contemplation, a precision that means that you will be heard when you speak because you will be speaking exactly your truth; and you will know when, and to whom, you are to express this truth. Perhaps you need to be honest with yourself. We can be clouded by too much communication or by too much noise, by others' ideas and opinions. Be quiet, and reflect upon your own thought process, allowing the stream of consciousness to reach its conclusion. This is not about telling pre-written stories but about finding clarity in the essence of your own true thought. Create the space, and take the time you need to communicate what it is you have discovered. Clarity of thought is enlightening for everyone around you.

## Truth

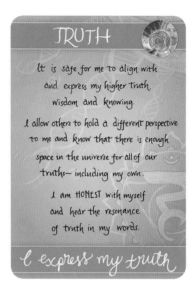

Truth carries a particular vibration. When I am working with clients and hear untruths, they feel jagged and jarring and disrupt the energy flow of the person speaking them. We can deceive ourselves, believing that we should be feeling or thinking certain things, but if what we say is not our higher truth, then we do ourselves a great disservice. There is a truth to be realized now. The truth can sometimes hurt and be temporarily disruptive, but being dishonest with yourself will not serve you in the long run. When we ignore our truth, we dishonour and disrespect ourselves. Coming into our truth is liberating and self-serving. It is what it is, and ultimately, it is empowering to stand in one's truth. The universe supports us to stand in our truth as we honour ourselves and experience the inevitable change that comes from being in one's truth. It is important to acknowledge that other people may have their own, different truth, which is equally valid, but that this does not have to detract from your own truth. Be courageously honest with yourself now.

## Space

We all need space to breathe, to grow, to move, to think, to be. Align with the belief that you have all the space you need, and begin to create this for yourself. Space within and space without is what is called for now. Empaths who are sensitive to other people's energy are in particular need of their own clear space to be able to reconnect with themselves. Clear the clutter, and take 15 minutes each day to be quiet in your own space, away from phones and distractions. Space enables the throat to relax and soften, so that we can be more receptive to subtle energies and connection to our higher or true selves, our desires, and our intuition. When we fear being alone, we can fill our space with noise and busyness. See creating space as a sacred ritual, space for magic to happen, for connection to our selves and to the wider universe around us. Cleansing your space with fresh air, the beat of a drum or vibration of a singing bowl, natural incense or essential oils may help you to find and honour the space you are looking for now. The most important suggestion I can make is to recognize when you do have space, and when you don't, then make space for yourself.

# Third Eye Chakra
## Aspects and Beliefs

## Protection

*All is perfect just as it is*

I release the need for armour and protection as I recognize that I am always guided and safe.

The more I let go of fear and mistrust, the more protected I feel. It is safe for me to choose love and possibility over fear and hopelessness.

I trust in my light, the divine light, and the wisdom that ensues from the alchemy of spirit and matter.

## Purity

*My intention is pure*

I release the need to control myself, my life and others around me.

I allow for and embrace purity of mind and vision.

I am honest, clear and pure in my intentions to serve myself and others to bring about peace in the world.

## Intuition

*I am guided*

I have intuition and know how to use it – I trust my intuition.

I listen to my inner visions, imaginings, messages and sense of knowing, allowing my intuition to guide me.

I release the 'need to know' and allow my intuition to develop at a pace that's right for me.

## Healing

*I am harmonious*

I see clearly how to bring harmony to pain, discomfort and issues of separation, and so I am healed.

I transcend the illusion of duality, seeing beyond the veil of divisive thoughts and behaviours.

I offer with confidence and integrity my visions for a brighter, more harmonious future.

## Peace of Mind

*I am peaceful*

I heal the poisons of my mind that limit and deny me by aligning with pure and honest thought and belief.

I joyfully recognize when I am thinking limiting thoughts from my conditioning, and realign with thoughts and beliefs that serve my growth and well-being.

I choose to question my perspective and think loving, supportive thoughts.

## Psychic Awareness

*I am psychic*

I open my third eye and allow visions of higher wisdom to be received and trusted.

I see clearly that which comes through my subtle senses to assist the alignment of my will with the divine will.

My psychic awareness is sacred – aligned only with the highest good for myself, others and the planet.

## Unity

*I unite*

I see the unity and harmony within the polarities that I am experiencing and choose to align with the centre point of balance, harmony and love for one and all.

I am open to seeing with fresh eyes, a more balanced perspective.

The truth of this matter lies in between the polarities within which I am resonating.

## Third Eye Chakra Main Card

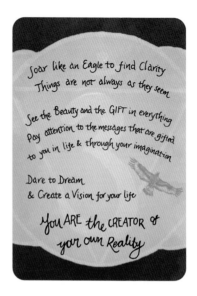

The third eye chakra card was inspired by my psychology background and my reiki teachings and practice. In essence, it is the learning that purifying the mind heals the body. Negative emotions, often anchored and perpetuated by thought, cause constriction and disruption to the body's energy flow, and therefore, its health. Depicted in the third eye artwork, Amitabha Buddha is the Peacock King deity who brings, and teaches about, immeasurable light and life and rides on the peacock here in his Western land of paradise.

The peacock symbology links also to the bird's ability to ingest the poisons of the snake (representative of the ego and the poisons of the mind). In East Indian folklore, it is believed that the transmuted toxicity gives birth to the peacock's most beautiful, iridescent colours (Ellis 2014). So this is the teaching of the peacock and the Peacock King: to purify the mind of the poisons of the ego self. Once cleared, the third eye begins to see with light and clarity that which was previously unseen. When our distortions are cleared, we can see clearly, recognizing the powerful creator within ourselves. As you begin to work with transmutation of the lower mind to a higher consciousness, a connection to the mystic realms develops, enabling you to create a vision for your life in accordance with the soul and akasha. Be open now to moving beyond the limits of time, space, and causality.

The two lotus petals remind us of duality, and draw us inwards to the meeting place of *ida* and *pingala*, in yogic thought, the two *nadi* channels by which *kundalini* energy rises, opening us to a higher consciousness. The petals attach to the ouroboros, the serpent representing unity, infinity, and wholeness, having met and devoured itself. It is the pure, alchemical process of meeting one's light and dark aspects, the assimilation and integration of the Yin and Yang that offers release and liberation from ourselves; in doing so, we are reborn. Perhaps you are in a cycle of completion and rebirth? The two ravens symbolize the mysticism you will experience now, as your true sense of self and the universal consciousness becomes visible to you. An expansion of reality is upon you. Watch and listen as the universe communicates with you.

## Protection

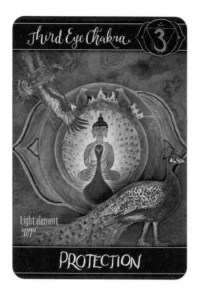

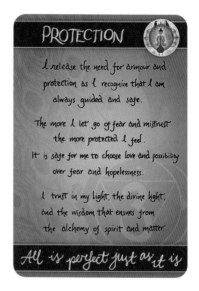

Seeking to find out what could go wrong serves neither your growth and development nor your sense of peace and wellbeing. A fundamental shift in perspective is being called for. You have been caught up in unnecessary thoughts for too long. What if you shifted your perception of danger and aligned yourself with safety? What if you knew that, ultimately, your spirit guides and ancestors will keep you safe—as will your own intuition—and that you can shift your own reality and release the need for so much protection? Protection is called for when we fear threat or danger. Choose safety and a vibration of love now. If that means making changes in yourself and your routine in the physical world, then make those changes. Trust in the process and the perfection of life itself. You are precious and exist here on Earth for good reason at this time. Focus on your purpose rather than on the obstacles around you.

## Purity

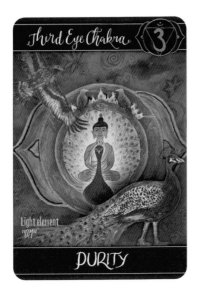

When we purify our mind and body, we allow more light to permeate our being, which both leads to and requires surrender, softening, and release. Your need to control (otherwise known as keeping yourself safe) may be getting in the way now of purifying harsh energies. It is safe to let go of control and purify your surroundings, body, mind, and intentions. Perhaps detoxification of negative energy or toxins is required to help you with this next step of development.

As the third eye opens, you will become more and more receptive to the stirrings of your unconscious and the visions of your higher consciousness. Take some time now to purify and become clear about your intentions. Intention is everything, the driver of life as we know it. Listen to your passion and to the bigger picture that is unfolding around you. Does your intention serve you, as well as the greater good? Are you being truly honest with yourself? Breathe deeply, and allow a little more movement in and around you to facilitate the vibration of purity into your life.

## Intuition

You are always feeling, sensing, and intuiting, whether you are aware of this or not. Don't doubt yourself so much, or question the validity of your intuitive hunches. When the world outside or inside you is so busy, it's hard to listen to the subtleties of intuition, so quieten your mind; you are being called to pay more attention to your intuition now. When you align with trusting your intuition, it will begin to speak more loudly to you. If you refuse to listen, it will persist. Paying attention to your intuition brings light into the darkness. Allow your inner callings to be present now by looking inside to find your answers. You are at one with the great cosmos, and she will commune with you, on the inside, when you quieten and go within. The answers are always inside rather than outside ourselves. Be wary of giving away your power and guidance to others. You are called to focus here because, with the help of your guides, you are capable of developing and trusting your own intuition.

## Healing

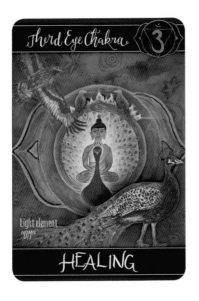

Healing is an essential part of our purpose, as we have long forgotten our divinity and our tremendous power. As we reconnect with our whole selves, we must go into the darkness and move through the birthing canal, like the butterfly pushing out of its cocoon. Be willing to see the harshness and judgements you have placed on the world around you. People are mostly unconscious, but it is time to rise, time for you to be a guiding light. Address your fears and feelings of separation, judgement, and condemnation, for when you judge and condemn yourself, you restrict your capacity to heal. Love is the answer. Love yourself, and love your brothers and sisters, for they too are finding their way back to the divine light. The more duality and separation you can heal, the lighter your load will be—and the more you will be the guiding and shining star that will bring peace, love, and harmony back to the planet.

## Peace of Mind

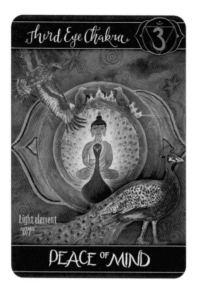
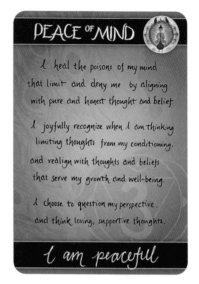

You are, and have always been, so much more than the conditioning you were born into. Perfection is encoded in your heart, and it is now your journey to return to this perfection, moving beyond the limits of your conscious mind, thoughts, and belief system. As you are doing now, actively rewrite your introjected beliefs so that you may find peace of mind. Your thoughts and beliefs can be wholly loving and supportive when you take the time to work through those that are toxic and poisonous. Like the glorious, iridescent colours of the peacock, inner peace enables you to shine your light. Choose to shift your perspective so that you may actively choose loving, peaceful thoughts, and see what becomes possible when you do so!

## Psychic Awareness

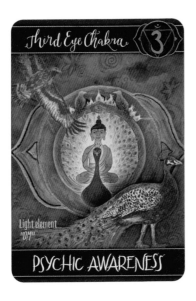
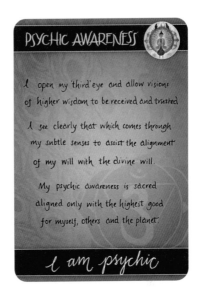

Let us shift the idea that magic is dark and dangerous, or that you will be hanged, drawn, and quartered for communicating with the consciousness of other realms or dimensions. We all have psychic ability, and you have picked this card because you have the potential to serve yourself, others, and the planet with your sacred gift. Remain grounded, and of heart, and you will be safe to open yourself to your psychic gifts. The opening of the third eye enables us to see deeply into the unconscious processes of the psyche, as well as receive higher wisdom and guidance from consciousness outside of our familiar time, space, and causality. Purify, and choose to connect only with guidance for your and others' highest good. A higher vision for your life enters now. It is time to lighten and play a little in order to develop your psychic abilities.

## Unity

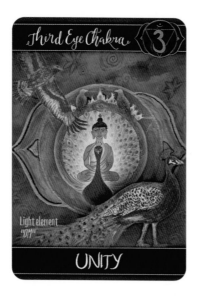

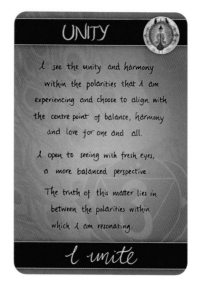

This card is really about moving out of the harsh ends of polarity now. We often experience life from two ends of the spectrum, being very connected or very lonely, very helpless or very powerful, very depressed or overspilling with joy. It is all there as vibration to be experienced, and when we are working with one vibration, we usually perceive the other end of the spectrum, too. It is helpful for you now to bring yourself into experiencing a more harmonious vibration, finding the midway or centre point of balance. Where all is possible, seeing a more balanced perspective brings peace, harmony, and less attachment to our experiences, which ultimately unites us with the energy vibration of love. Love is our natural state of being. Let go of the dramas, the things in life that cause you pain, and come into the blessed unity of the one truth, heart, and mind for all.

# Crown Chakra
## Aspects and Beliefs

### Possibility

*All is possible*

All is possible for me in this universe of infinite potential.

I release all conditioning and limits that I have placed in my path unknowingly.

I believe, invest and intend in the possibility of a positive, peaceful and loving outcome.

### Connection

*I am always connected*

I recognize the inter-connectedness of all of life.

I honour my connection to 'All That Is'. I embody universal love.
I am worthy of God's unconditional love.

I am open to new connections and possibilities as I explore the gift of consciousness.

### Divine Will

*I allow the unfolding*

I align my will with the divine will, allowing wisdom from the higher realms to support and guide my evolution on this earth.

I grow when I settle into the service of myself and others.

I leave space for the magic of the universe to play in my life.

## Integrity

*I have integrity*

I am aligned with my higher truth and am deeply and lovingly honest with myself.

I listen to the truth in my heart and know what is right within me, aware that many truths can exist.

I am ethical and integrous in my actions.

## Knowing

*I am wise*

For the greatest good of all, I trust my knowledge and wisdom, and the higher knowledge and wisdom available to me.

I am an aspect of universal consciousness – I know myself to be part of the whole.

I now grow beyond my previous experiences.

## Consciousness

*I am conscious*

I surrender the struggle of my ego and conditioning and allow guidance and knowledge to raise my consciousness.

Knowing that I am enough, I allow the unfolding of my inner magnificence and beauty.

I practice stillness and emptiness, surrendering to higher consciousness in and around me.

## We

*We are one*

I am blessed to be part of the One. I honour and cherish my brothers and sisters past, present and future who journey with me.

Difference and polarity are not a threat but an alternative view and experience.

I embrace the shared experience of myself and others as eternal beings.

## Crown Chakra Main Card

As Shakti, the primordial cosmic energy, rises in the form of kundalini, the divine feminine awakens us, shooting up the spine through the crown to the cosmos (the divine father). Of course, the divine feminine and masculine cannot be separate, nor exist without the other. It is at the crown that we come into unity, into the interconnectedness of all things. The Borromean Rings in the centre of the picture have represented, through time and across many civilizations—ancient Buddhist art, India, Norse stone inscriptions, and throughout Europe—the interlocking of three divine aspects of the whole. This symbolic link represents the strength in unity: the central triangle within the circles forms a powerful transformational energy arising from the three complementary forces of sacred life. If one circle were to be cut, the others would separate and fall apart. The Borromean Rings remind us of the "we" that, together, forms the whole we often seek.

The Christian holy trinity of the Father, Son, and Holy Spirit has been represented through these interconnected circles. This divine trinity has similar expression in other forms across religion and culture, and when we look closer, the three is split into six; into male and female counterparts, the foundation for the flower of life, where six circles connect around a single circle, or point of creation. In the Hindu *trimurti* of supreme divinity, we find Shiva, Brahma, and Vishnu, representing the cosmic functions of

238

destruction, creation, and preservation, and their feminine complements Parvati, Saraswati, and Lakshmi. In the angelic realm, we find Archangels Gabriel, Michael, and Chamuel, and the feminine aspects Archeia: Faith, Hope, and Charity. These cosmic forces of life together represent the whole. It is this whole, the One, or the Supreme God, Dattatraya, Shri Lalitla Deva, Great Spirit, whatever we wish to call All-That-Is, that we become humbled by and remember we are part of as we raise our kundalini and expand our heart consciousness through the crown chakra.

Metatron—depicted as Thoth, the record keeper of universal wisdom in the sacred land of Egypt—is the bringer of consciousness to this realm, the scriber of truth, and the path to enlightenment. He is depicted here carrying his emerald tablet of ancient wisdom. Thoth is the arbiter of good and bad, able to sit in between the polarities of both and see the whole, in balance, unity and oneness: the zero-point from which great creation springs forth. The powerful and mystical divine goddess and teacher of wisdom and esotericism Isis, the mother of Horus, wife and goddess protector of the kingdom, is depicted in union with Thoth on the crown chakra card, offering you her healing hand. These teachers of healing, medicine, and great loving wisdom encourage you to be empowered now—to know your strengths and work with universal truth and magic for the healing and enlightenment of one and all.

The opening of the crown chakra is met in this picture with the third element, the light of the dove, bringing in the form of the holy spirit or messenger the energies and enlightenment of heaven to all sentient beings on Earth.

## Possibility

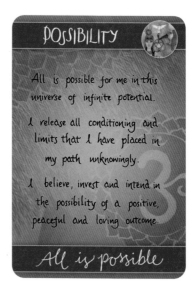

All truly is possible. Open and expand your mind and knowing to these beliefs. We do not need to know the how, just that all is possible. Allow inspired thought and action to move you towards your goals. Release and transmute limitation, for it no longer serves you or the greater good. Ponder your situation now—how could it work out better than imagined if all were possible? Expand your imaginings, and maybe sit with paper and pen and allow the universe to play a little in your creations. When we clear the fears and blocks to our soul's reconnection and expression, we can recognize fully that all is possible. Remember the driving forces of love, purity, justice, and truth. Align and purify your intentions, and let the possibilities and magic happen for you, with you, and through you now.

## Connection

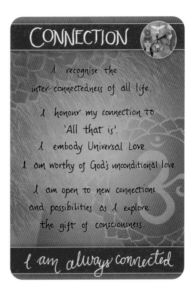

You are the universe in all its glory; you can never be separate from it. You make an imprint upon the universe, and it imprints upon you. What you are experiencing may well be a reflection of you, your beliefs, and expectations. Raise your vibration now by recognizing your connection to All That Is, and embody the universal divine love that is available for you to connect with. Mother/Father God loves you unconditionally and seeks to pour love into your brothers and sisters on Earth through you, but you must recognize that you are already connected, even through thought and intent. Meditate or sit quietly, and feel the expanse of energy around you as you explore and open to a deeper and lighter consciousness. If you are feeling disconnected at this time, forgive yourself, and connect to the spark of the divine in your heart that is your essential being. Breathe life into this spark, and feel your light grow. It is in all of us, and you are loved more than you can ever know.

## Divine Will

It may be time to stop battling, attaching to, or pushing so hard with something you are trying to achieve. There may be an easier way or a little insight to be gained now. You have free will but you may be pushing towards something that is not meant for your soul's purpose, or calling. We all have missions, learning, and healing to do, but you may be helped now by checking in with yourself to ascertain whether this course of action and persistence is aligned with the divine will for you. Are you truly serving yourself and others now? The late self-help author and speaker Wayne Dyer frequently used the expression "Let go, and let God". This is what is being called for now. Let go a little so that there is room for your team of spirit guides and angels to play and support you now. Are you asking for their help? You will soon find a little more clarity. Then call upon hope, faith, and charity to support you along your path. A little re-jig is necessary now so that your will may be aligned with the divine will.

## Integrity

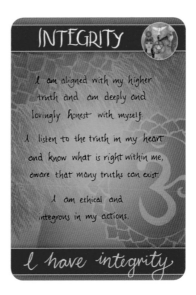

Be brave in your ability to stand in your truth. Perhaps your integrity has been questioned in the past, or maybe you have behaved without integrity and are using this against yourself now, doubting who you are. We can all slip and behave in ways we think will serve others rather than ourselves; ultimately, though, stepping out of our truth is always a disservice. Walking the pathway of the warrior in love and truth can be a lonely one. Know that you are being supported right now, and that you are not alone on your mission. Call upon Archangels Michael or Raphael, or beautiful Mother Mary, now for help with finding the truth in your heart and the courage to act in accordance with your truth. You have integrity. Recognize this in yourself, and others will see it too.

## Knowing

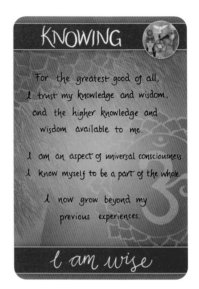

For the greater good of all, you must now come to trust your knowledge and wisdom. There are new insights and doors of knowledge opening up to you now. It is time to be curious and trust in your experiences. There is knowledge encoded in your state of being and much universal wisdom to be shared at this time of great awakening. Perhaps you have always known that there was more to life than we had previously been aware of. As you expand your consciousness now, you will become aware of this knowledge and have a sense of knowing. Know that you belong and are a necessary part of divine consciousness. Recognize your wisdom, and if you are drawn to share your knowledge with others, now is the time to do so. You are wise beyond your years.

## Consciousness

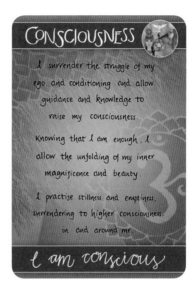

Your ego and inner childhood hurts are still trying to protect you, yet your soul is longing to see and experience itself more fully. It is time for you to contemplate letting go of the hurt, anger, shame, or guilt your personality and ego are trapping inside you. Breathe and release, as you are much more than your stories of old. Your experiences are valid. Your soul has experienced these feelings before, and deep healing is now required at the source of these vibrations, so that you may heal the soul fragments that still hurt and transcend your current reality. You may become conscious of past experiences now that will help you make sense of your current life situation. Regardless of the hurts, you are beautiful; regardless of the fear and pain, you are loved unconditionally. Love yourself deeply now, and raise your consciousness to enable integration, as you evolve and emerge more fully and completely than ever before. Go within. Transcendence to a higher consciousness is upon you.

## We

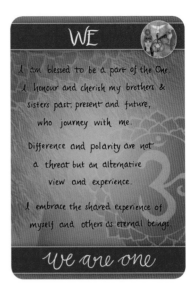

The thousand-petalled lotus is unfolding for you now, with you at its centre. All around you is you as I, and I as we, as you recognize yourself in others and they recognize themselves in you. Access to higher dimensions is helping you now to transcend time and space, as we exist in the here and now; all being present with us in this moment. As you connect with your place called home, bring it down to Earth so that it may be lived here. Be in your "unity consciousness", aware of duality and polarity but not attaching to it, for your liberation will free others. Resist judgement of others, or you will fall again into duality, but bring the love and compassion of higher realms to Earth, to Earth's sentient beings. We are all journeying together, and together we unite. May you be the light, the peace, the love, and the god/goddess that awakens our hearts and minds to the galactic loving consciousness of the universe.

## Introducing Your Chakra Power Animals

The animals listed here and depicted in the chakra cards carry a particular vibration. If you wish to temporarily shift the way you feel, in order to help you to stay positively focused and move away from negativity, you can imagine yourself to be one of these animals or an animal of your choosing. This is an effective technique for changing course if you have been allowing a negative chain of thought to flow. Tell yourself, "Stop!", "Cancel that!", or "Delete!", and choose a different energy to align with. Imagine being this energy for a minute or so, until your feeling has changed.

### ROOT CHAKRA | The Elephant

The elephant is a symbol of the stability that family can bring. It is a loyal animal, with strength, sensitivity, and focus. This animal has longevity and staying power and helps drive us towards what we need to address. Call upon the elephant for steady wisdom and focus. She can awaken the divine feminine in our lives and will shelter us from harm.

### The Snake

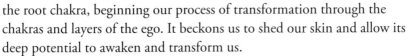

The snake lives on—and moves along —the ground, and can be called upon to assist us with grounding ourselves in primordial earth energy. The Snake represents the kundalini energy that awakens and opens the root chakra, beginning our process of transformation through the chakras and layers of the ego. It beckons us to shed our skin and allow its deep potential to awaken and transform us.

### SACRAL CHAKRA | The Dolphin

The dolphin is a highly evolved creature, sensitive and harmonious in its nature. Its spirited being reminds us to connect with the lightness of life and encourages us to play wholeheartedly. Joy and love are our natural state of being.

These beautiful and gifted creatures are powerful cosmic co-creators of joy, generosity, and connection.

### The Whale

The whale symbolizes our deep soul's nature and urges. Its beautiful and haunting song echoes deeply from its belly. Guardian of the oceans, keeper of spiritual wisdom, this animal holds a steady presence for us all. Whale teaches us to dive deep into the heart of the matter to find the eternal wisdom of all that has gone before and all that will follow.

### SOLAR PLEXUS CHAKRA | The Bear

The bear teaches us to have boundaries. He allows us to be steady, find our strength, and stand our ground. Bear is a protector and will shield us from what we need not engage with. He is an arbiter of justice and will help us to find our personal authority. If you need to stand up and take the lead on matters close to the heart, call upon bear for help.

### The Lion

The lion need not fear or attack, as he knows his own strength and capability. He, like the bear, stands his ground and protects his pride of lions. Lion exudes courage and represents the ultimate power within the animal kingdom. He is intuitive, assertive, and fully present in the power of now. The lion is wise beyond his ancestral years, an emblem of self-mastery.

## HEART CHAKRA | The Dove

Representing the spirit messenger,
the dove symbolizes the purity
and truth of the divine. A
bridge between worlds, the
dove brings light into the
recesses of our shadows in times
of need. Calming the mind, dove
helps us to transcend the transient
stories and reside in our heart's divine
dwelling place. Dove is the embodiment
of peace and tranquillity—the heart's desire.

### The Deer

The deer is an instinctual sensing and
feeling animal. It has a gentle energy
and is intuitive by nature. It lives
through the sensing and intuiting of
its heart and has a magical essence that
connects us to life's mysteries. Deer
helps us to find our inner grace and
gentleness, guiding us towards our
next move, ahead of time. Call upon
deer to come back to the essence of
innocence.

## THROAT CHAKRA | The Wolf

Wolf will always assist you to howl,
from deep within your belly, your inner
expressions into the outer world. The
refined truth is expressed through the
wolf, and its echoes are heard. Wolf is a
loyal guardian, a friend always bringing
us back to our truth when we are
pulled to stray. If protection, an ally,
or guidance is needed to help you
walk your own path, call upon the
wolf to light the way.

### The Hummingbird

The blue-throated hummingbird teaches us how to sing with joy. Its light vibrations and the hum of its wings clear the reverberations of old, enabling us to fine-tune our own voices to the sound of our highest expression. Hummingbird chirps and awakens, elevating us to recognize the beauty in and around us—its colourful throat uninhibited and its flight as free as the morning sky.

### THIRD EYE CHAKRA | The Eagle

As the eagle soars from the greatest heights, its perception is enlightened. A spirit messenger, the eagle brings news of change and possibility and inspires through its strength of conviction. Its ancient origins can help you to acquire a higher perspective, bringing forth its wisdom from the higher realms to this earthly plane. This bird of great strength and foresight has extraordinary vision, enabling you to find the treasures in your own life.

### The Peacock

Impervious to the poison of the snake, the peacock stands fearless in all its glory. With its ability to transmute toxins, the peacock calls us to step forward without apology and heal conflicts of duality. This bird will enable us to grow beyond our limits into our true authentic power, in service to others. Its radiant beauty and poise teaches us how to recognize, honour, and love ourselves.

**CROWN CHAKRA | The Swan**

The swan signifies strength, beauty, and grace. It glides with ease through the water and reminds us to steady our flow. The swan is a carrier of the extraordinary, a reflection of divine love, with the ability to bring us to a point of inner stillness and tranquillity. An omen for lasting romance and true love, the swan offers reassurance about our sacred union and creative pursuits. Call on swan to help find your inner glow, grace, and beauty.

### The Rainbow Butterfly

The rainbow butterfly is the ultimate representation of the spectrum of light that together creates the magnificent whole. It is birthed through rapid and radical transformation and symbolizes our ability to do the same. The butterfly has a lightness of being, encouraging us to embrace change and surrender to the divine will. The rainbow butterfly reminds us to have faith during times of transition and growth.

# Resources

# Five Healing InSight Case Studies

The following case studies give real-life examples of the process in action. Whilst I aim to keep it simple, the mind-body is complex, and we have many stories, interwoven ideas, and perceptions of reality. As you are likely to come up against yourself from time to time when working with the system, I have kept the content "real" with the following cases.

Some of them are big life issues that have taken a significant amount of processing. I've included forgiveness protocols, and the manifestation process, so you can see how that is done. More complete processes are on the Healing InSight website and the YouTube channel for you to be used as resource examples.

The following, very personal accounts are given to help with your deeper understanding of the Healing InSight method and its process. I love this work; I live it, practise it, and I am used to energy clearing and dealing with the difficult stuff—it made me the person I am today. The people in the case studies are real people; some completely new to energy work, all relatively new to the system, but each and every one has offered you their very personal experience and journey for mine and your behalf.

I thank them sincerely for sharing.

## ANDY
### Feeling a Burden and Worried About Letting People Down

Using the Healing InSight method described earlier, Andy explored and muscle-tested to find several limiting beliefs that were being played out in his life, causing him to feel inadequate and disempowered. In his words, he was afraid of "wasting people's time" and "getting in the way of other people's success, especially at work".

Andy muscle-tested "yes" to the following negative beliefs: "I am a failure", "I let people down", and "I make things worse"; he tested "no" to the following positive beliefs: "I am and always have been a success", "I am competent and capable", "I am reliable, dependable, and appreciated", and "I make things better."

There are several different beliefs here, so we worked with one at a time. I describe the first one here; the others can be found on the Healing InSight website for reference.

In addressing the first belief ("I am and always have been a success"), Andy muscle-tested that it was for his highest and best good to align with this positive belief now, and he gave full permission to go ahead and balance for it. Usually, we are then directed to the Simple or Advanced Method to go ahead; however, this time, we got a "no" for the Simple Method, and a "no" in the muscle test for use of the Advanced Method. We then asked whether to use the Life Issue process, which was a "yes".

On reflection, it is easy to see that many of these beliefs are tied up with each other and, whilst we may have collapsed one table leg (or belief) at a time, we would have had many table legs to deal with. The Life Issue Alignment is very similar in terms of process to the Advanced Method, but it has a more general approach. When there is an issue that is difficult to put into words or to fully get hold of (from the unconscious or subconscious mind), it's useful to use the life issue alignment because your higher self does know what is best for you and knows where your blocks and limits lie. Whilst we were looking at several specific beliefs, our intention was to clear a bigger issue. Ultimately, the system showed us that we needed to work more globally.

In letting go of the specific beliefs and addressing this as a life issue, Andy went ahead to muscle-test to find his first priority belief(s). This was in the Sacral chakra, the aspect was Emotions, and the belief was number one:

*It is safe for me to feel emotion as I experience relationship with myself, others, and the universe.*

Andy went ahead and activated the hemispheres of the brain relatively easily and peacefully. When he was visualizing and embodying the belief, he described seeing himself as a child in a shop where he had previously felt like a burden asking for something, that it was okay for his caregiver to be upset with him and that he shouldn't blame himself for their reactions. He had the sense that it was good to know that he "could have feelings about things", almost as if previously he had denied himself the right to having feelings about certain events. Then came the interesting phenomena, as the resistance started to arise and Andy was doubting that he had picked the correct belief—that he was failing—and wasting my time. Andy continued, grounded the belief and gave a large yawn as we moved on.

There was a second priority belief to align with in order to resolve the life issue. It was located in the Root chakra, the aspect was Grounding, and the beliefs were Beliefs One and Four. (NOTE: When one or more beliefs are selected, we read them together in one long string of words.)

*I am anchored into my physical existence and resonate in perfect harmony with the physical world; I am earthed.*

Again the hemispheres balanced relatively easily. When Andy brought the belief into his body and began the visualization process, he described himself as being "...fully tuned in to the earth—like there's nowhere else I need to be. I'm fully focused here and feel the weight and density of Earth, like I'm locked into this density. It feels good and solid, I feel present, harmonious with my environment." He went on to say "I feel safe, safe from energetic disturbances, like if lightning came down it would just pass straight through me ...[big yawn] ...I get it now."

These kinds of realizations, or recognitions, let you know that you have fully aligned with the belief. Staying with the visualizations and observing the belief, perhaps speaking it or recognizing it, allows the resonance to evolve and take hold.

We muscle-tested again and found that there was another priority belief to align with in order to resolve this life issue. This belief was found in the Root chakra, Abundance aspect, and the beliefs were Beliefs One, Two, Three, and Four:

*I gather easily and effortlessly all that I need to support, nourish, and comfort me.*
*I focus my attention upon all that I am grateful for. There is an abundance of nourishment, support, and love for me. I have.*

Abundance had been an issue for Andy for some time and was showing up here linked to his sense of burden and failure. I noticed that, as Andy was working through the activation of his hemispheres in relation to these beliefs, he began to build more momentum with the words, and the energy of the words also had a rhythm, a clearer meaning. I have noticed this a lot—when the belief starts to align, the words start to make sense and take on an energy and momentum of their own, as if coming to life. A big yawn, and he was aligned.

This seemed like an exciting realignment for Andy. As he came to his vision, he described seeing a computer game, that he could go around all of the levels, and everything he needed was just there for the taking. His realization was in the key of Gratitude and saw a feedback loop of "I am grateful; therefore, I have; therefore, I am grateful; therefore, I have...", and so on. He said: "I'm recognizing that it's all there. There is so much love. Why would I doubt that I am alone? It's a 'having' universe ... it shows up when you tune in to it ... It feels like 'yes, of course'... feels like a relief, a joy. It's exciting, like tuning in to what I already knew."

This is the wonderful phenomenon that can occur with the Healing InSight realignments: We can, over time, become distorted and removed from our higher truth, but when we realign with it (hopefully, as reflected in the channelled beliefs), it is like coming home to our deepest sense of knowing. It is such a joy and privilege for me to watch people clearing the cobwebs and reconnecting with their divine wisdom. Andy grounded the belief and tested to ascertain whether there was another priority belief to align with.

The fourth priority belief to align with in order to resolve the life issue was found in the Solar Plexus chakra, the aspect was Authentic Power, and it involved Beliefs One and Three:

*My authentic power is achieved through self-esteem, love, truth, and authenticity.*

*It is safe for me to be powerful. I think and speak affirming, supportive words and imagine a life I love.*

Again this balance came in relatively easily, Andy repeated the belief, focusing upon each hand until the hemispheres activated (noticed through sensation in each hemisphere of the brain), then spent time using the infinity harmonizing movement to balance both the activated hemispheres in relation to this belief.

As he brought the belief into his body and conducted the visualization, he noticed that it was "an easy place to be" .... "It just feels easy; it feels great ... I feel bigger ... truer. I feel limitless ... I feel powerful but very gentle at the same time ... I feel calmer, bigger, more real, more relaxed." When asked where he felt this (to help him to recognize and anchor this feeling), he noticed it in his solar plexus, heart, and throat, then noticed the feeling in his third eye, too. It is useful to notice where in the body one feels the sensations as it can help you to tune in to the feeling a little more.

A fifth priority belief was then identified in Andy's Throat chakra, Self-Expression aspect, Beliefs One and Four:

*The passion felt in me cannot help but be expressed, as I use my voice to put my message, wisdom, and teaching out into the world. I speak up.*

As Andy was working through these beliefs, he was getting the awareness that he doesn't have to focus his attention upon being a "nice person". He commented, "It's not about me being accepted" and recalled several people in his life who have rejected him due to his unique ideas, which differ from the mass consciousness. Andy continued: "I can see that I still need to speak up, even if others don't like it ... I don't need to withdraw back into the world ... I feel good about this ... I'm noticing that it's difficult for me to speak up at home. I have conversations with people inside my head ... and when I do speak up, I never really say what I meant to."

Andy needed to become aware of this and of his patterns before he was able to let them go. He needed reminding to return to the beliefs, as sometimes the old stories want to keep on being told and acknowledged. Once aligned and in the belief embodiment visualization process, he reported: "It's like I'm singing a new tune ... I can feel the resonance emanating from me ... I can see it's like coloured light emanating out of my sacral and throat chakras and then my heart, too, and when I transmit it—I think it's my passion—when I emit it and people listen, it's like they light up too with the same resonance and colours; something lights up in them. I transmit it through the voice— like the voice is a carrier of vibration, and if they're willing to hear it, they can receive it ... I feel aligned with wanting to do that ... It feels like my purpose, my wanting to speak up."

He had the insight that he needed to stay steady to his core vibration and not try to be liked for his message, not try to remain in favour, and for his words to be less about him and more about the message that he wishes to convey. He saw, finally, that his message is one of warmth, one of conveying the truth of unconditional love as a way of life, a way of being our whole selves.

Working on ourselves and going through these shifts is hard work, it is tiring, and doesn't always leave one feeling elated. When we let go, we come into emptiness and generally just feel like a big rest or sleep. This is a good idea, as it allows for assimilation of all of the changes that have taken place. We did break here and came back to the process, which is absolutely fine to do. When the body becomes tired or dehydrated, muscle testing can feel compromised, so listen to your body and take your time. These are big changes that could take years of therapy to shift that you are changing in a matter of minutes, or perhaps hours. For anyone who is very sensitive or suffers with low energy, it may be beneficial for you to keep to one or two realignments a day.

At our next session, Andy muscle-tested to align with the priority belief, which was in the Sacral chakra, aspect Potential, and Belief One:

*I am alive with potential and fertile with possibility.*

Andy began to visualize drawing the infinity symbol in the hemispheres of his brain with his hand here, which activated the hemispheres very quickly, and so thought that he was aligned. In his visualization he saw a box, which he opened to find a broom. He began sweeping things away but felt like he was busy sweeping up everyone else's mess, feeling like a janitor and a little uninspired. He saw that he had spent much of his life helping other people to clean up their mess, or helping others with their failing projects. He saw what he had been doing and realized that this was not what he wanted, and certainly wasn't feeling alive with potential and possibility. He muscle-tested the belief—which he had not come into alignment with, so he took his time and realigned again, this time more slowly and with more intention.

In this visualization, he saw a tunnel descending. When he followed it in, he found a wagon. He went deeper and stopped and saw a load of treasure piling into his wagon, though it was grey. He wasn't sure that this belonged to him and decided that he had been carrying other people's treasure and tipped it out—the moment he did this, he saw gold and colours. There was his own treasure at the very bottom of everyone else's. He said: "I'm loving it …. I feel wonder …. It feels like me …. It's familiar …. It's like finding a baby …. It is truth …. It has value. I can feel its value."

Andy grounded the belief. Again, his body began to ache, and he had the sense that he wanted to stop. This is quite common: just before the end is near, the client senses that it's not working or their goal can't be achieved. This is our old friend Resistance again. I suggest that you muscle-test to see if there is another belief to align with, then decide if you wish to continue. Everything has a beginning, middle, and end. Remember: we are working with Andy's sense of being a burden and a failure and wasting people's time. Knowing this, I felt that it was important to see this through to completion. Here's what happened.

Andy had one more set of beliefs to align with. These were in the Sacral chakra, the Letting Go aspect, and Beliefs One and Two:

*I release repressed or trapped emotions and their associated feelings with ease and grace. Where appropriate, I let go of those people and situations that perpetuate hurt and unease.*

The left hemisphere activated in accordance with the belief fairly quickly, and as the right hemisphere began to activate, Andy saw birds, like bats, flying away.

He said: "Emotion is coming up, sensation … It's rising into my face and head … my chest, and back … It feels like pressure—like there was a heavy mass in my head, but when I breathe, the heavy mass dissolves into little bats that fly away … like washing away deposits … Now it's pressure-washing my aura from the inside out. It's satisfying. It doesn't go easily, but when it goes, it goes up and out of me. I realize that I'm not getting rid of it … but I'm not letting it stick to my body, I'm letting it go up into a higher aspect of myself, so I can process it another time."

Then after more observing and allowing, he commented: "There's a geyser, a huge jet of water pushing up a big cloud above my head. I'm still feeling emotion … feeling upset. There's a small child sitting clutching his knees … It's me, and I'm comforting him now, and it's just love. It's pink like Turkish Delight. It feels less heavy now … [big yawn], and now I see a familiar image. I've seen this before. It's me as a wretched shrivelled-up prune of a person, but the pressure washer is cleaning me up and showing me that inside I am shiny and chrome at my core ... I'm not horrible and disgusting ... I'm shiny, and I refuse to be dumped on ... Things slide straight off ... [big yawn]."

This was a big process for Andy, a left-brain dominant thinker who experienced a deep cleansing of both old emotion and painful distorted perceptions of self. The last alignment tends to be the big or emotional one, and indeed, this was the case here. The life issue was now testing as resolved.

Andy now muscle-tested his initial limiting beliefs—some had shifted, and others still applied. This was a lot of work, and there were still beliefs that needed to change. Do take heart if this happens. You have been running a lifetime or more of these beliefs and experiences. Changing one belief (or in this instance, seven) doesn't change the whole field. However, I urge you to take the time to be thorough; persistence and fine tuning can change everything! The negative beliefs need to be cleared in order for you to feel the benefit; it is not enough to just install positive beliefs. Muscle-test to see if the Manifestation process is needed.

You can follow what happened next on the website. Thanks for sharing, Andy.

## NATASHA
### Loss of Soulmate and Relationship Pain

Natasha attended the Healing InSight workshop and had been using the system regularly and successfully to help her through some life changes. She had moved house and changed careers after a difficult divorce, and a life of renewed contentment was growing. She had called in her soulmate and felt upon meeting him that he was "the one".

Although the relationship was intensely beautiful—as soulmate relationships can be—it was also accompanied by complications and set back by prior work commitments on his part. This meant that, unless their plans were changed, the two could not be in relationship with each other. Their conscious separation to prevent future heartache was itself causing much hurt, pain, confusion, and feelings of loss and rejection. Her soulmate's decision was out of her control. He had to make the choice to follow his heart's desire for this new love, or to follow through with promises, commitments, and his pursuit of what he perceived to be happiness and success.

It is very difficult when we love someone and perceive that they are hurting themselves (and us in the process), stuck in their ego's fears and limiting beliefs but not doing their inner work. We cannot make another person change or make better decisions for them. We can only do our own work and hold a space for someone to step into. People may not step into the higher versions of themselves, and we must then recognize that their behaviour is ultimately what counts and impacts us.

As an aside from this story, I have seen many a person stay in a difficult, perhaps undermining or disempowering relationship because of hope, promises, a few kind—or harsh—yet manipulative words, and being given "just enough" to stay. This is not what was happening here, but the gentleman's behaviour was triggering Natasha's hurt and rejection, and ultimately the emotional pain was too great, leaving Natasha wanting to find relief.

Natasha first identified her emotions as "confusion, hurt, deep upset, and rejection" and was aware of strong sensations in her solar plexus, sacral area, and throat. Her throat was very tight, and she was so uncomfortable within herself that she decided that she needed to let the whole situation and relationship go.

She began to work with the Letting Go belief in the sacral chakra:

*Where appropriate, I let go of those people and situations that perpetuate hurt and unease.*

Natasha muscle-tested "no" to the first permission statement, indicating that it was not for her highest and best good to align with this belief now. She intuitively asked herself, "Why not?" and became aware of the tears and tightness in her throat, and that she had been coughing and irritated in her throat for the last week. She thought, "I need to speak my truth", so she muscle-tested for the belief:

*I speak my truth with grace and ease.*

This belief was currently a "no", indicating that she did not believe this to be true at present, so Natasha went ahead, getting a "yes" in her permission statements that it was for her highest and best good to align with the belief, and a "yes" to having full permission on all levels to align with the belief now, using the Simple Method.

Natasha went ahead and brought herself into alignment with this belief using the Simple Method. NOTE: She could have used the life review method to muscle-test in order to find the "priority belief" to align with to clear the feelings in her throat. Following your intuition, however, is always beneficial and will help you to develop a more intimate relationship with yourself. Getting to know and love ourselves is the greatest gift we can offer ourselves after all.

Natasha went through a long and emotionally painful Simple Method balance, releasing many tears that had been caught up in her throat. I always take my hat off to those who are willing to go through and heal their pain. It is not easy, but passing through the dark birth canal of transformation is one of the most beautiful experiences of honouring our human psyche and our choice to incarnate, heal, and evolve. Natasha described a lot of resistance to the new belief and pain of the old belief ("to be silenced in my truth") arising in her body. Her arms were heavy and began to shake with jerky releasing movements as the tears streamed down her face. She bravely persisted, her left hemisphere activated, followed by the activation of the right hemisphere, a little less of a painful process. Natasha continued until the emotions had all subsided, her voice stabilized, and she felt peaceful. Natasha brought the belief into her body and allowed the resonance of the new belief, "I speak my truth with ease and grace," being able to see and sense what this new belief would look and feel like.

She then went back to the belief "Where appropriate I let go of those people and situations that perpetuate hurt and unease", but still she muscle-tested that it was not for her highest and best good to align with this positive belief now. Natasha began to get frustrated with these road blocks, as she was desperately trying to serve herself and ease her painful heart.

She tuned in to herself to see what else needed to be done first and was guided to Forgiveness, a wise aspect to focus upon if one wants to let go of a hurtful relationship. The belief statement here was a simple: "I forgive myself and others." Natasha also got a "no" in her first permission statement (that it was not for her highest and best good to align with this belief now). It may have made sense to be more specific here. If we need to forgive a person, our feelings are of course our own, but we must forgive them for the behaviours that have triggered the specific feelings we have about that. For example, "I forgive [name] for the anger, ignorance, and/or rejection that triggered the hurt, pain, loss, and/or abandonment I feel."

Frustrated with the difficulty in clearing her pain, she went back into her body to see what it was telling her. The most prominent sensation was in her solar plexus. The feeling, when she allowed and observed it, was fear. This is likely the hidden gain of not letting go and not forgiving, for if she was to forgive and let go, she would be "alone without love" again. Her fear of being alone was causing much pain, rejection, and "aloneness", however. Natasha muscle-tested the statement that the issue was located in her solar plexus and got a "yes". She then turned to the Solar Plexus aspects and muscle-tested for Free Will and found that she needed to align with priority Beliefs Two and Three:

*As I face my life lessons and learn from my experiences, I realize that there is really never a wrong decision. I trust the decisions I make and choose love, forgiveness, and expansion over fear and lack every time. I always have a choice.*

How appropriate! Natasha went ahead and brought herself into alignment with these belief statements, activating each hemisphere and, in fact, having a similar experience to the last difficult alignment— her arms shaking and jerking, and tears, emotion, and pain rising and releasing. As a result of staying with and working through the process, Natasha became calmer—her emotions settled, her voice steadied and normalized, and in the visualization process, she felt positive, clearer, and could no longer locate any feelings of fear.

Natasha then went back to the issue of forgiveness and this time specified that she wanted to forgive her soulmate (we'll call him Simon), also being specific about what it was that she wanted to forgive. Her belief statement was "I forgive Simon for all of the pain and fear I feel with his decision", realizing that it was his decision to choose his prior commitments over her that was causing her (and him) so much distress.

Natasha had a clear run at this Simple Method, her permission statements all supporting the alignment. This was a relatively straightforward belief realignment. Natasha had previously experienced the loss of a significant relationship and was able during the aligning process to recognize her fear of spending years grieving the loss of this significant relationship. Once aligned, Natasha reported an overall feeling of release. She described "feeling freer and less held by [the issue] ...like an energy cord seems to be detached .... The whole issue feels so different."

Natasha then tested the initial Letting Go belief, which had aligned, so her initial intention to release the pain and let go of the relationship had been successful. She completed the manifestation process to forgive Simon a few days later, as her feelings were still raw and surfacing. This process helped her head to align, which was fearful of being alone and still carrying confusion. In terms of forgiving him she came into strong feelings of freedom, warmth, being empowered, and open in her previously constricted solar plexus. In her vision she could happily see and smile at him. I recommended that she muscle-test to see if she needed to do the manifestation process for the actual Letting Go belief as well.

Hopefully, if the relationship is meant to be, Simon will honour his true feelings; however, Natasha is now free and has begun to heal her hurt and can perhaps choose a relationship that is loving and easy. Natasha aligned with:

*I am worthy and deserving of having a wonderful, loving, committed, joyous relationship.*

She also went on to align with the beliefs:

*I am wholly available for a wonderful, loving, committed, easy, and joyous relationship.*
*It is safe, possible, and appropriate for me to have a wonderful, loving, committed, easy, and joyous relationship.*
*I am ready, willing, and able to have a wonderful, loving, committed, easy, and joyous relationship*
*I now have a wonderful, loving, and easy, committed, joyous relationship.*

I am wishing and intending for Natasha that she find a well-deserved "wonderful, loving, easy, committed, and joyous relationship"! Whether it be with Simon or someone else, she has cleared her own limits and blocks to having a good relationship and has honoured herself with self-love.

# CHRIS

## Clearing Fear and Forgiving His Angry and Unpredictable Mother

Chris had been coming to see me for some time for help with feelings of being stuck in a perpetual cycle of fear. From a very young age, his mother had controlled him through fear. Her anger often came out of nowhere, and he and his sister both silenced and buried themselves and their emotions. The world was a dangerous place for them to exist in, and any joy or expression were squashed, devalued, and criticized.

Chris lived with this tight, uncomfortable feeling in his solar plexus, and had a hard time engaging with the world, or indeed, doing anything that could be criticized or cause upset, anger, and rejection. Every day life became more bearable as Chris began to know and honour himself, and he had taken up activities and interests that served him and made him feel good; however, he was still easily triggered into this tight, uncomfortable, stuck place of procrastination, which prevented him from truly engaging with life and "getting things done".

So we looked at the feelings, which were largely the same feelings of fear he had been carrying for years: fear of being criticized, ridiculed, or dismissed; fear of being squashed and getting things wrong. These feelings were all tied up in how he had felt as a child and were all still in existence due to the unresolved traumas and attachment he had to memories of his mother.

True forgiveness is the greatest gift to self. It is remarkable in terms of freeing all of the emotional energy tied up in our attachment with another. When we have had a difficult relationship, we can hold onto all of the feelings that have been created and left unresolved. It's a little like a washing line between two people, and our (often dirty) washing is still hanging there, waiting to be taken off. When we forgive—deeply, honestly, and specifically—for the damage that has been done, we pull down that washing line and the person can be released, or at least, the washing line can be cleared of all of its dirty washing.

We developed a rather long, but all-encompassing statement about forgiving the mother for her specific behaviours that triggered these feelings in Chris. It looked like this:

*I forgive my mother for being critical, angry, unloving, damaged, volatile, and unpredictable, and for using fear and anger to control me and for devaluing me, which triggered my feelings of inadequacy, incompetence, fear, hurt, shame, mistrust, devalue, and anger and made me feel unsafe, unstable, and have poor self-worth and a poor self-identity.*

It is a relatively long statement, but the essence and intention are clear and all of the important aspects of both her behaviour and Chris' feelings have been stated.

Chris went on to muscle-test his permission statements, getting a "yes" to both that it was for his highest and best good to align with the forgiveness belief now and that he gave his full permission to align with this belief on all levels.

The first priority belief was muscle-tested to be in the Sacral chakra, the aspect was Letting Go, and the Beliefs One and Three:

*I release repressed or trapped emotions and their associated beliefs with ease and grace. I release my investment in staying safe and stuck. I surrender, trust, and allow the light to guide me.*

Chris had held onto his fear and safety patterns his whole life, so this took time, perhaps 10 minutes of repeating the belief, softening, breathing, persisting through uncomfortable sensations for the left hemisphere to come into alignment. The right hemisphere happened more quickly, and momentum and congruence built up with the whole-brain integration process (focusing on the whole body whilst performing the infinity harmonizing movement, after activating each hemisphere).

Interestingly, when Chris came into his visualization, he didn't get a clear feeling. Perhaps he could have stayed with the alignment process a little longer. I would suggest that if you are not sure you are done/ aligned, keep going. Chris was in my presence, so the observer effect can cause someone to rush a little, or want to please/not fail. If you are in an advanced process, feel that your alignment is complete, but the visualization doesn't feel clear, do not worry; you are in the middle of a process, so be with what-is, observe, and allow.

For Chris, as he came to bring the belief into his body, he became tight in his solar plexus and had the thought that it was hard to trust the possibility of surrender. His legs became shaky. We muscle-tested to ensure that he had aligned with the belief, which he had, so we continued to see what other layers were there in relation to forgiving his mother.

The next priority belief that was identified was in the Root chakra, the aspect was Grounding, and Beliefs Two and Three.

*I am of the earth as I am of heaven. I root down and yield to the world around me. I connect with the life giving energies of the earth and lovingly release lower vibrations to Gaia to be transformed.*

These belief statements aligned more quickly. Chris began to see a dark red colour, which got lighter in the visualization, he began to see this red turn into a fire in his roots and see "things moving down ... into the fire". Fire is typically the element of transformation. The image then went black ... perhaps to ashes, as fire always burns out. Chris felt like something was blocking his view, but he could see green around the edges of his vision. He reported feeling better, grounded, his legs stable.

Chris did not have any other beliefs to align with, and when he muscle-tested the initial forgiveness statement, he had come into alignment with it. He continued with the Belief Embodiment Visualization process and saw a black ball representing his attachment to the hurt, anger, and fear he had felt about his mother's behaviours, then saw the mud rising to "gobble it up". He felt okay; the solar plexus feeling was less tight. It seemed that although this was clearer, easier, and a release had been witnessed, there could have been a greater sense of relief. We muscle-tested to see if the Manifestation process was needed, and it was.

In the Manifestation process, we muscle-test the belief with our hands on our heads, hearts, and gut to see which of these aspects of the self are in agreement with or are resisting the changes we have instigated. In Chris's case, the head and the heart were resisting, and the gut was aligned. In listening to each, this is what they showed him:

The head saw darkness and then flashes of red, saying "I don't trust it ... [remembering the memories of anger] ... anger explodes at any moment".

The heart saw a large built-up street. Chris noticed that there was no grass allowed to grow. As he observed, the scene shifted, and he moved onto a large grassy area—green, the colour of the heart, the grass perhaps representing life, new beginnings. It was interesting to notice here that the heart came into alignment when it was given attention.

The gut showed Chris a vision of blue water running freely down a pipe ("It's just free; it's letting go"). The element Water is connected to the lower *dan tian* and sacral chakra that governs the gut, also the centre for emotion, which is perhaps what Chris visualized to be running free.

In returning to the head, to inform it of what the heart and gut saw and felt, Chris saw the red room but calmly walked out of it into a blue room and spent a little time here and felt calmer, as if he recognized that he had a choice. This indicated to me that he had moved out of his freeze response into calm and was able to find movement. He muscle-tested the heart, head, and gut and found that all were now in coherence with the Forgiveness belief. His Grand Manifestation visualization brought further shaking and fear: he saw a light background with a bug flying around. The bug eventually began to be caught up in the background, leaving Chris feeling lighter and brighter.

The following day, Chris told me that in his dream, he had visited his three-year-old self, who was busy collecting scissors and sharp objects to protect himself. Chris asked the child to give him the sharp objects and promised that he would protect him now. The child handed over the objects happily. Chris then saw his teenage self in a rage. It had never been safe for Chris to feel anger, nor was he allowed to be angry, so this was a significant release of repressed emotion within the dream. Adult Chris was surprised at the level of anger and within the dream, was able to help his teenage self release the feelings quickly. The following morning, Chris was able to respond to his ex-wife on his own terms, which he had usually struggled to do.

Although uncomfortable, this is crucial work for Chris. He must learn to have anger and express it without harm. Having anger allows him to move out of the terrifying freeze response into fight-or-flight, if need be, but hopefully into self-empowerment, being able to assert boundaries, and the possibility of safety. Time will tell how these beliefs manifest. It may not always be a complete and immediate resolution; however, it is always apparent that working with the system provides movement and release of resistant limiting patterns, as reality catches up with the energetic shifts.

## SOPHIA

**Finding Freedom through Forgiveness**

Sophia had been let down by a string of men in her life, beginning with her dad, step-dad, boyfriend, then husband. Searching for love and to know her worth, Sophia has been on an incredible journey of awakening and self-love, but the desire to still find love from her ex-husband, who had betrayed her and was still giving mixed messages, caused a lot of hurt, sadness, and confusion.

Sophia recognized that she was still, on one level, searching for self-worth from the present-but-rejecting or absent men in her life. She was ready to release her attachment to her need to know that she was important and lovable from these sources of pain in her life, so she worked with the Forgiveness protocol (see Resources).

Sophia devised three statements to work with forgiveness of her dad, her step-dad, and her ex-husband. These address the behaviours and things that needed to be forgiven that triggered in Sophia the emotions associated with each of these people.

Her first statement was as follows:

*I forgive my dad for not being loving; for being critical; for not complementing me or saying that he loved me; for saying hurtful, untrue things; for sometimes cutting me out of his life; for talking to me like a staff/employee; for the instability and manipulation that triggered in me confusion, hurt, loneliness, a lack of self-esteem, and a deep desire for love.*

Sophia went on to muscle-test her permission statements. She was guided to do the Advanced process, beginning with the Sacral chakra, aspect Self-Worth, and Beliefs One, Two, and Four:

*I am worthy. I listen to my needs and desires and honour myself. I give myself the time, space, and loving kindness I need to manifest all I am. I nurture.*

As she stated this, Sophia experienced immediate nausea and pain in her stomach. Her throat tightened, and she felt a heavy sensation in her shoulders. She kept working through the process of activating the right hemisphere, feeling fuzziness in her head until she felt the right hemisphere activate; she then moved to activate the left hemisphere, and tears came when she realized what it was to feel self-worth. Her hemispheres now were both aligned and activated. In the Visualization process, she saw herself being enveloped by a pink cloud, the energy of unconditional love.

The next alignment was in the Root chakra, aspect Stability, encompassing Beliefs One, Two, Three, and Four:

*I allow myself to give and receive support. I trust in the pathway that unfolds before me. I recognize the interconnectedness of all things. I lovingly support myself with kind thoughts of encouragement, compassion, and understanding. I am supported.*

As she aligned with these beliefs, Sophia again experienced instant nausea and pain in her stomach. This pain increased, and her voice became strained, followed by a sharp electric shock-type pain in her left knee. As the beliefs settled, Sophia began burping, a form of release; her voice came into a regular, clearer tone, and she began to feel a sense of acceptance, as it fully aligned. Her visualization included seeing the roots of a tree taking hold in the earth and stepping stones across a river. Trees can often represent feeling rooted and stable, and there lies the pathway ahead across the river.

Through further muscle-testing, she discovered another belief to align with in the Solar Plexus chakra, aspect Boundaries, and again, Beliefs One, Two, Three, and Four. (Sophia had an instant headache reaction and resistance to working with this belief even before she had read what it entailed. We truly are so much more than our conscious mind's awareness!)

*I stand my ground where and when I need to. I recognize that my truth is just as valid as other people's truth and assert myself appropriately. I trust in and expect a positive outcome and have the strength and kindness needed to enable me to stand my ground. I stand my ground.*

Emotions began to come up about her current relationship and boundaries with her ex-husband, as Sophia activated the left hemisphere. Sophia persisted through the emotion, repeating the beliefs and performing the infinity harmonizing movement. She activated the left hemisphere and moved to the right. Just before the complete alignment came in, she noticed an activated "wide brain feeling ...with tingling and heaviness". As this lightened, she noticed an easiness and an increase in the momentum of the words and stability in her voice. Her visualization with this belief was lovely and clear. She saw in her mind's eye a line drawn in front of her and heard the words "My boundaries make me strong".

The next belief that Sophia muscle-tested to align with was in the Heart chakra, in the aspect Forgiveness, Beliefs One, Two, Three, and Four.

*I forgive myself for my imperfections, do my best, and find contentment with this. I am good enough. I recognize my hurts and nurture my inner child with all that she/he needs. I forgive others for their preconceptions, judgements, and behaviours, trusting that we are all doing our best with our current levels of awareness and patterning. I forgive.*

As she stated this, Sophia began to be aware of a heaviness in her head, which radiated down to her neck and shoulders. She activated the left, then right hemisphere, and in the Whole-Body Awareness process (using the infinity harmonizing move whilst repeating the belief with a whole-body awareness), the heaviness started to lift and Sophia began to feel herself taking root, grounding. This visualization took a little longer to present itself. Settling into what this meant and felt like, Sophia began to see a white dove and white light, a beautiful energy of spirit, connecting to and embodying this process of forgiveness for her.

When Sophia tested the presence of Beliefs One, Two, Three, and Four, she found that number four—"I forgive"—had not yet aligned. She correctly checked in with her intuition and asked herself why? It came to her awareness that she did not want to condone conflict. Sophia was drawn to muscle-test whether it was safe for her to forgive, and she got a "yes". Then she muscle-tested "I am able to forgive" and got a "yes". This awareness was then enough to bring the forgiveness to her father into alignment. She did forgive her dad, which was confirmed with the muscle test.

Sophia didn't continue to do a last Visualization process, which would normally be recommended. She muscle-tested to see if she needed to do the Manifestation process, which she did.

She read out her belief and muscle-tested her gut (testing "no"—not aligned), her heart (testing "no"—not aligned), and her head (testing "yes"—aligned). We always first tend to the aspect(s) that are not aligned to see where the resistance is. When Sophia put her hands on her gut to tune in to what her gut had to show her, she had butterflies in her stomach, apprehension that it wasn't safe to forgive him, and the question arose of how she would protect herself from being rejected again if she forgave her father? She acknowledged, heard, and accepted the gut's concerns.

She then took a few deep breaths and put her hands on her heart to see what it had to show her. Sophia saw herself as a little girl who was sad and resisted forgiving because she "wanted her daddy". Sophia acknowledged her inner child's feelings and needs. When testing the aligned head and intuiting how the head felt about the act of forgiveness, she saw him there smiling at her and got a sense that "he really did the best he could"and that "there was love". She saw happy, forgotten memories from past holidays and precious time spent with him, which had been clouded by the hurt. There was serenity. The head informed her of how much he had taught her and brought good things into her life. She remembered his qualities and that he never shirked his responsibilities.

This information was then fed back to the resistant heart and gut. The heart then unfolded "like a warm blanket", and she saw more memories of the things he had done with her, such as the horse riding lessons he had taken her to. The heart was aligned.

The gut didn't see much, so she turned back to the heart and the head to see if they could offer the gut help, connecting again with the happy memories of her dad and the time they had shared. Then, returning to the gut, she noticed a smell, a freshness, like grass in the spring or a new start. Sophia described warmth in her spine and tingling in her legs. The gut had aligned. In her Grand Manifestation Visualization, after tapping on the third eye and stimulating the pineal gland, she had a vision of an eagle soaring above, looking down with huge expansive wings. She began to feel the power, strength, and expanse of the eagle and the freedom to fly.

Over the next few days, Sophia worked on Advanced Forgiveness protocols for both her step-dad and her ex-husband, then spontaneously booked a ticket to her favourite place in the world for the following weekend. The accounts are both touching and demonstrative of the power of working with the Healing InSight system, using the Forgiveness protocol to enable a healing and a deeper reconnection with one's loving self and personal power.

## ROISIN
### A Simple Method Balance about Earning What I Am Worth

Roisin worked hard. A highly capable, dedicated woman, she always went above and beyond, doing her best and whatever was needed. She worked among more highly paid people, doing some of their jobs without acknowledgement or financial reward. Roisin developed a belief to acknowledge her worth and financial recognition in accordance with this:

*I recognize my full value and worth in all areas of my life, including my professional life and capabilities, and earn good money that reflects my skills, efforts, and worth.*

Roisin could go ahead and align with this using the Simple Method and focused upon the left hemisphere first. As she read out the belief, she began to feel nervous in her stomach, but continued with the process. The first hemispheric activation took a little while, but the second was quicker. The words building momentum, she took a few deep breaths and got a sense of the belief aligning.

In the visualization, Roisin's tummy was a little nervous again initially, but this cleared as she began to stand taller. She kept repeating, "I need to hold my head up high ... I can relax ... courage will come from within."

She had the sense that she could be more confident, that she could "take it or leave it", that she didn't have to screw herself up to prove herself or please others. "I don't care ... I see my head is up high ...the nitty-gritty doesn't matter ... my spiritual work is more important. I have to listen to myself more." This was lovely insight and realization for Roisin. As she grounded the belief, there was a sense of light moving down through her body all the way to the earth.

She muscle-tested to find out if the Manifestation process was needed, which it was. Her head, heart, and gut all tested as being positively aligned, so we looked at what each one had to say. Her gut was the one that had a few concerns; namely, a little anxious feeling that she might get hurt if she recognized her worth. The heart reassured her that she would be fine if she continued to listen to her higher self and wisdom. The head showed her the way forward. She would have to make some changes in her life and have tricky conversations with people she cared about, but the message was strong: "Hold your head up high and you will be fine."

The gut, having heard the insights and feelings of the head, began to come on board. This took a little time, but Roisin observed, allowed, and began to see the vision board of self-worth and feel it in her body. Her gut began to feel better, and a good feeling filled her body, as she said: "I put my head to the white light ...standing tall ...speaking my truth and not being afraid." This allowed Roisin to step into what felt more open and possible.

# Healing InSight Method Q & A

This book is a journey of personal transformation, which you are invited to take. Humans are complex. We are attempting radical change—the soul longs for evolution. So what if things don't go to plan? In this section, I've listed the common issues that come up in the form of a Q&A; there is a more in-depth Q&A on the website. As we travel alongside each other, more questions may be thrown up, which I look forward to resolving with you. The book is just the beginning.

## 1. What if I don't get a clear muscle test?

Drink water, rehydrate, and loosen up. Come out of your analytical mind by practising a little qigong. Shaking, earthing, and performing the Heaven and Earth movement should set you up to muscle-test. If this fails, address your beliefs around muscle testing by using the statement: "I always muscle-test easily and accurately" This is about you being in touch with yourself. You may just need to clear some built-up resistance and unwind your body first. Bring your mind inward, and sense. The more you attune, the easier it becomes. Don't decide that you can't do it! Just teach your body how to. Intend that you can. Don't confuse yourself, and double check everything.

## 2. What if my sway test is backward = "yes" and forward = "no"?

This is absolutely fine. You are muscle-testing for your "yes" and "no", and have found what they are for you. You can confirm by testing for truths, such as "My name is _____ (insert your own name), then again with a statement that is not your truth. This helps confirm your "yes" and "no". Occasionally, the word "yes" has negative connotations for people and can lead to a weak muscle test. The above exercise can teach your body to muscle-test more accurately.

**3.  What if it is not for my highest and best good to align with my chosen belief?**

Ask yourself why. Do you need to change the wording of the belief? Do you have to prioritize something else first? If you ask, it is usually given, and you will find a way forward. If you're truly getting nothing, then listen and respect your higher wisdom. More often than not, awareness will come to mind and, once this has occurred, it is enough for the higher self to permit the alignment. It may simply be a case of "not now, there isn't enough time" or "the conditions are not right". The higher self wants you to evolve and will not block your healing without good reason. Be curious.

**4.  What if I do not give my full permission to align with my chosen belief?**

As above, ask "why?" You will more likely gain unconscious awareness here from an aspect of yourself that needs to get on board with the shift. Resistance to the new alignment may begin to surface here, so check to intuit what that resistance is, acknowledge it, and retest for permission. If it is a repeat "no", work with the resistant belief.

**5.  What if it is not for my highest and best good to use the Simple or the Advanced Method?**

If your muscle test indicates not to do either the Simple or the Advanced Method, try the life review process instead. You may not have pinpointed the best belief for you, but your intention knows what you need to clear. The life review process is a more generic way in.

**6.  What if one of my hemispheres won't activate?**

You are likely caught up in resistance, so soften, soften, soften. Breathe, allow, observe, and stay focused on your intention to align with the belief. Read the belief out loud. If excess energy arises and feels blocked or painful, use the grounding posture, breathe, soften your knees and your stomach, and come back to it. If you are really just stuck and nothing is happening (which is never really the case), soften and bear witness to the resistance, then place the hand of the hemisphere you are activating on that hemisphere to encourage blood flow here. Keep repeating the belief, and come back to the movement. This will increase blood flow to the brain. As we do want to activate the hemisphere in relation to the belief, don't stay here for too long; just give it a helping hand. This is helpful if you are one-hemisphere dominant.

**7. What if other thoughts, memories, and beliefs come into my mind when I'm doing the method?**

With the Healing InSight method, when people have been realigning themselves with a helpful belief, they sometimes get a mental snapshot of memory from the time they developed the unhelpful and limiting belief. Nothing needs to be done with this information, other than recognize and allow it. When working with the system, you are engaged in a process of change, and bringing memories into consciousness is part of allowing the release and realignment with something new and positive. If other beliefs arise that need to be aligned, write them down, but don't interrupt your process. Often becoming aware of another old belief helps align the one in process.

**8. What if I've muscle-tested for a chakra using the Advanced Method yet none of the aspects of this chakra are testing "yes"?**

Retest that the priority belief is in this chakra. If "yes", align with the affirmation on the main root card using the present tense ("I am").

**9. What if I don't believe that it is safe or appropriate for me to align with my chosen belief?**

We may resist aligning with something we don't believe is true for good reason. The hidden gains from holding on usually involve safety. When we programme in a belief, we are opening ourselves up to the potential of that new reality. We may not be in the new reality immediately, but there's no need to avoid aligning with the new belief if it means we open up to the shift. Energy changes immediately, but physical reality operates in time and space and has to catch up. When I came to write this book and hit writer's block, I aligned with the statement "I am a successful author". When I doubted my healing gifts, I aligned with "I am an amazing healer". These helped me to come into alignment with my potential, clearing the conditioned, "Who do you think you are?" type of limitation.

When we first learn to drive, we don't know how to do it, but it doesn't mean that we won't be able to. If I believe that "I am a bad or dangerous driver" or won't learn because "the roads are not safe", I'm more likely to create a field for that experience and drive badly, or notice all of the dangerous events on the road. If I change my beliefs in alignment with "I am a good driver; the roads are safe", I will feel more relaxed, think more clearly, and likely drive well. Athletes cultivate a winning mindset in order to reach their potential.

It is important to change those beliefs that don't serve us. One positive belief that is difficult for many people to align with is "I am safe" or "The world is a safe place". The inclination to worry is a result of trying to keep ourselves safe and prepared for every eventuality. The attention is on what can go wrong. The fear behind worry is that "Bad things will happen if I let go of control" based on the premise that "I/the world is unsafe". In this universe of infinite potential, it is true: the world is unsafe. It is also true that "The world is a safe place/I am safe". The former keeps us on guard, stressed, and everything that comes with that; the latter relaxes and aligns us with the reality in which we are safe. It is our free will to choose love over fear, and if we can create our reality, which would you rather step into? Practise feeling contentment, safety, stability, peace, love, and trust to fully align with safety. Don't let the story of your past or your ancestors dictate your future. We are going through a paradigm shift; it's okay to let go of fear.

### 10. What if I can't do the movement?

Executing the movement can be tricky for some people. It may mean that you are not fully in balance with the left and right aspects of yourself, or of your physical or spiritual aspects. You may be rejecting part of yourself, which is preventing you from feeling whole. Look at this list and see if any items speak to you:

- Masculine self versus feminine self
- Creative/expressive/emotional self versus rational/logical self
- Spiritual self versus physical self
- Future self versus past self.

I suggest that you practise drawing the infinity harmonizing symbol while thinking about the rejected part of yourself, and welcome in that aspect so that you may feel whole.

I worked with one lady who could not use the symbol. She identified that she rejected her feminine self, and when asked why discovered that she believed women to be weak and needy, which was not okay; moreover, she felt that if she embraced her feminine self, she would not do well in business. We discussed whether it was possible to be both feminine and strong, and she agreed it was. We discussed if it was okay for her to have needs (be vulnerable), and she agreed it was. We then used the belief statement "I balance the masculine and feminine aspects of myself and welcome my feminine self into my whole being". Although the movement she made was a little clumsy, the belief did align when she used the Simple Method and Manifestation process, and the movement became much smoother and easier for her to follow. She had not realized that she was denying this aspect of herself to the extent she was, and felt a renewed sense of wholeness.

### 11. What if I don't feel better and the system seems not to be working?

Sometimes, it can feel like the Healing InSight system is not working, leading you to blame the system or yourself. Remember: it *is* working, but this joyous thing called resistance (which may actually feel more like a sledgehammer or brick wall) is trying to keep us safe by keeping us aligned with earlier decisions we made about the world or to release them.

Try not to judge yourself or the system. This is not your higher self speaking, although it may feel like it; it is your subconscious programming. Trust the process, and follow the tips in question six above. If there's a lot of resistance, you're clearing a big issue and will feel clearer soon! Be patient, and remember how long you have been practising the opposite. Love and support yourself in reaching your *intended* positive new belief.

### 12. What if I enter a healing crisis?

A healing crisis may occur when we purge something that doesn't serve us and that we have been holding onto for a long time. It may feel like your body is beginning to react, go into shock, as if we don't know who we are without the problem. Take your time with the amount of processing you are doing, and don't leave a process incomplete. Take a break, by all means, but return to see it through to completion, including the use of the Manifestation process. If you hit a healing crisis, seek help from a practitioner, healer, or therapist. This can be done via video link, if need be, or get support through the available Healing InSight channels. It usually means that you are hitting the nail on the head and those things that were keeping you stuck are shattering. It is okay to go into the shadows; if you are willing to stick with it, you'll come through by relaxing into the process. Remember: your soul is leading you through your unconscious drives to places you need to revisit. Trust your intuition that you are exactly where you need to be as you move through your fears and challenges.

# Healing InSight Worksheets

## Forgiveness Protocol Worksheet

First, look at the way the person you would like to forgive makes you feel. Hold them in your imagination, and list (place on "the washing line") all of the feelings or things you recognize in yourself as difficulty, pain, contraction (being less than you are), as a consequence of this relationship.

Below is a list of the feelings I have when I imagine you, or consequences and subsequent behaviours in my life, because of how you made me feel. These are:

**Me**                                                                                           **Them**

_____

_____

_____

_____

_____

☐    I acknowledge that these are my own feelings, behaviours, or life issues.
☐    I intend to release myself from my attachment to you and these feelings, behaviours, or life issues.

The following is a list of all of the things you did or didn't do, including a list of your negative attributes, which triggered in me feelings, behaviours, and life consequences:

_____

_____

_____

_____

_____

_____

_____

_____

**My Forgiveness Statement**

I forgive you:

_____

for your (include the feelings, behaviours, and events you identified in the other person above):

_____

_____

_____

that triggered me to feel/experience:

_____

Once you have your statement, muscle-test using the Healing InSight system to see if it is for your highest and best good to align with this belief statement. Change it, if necessary, and continue to use a Healing InSight Simple or Advanced Method process. You will likely need to use the Advanced process and may also need to follow up with the Manifestation process, so check at the end to see if this is so. Once you have forgiven, you should be able to let go and may wish to finish with a letting-go belief.

## Healing InSight Life Review Worksheet

The Healing Insight Life Review is to enable you to evaluate your own life within the scope of the holistic chakra system, as reflected by the chakra aspects. You can work through the review and reflect upon the aspects and the polarities I have selected (the expansive statements and the limiting statements), scoring where you sit on each polarity's continuum, and then highlighting—perhaps circling—the ones you would like to address in terms of belief change. You may also muscle-test through the expansive and limiting statements, and record a "yes" or "no" for each. We would be hoping to find a "yes" for the expansive and a "no" for the limiting statemens.

Our collective and familial conditioning, however, means that this is rarely the case. Circle the statements you would like to change, and use the system to align with the expansive beliefs. As always, there should be no judgement placed on your discoveries. The purpose is to enable you to dive into the development of self-awareness and self-love as you journey to become more joyous more of the time. Wishing you all the compassion, patience, and kindness you need to transform your life into one of joy, health, wealth, and bliss.

| Expansive Beliefs | Chakra Aspect | Limiting Beliefs |
|---|---|---|
| | **Grounded** | |
| I am grounded | | I am unanchored |
| I am connected to my roots | | I am always searching |
| | **Natural World** | |
| I work with nature | | I am disconnected from nature |
| I flex | | I fight |
| | **Capability** | |
| I am capable | | I am incapable |
| I am strong | | I am weak |
| | **Stability** | |
| I am stable | | I am unstable |
| I am supported | | I am unsupported |
| | **Abundance** | |
| I have | | I lack |
| I am wealthy | | I am poor |
| | **Physical Body** | |
| I love my body | | I hate my body |
| I love myself | | I reject myself |
| | **Safety** | |
| I am safe | | I am unsafe |
| I am loved | | I am vulnerable |
| | **Letting go** | |
| I let go easily | | I hold on |
| I am free | | I am stuck |
| | **Emotions** | |
| I feel | | I am numb |
| Emotions help me | | Emotions cripple me |
| | **Potential** | |
| I am full of potential | | I am useless |
| All is possible | | I am blocked |
| | **Self-Worth** | |
| I am worthy | | I am unworthy |
| I honour my whole self | | I reject myself |
| | **Creativity** | |
| I create | | I procrastinate |
| I play | | I struggle |

| Expansive Beliefs | Chakra Aspect | Limiting Beliefs |
|---|---|---|

### Instinct

I follow my instincts .................................................... I ignore my inner voice
I sense and feel ................................................................ I must please others

### Sensuality

Pleasure is good ............................................................................ Pleasure is bad
My natural state is joy ........................................... My natural state is pain

### Authentic Power

I own my power ...................................................... I give away my power
I trust in power ......................................................... Power is dangerous

### Courage

I am courageous ......................................................................... I am scared
I am possible ............................................................................................ I can't

### Individuation

I accept my uniqueness ............................................... My difference hurts me
I succeed as me ................................................................. I hide my true self

### Greatness

I am amazing ....................................................................................... I am bad
I am good enough ............................................................................ I'm inadequate

### Boundaries

I stand my ground ........................................................... I am walked over
I can say yes and no ................................................. I mustn't cause upset

### Free Will

I am free to choose ............................................................. I am controlled
I move beyond limitation ........................................................ I am limited

### Autonomy

I am free ............................................................................................ I am trapped
I am independent ........................................................................ I am dependant

### Loving Relationships

I have love ......................................................................................... I lack love
I choose love ................................................................................... I choose hurt

### Openness

I am open ........................................................................................... I am closed
I give lovingly .................................................................................... I withhold

### Forgiveness

I forgive ................................................................................................... I blame
I understand .................................................................................... I disapprove

| Expansive Beliefs | Chakra Aspect | Limiting Beliefs |
|---|---|---|
| | Gratitude | |
| I am grateful | | I am selfish/ungrateful |
| I lovingly receive | | I isolate myself |
| | Harmony | |
| I am harmonious | | I am discordant |
| I am balanced | | I am imbalanced |
| | Ease & Grace | |
| I am graceful | | I am clumsy |
| Life is easy for me | | Life is difficult for me |
| | Compassion | |
| I am compassionate | | I am judgemental |
| I love others | | I hurt others |
| | Self-Expression | |
| I express myself | | I deny myself |
| I say how I feel | | I silence myself |
| | Communication | |
| I collaborate | | I dictate |
| I communicate | | I suppress myself |
| | Freedom | |
| I am healed | | I am sick |
| I am free | | I am stuck |
| | Transmutation | |
| I transform | | I resist change |
| I release | | I hold on |
| | Clarity | |
| I have clarity | | I have confusion |
| I am clear | | I am clouded |
| | Truth | |
| I know my truth | | I misunderstand myself |
| I am honest | | I am dishonest |
| | Space | |
| I have space in my life | | I am weighed down |
| I am spacious | | I am dense |
| | Protection | |
| I am protected | | I need protection |
| The world is safe | | The world is dangerous |
| | Purity | |
| I am pure | | I am toxic |
| My mind is quiet | | My mind is noisy |

| Expansive Beliefs | Chakra Aspect | Limiting Beliefs |
|---|---|---|
| | **Intuition** | |
| I am intuitive | | I can't feel, hear, or see |
| I am guided | | I am alone |
| | **Healing** | |
| I am part of the divine | | I am separate |
| I am whole | | I am fragmented |
| | **Peace of Mind** | |
| My thoughts are peaceful | | My thoughts cause pain |
| I bring peace | | I cause disruption |
| | **Psychic Awareness** | |
| I trust my visions | | I have false imaginings |
| I am the light | | I attract the dark |
| | **Unity** | |
| I seek to unite | | I seek to divide |
| I find balance | | I am extreme |
| | **Possibility** | |
| I am possible | | I am impossible |
| All is possible | | I resist my potential |
| | **Connection** | |
| I am connected | | I am disconnected |
| I am love | | I am loved conditionally |
| | **Divine Will** | |
| I follow my purpose | | I am off purpose |
| I am of service | | I hold on |
| | **Integrity** | |
| I am true to myself | | I am dishonest |
| I know who I am | | I am lost |
| | **Knowing** | |
| I know what is right for me | | I am confused |
| I am wise | | I am stupid |
| | **Consciousness** | |
| I am divine | | I am unaware |
| I am awake and expanding | | I am asleep |
| | **We** | |
| I love you | | I fear you |
| You are a gift | | You limit me |

# Qigong Practices

Whenever I begin a qigong class, we always ground and anchor into Wuji: we connect to our bodies (feet, legs, pelvis, stomach, spine, neck, head), our breath, our lower *dan tian* (or *hara*, just below the navel) and middle *dan tian* (heart), then we connect to the energies of Earth, then the Heavens, recognizing ourselves, with increased awareness, as an empty vessel between both.

Chapter 7 has a detailed description of how to settle into Wuji. This standing posture is both beneficial and meditative in its own right, a practice of surrender, of letting go to the energy flow. Once we are anchored into Wuji, we perform three warm-up exercises that are also taken from qigong. These are hip circles, spinal turns, and shaking. I include them here as I would not be without them, and I know them to be great for tension release and energy flow.

I close this section with a meditation that I think you will find very useful to include in the qigong practices that support the healing work in this book. I have posted other useful meditations on my website that I encourage you to include in your healing work.

## Hip Circles

1. Depending on your gender:
   - Ladies, bring your right hand to your stomach, palm facing into the lower *dan tian* (just below the navel), and place your left palm over the top of the right, palm facing inward.
   - Gentlemen, bring your left hand to your stomach, palm facing into the lower *dan tian*, and place your right palm over the top of the left, palm facing inward.
2. Keeping your feet parallel and knees soft, begin to circle your hips around in an anticlockwise direction, slowly and gently, noticing the sensation, the smoothness, and the bumpiness of the hip as you circle. The body is engaged in a gentle spiral here, and movement begins to flow, releasing not only the hips but

the knees, legs, and spine up to the nape of the neck. Make the movement as small or as big as feels good. Play, observe, and get to tune into and listen to what your body likes. We're working with the Water element here, so perhaps imagine circling in a pool of water, or imagine the hip joint moving gracefully through the synovial fluid that surrounds it. This is a wonderful movement for anybody, but is particularly helpful if one's work involves sitting for long periods throughout the day.

3. After about five minutes, follow a figure of eight (our infinity harmonizing shape) with the hips, to enable us to change direction and begin circling in a clockwise direction. Again, observe, allow, and observe again, bringing awareness into the body. Notice how the movement feels in this direction, and take time to unwind tensions and release. All of this time, energy is gathering in the lower *dan tian* through the alignment of two important energy points in the palms—the *lao gongs* and the lower *dan tian* (your deepest reservoir of resource). You might notice heat building in this area as energy begins to gather and move through the body as it spirals.

4. Once unwound, bring the circling movement back to the centre, back to stillness and the Wuji standing posture.

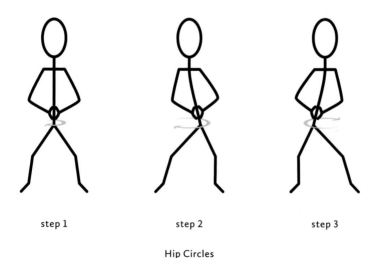

step 1          step 2          step 3

Hip Circles

## Spinal Turns

Spinal turns offer us many benefits, including the release and movement of the spine from the sacrum all the way to the base of the skull. As we build momentum, the arms will begin to tap on the kidneys (liver, stomach, and spleen), which also bring great benefits. I actually moved into a past life regression and clearing from doing this movement at home.

The kidneys store old patterns and memories and are essential for the flow of our life force and feeling of vitality. When we carry holding patterns, especially in the shoulders—as most of us do—spinal turns can be a lovely practice to teach the body how to let this go, an active practice of surrender as we find freedom of movement within the body. Here's how:

1. Enter into Wuji, if you are not there already. Remember knees are soft and open, hips are loose, pelvis is neutrally hanging, feet are rooted, and there is a sense of rising through, or noticing the space in between the vertebrae in the spine.
2. Turn the eyes and head slowly to face the left, then the right. Continue with this movement, allowing the shoulders to follow, sensing the movement and twist in the upper spine.
3. Keeping the hips facing forward following the Wuji stance, begin to build speed and momentum with this practice, allowing the arms to hang loosely by the sides. The muscles of the arms and shoulders are as relaxed as possible.
4. Reminding yourself to keep the knees softly bent and the hips facing forward, as if sitting on a horse, continue building momentum. When the hips are facing forward and not twisting with the movement, it allows the lower spine to twist. If we turn the hips, the lower spine remains still.
5. As the momentum has built, it is as if we are swinging like a pendulum between the left and right. We can now allow the back of the hand to tap gently on the kidneys as we turn. The hand at the front of the body can fall onto the liver or stomach and spleen.
6. Allow the head/eyes to turn as far as is comfortable for optimal spinal release.
7. Bring the movement slowly into stillness.

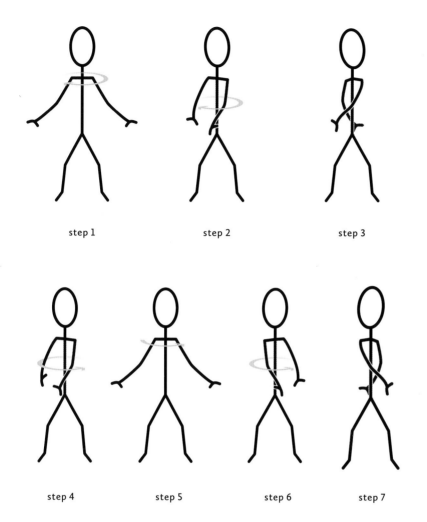

step 1          step 2          step 3

step 4          step 5          step 6          step 7

Spinal Turns 1-7

## Shaking

The body loves to shake! When we can get past feeling self-conscious in class and give ourselves permission to shake, we feel the release and tension literally leaving our bodies and become aware of where we are holding tension. Shaking brings our awareness into the body and becomes quite a meditative practice. After a good shake, you may feel that it is time to move on, but the body may protest, as it needs more to come into stillness. Play with this one. There are huge benefits to shaking, including—so I was told by a yogi many moons ago—increased bone density.

1. Begin in the Wuji standing posture, earthed and connected through the central channel to the heavens. Arms and shoulders are loose. All muscles are relaxed, including those of the jaw.
2. Do a vertical shake, bouncing from the knees. I like to do this to music and enjoy Katie Hope's Tai Chi album, track four, and Taylor Swift's Shake It Off.
3. Give yourself permission to shake it off, all of it, from anywhere you notice tension. Shake off down the arms and fingers, and through the legs and feet, into the earth.
4. Gently come back to stillness, and kick off from the ankles and toes any remaining tension.

 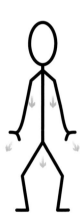

Shaking

## Lung Openers

Lung openers are brilliant for regulating the breath. This is especially useful if meditation is something you struggle with. The breath is key to disrupting the fight-or-flight response, so if you find yourself in a fear or stress response frequently, lung openers are a lovely way to teach your body how to deepen and lengthen the breath without really focusing on it or trying to manipulate the breath into slowing down, which can sometimes cause anxiety. Proper breathing technique is vital for health. Many of us shallow-breathe and have stagnant air in the bottom of our lungs that doesn't get emptied out. When the stomach is tight, the diaphragm rises, and we breathe into the top half of our lungs. When the stomach relaxes, and the air fully empties out, we can take in a full breath and fill our lungs. Go at your own pace with this one until you can slow down your breath in time with the movement. The exhale is key to a fresh new breath of *qi*. Here's how it goes:

1. Stand in Wuji, with your hands by your sides, and bring your index finger and thumb together.
2. Breathe out. On the inhale, lead with your wrists, drawing the hands and finger and thumb (large intestine and lung meridians) up to the heavens. Allow your eyes and head to follow.
3. Release the finger and thumb lock, so that the hands are soft and open, and allow the elbows and knees to soften. Your whole body begins to draw down towards the earth, returning to a slightly lower version of Wuji.
4. Put your finger and thumb together again, and on the inhale, breathe in as you raise the arms, opening the lungs fully.
5. Release the fingers, soften the hands, and draw the elbows and knees back down towards the earth as you fully exhale.
6. Continue with this rise and fall, inhaling on the rise, arms extending upwards, and exhaling on the fall, muscles soft and relaxed.
7. Exhale more fully than you think you can. This will allow you a full inhale.
8. Begin to pause as you reach the heavens, perhaps imagining the moon and its silvery-white glow lighting up your lungs—as if for a moment, you are holding the moon between your hands.
9. After several lung openers, come back into Wuji.

step 1          step 2          step 3          step 4

Lung Openers

## Balancing Heaven and Earth

When we feel scattered, disjointed, and out of sorts, Balancing Heaven and Earth is a lovely way of bringing us back to a calm, gently energized place (as is the harmonizing infinity movement). This movement helps release excess energy and open the flow of energy through important meridians. We access more strength as we open the shoulder and the meridians that run from the hands, find a posture, and breathe for a short time as our bodies reconnect and balance the opposing yin and yang forces in our bodies and mind. We repeat this opening and balancing with the opposite hands, and so on.

1. Stand in Wuji.
2. Bring your hands into the Holding the Ball position in front of your lower *dan tian* (palms are beaming into the lower *dan tian*, sensing and sitting on the edge of its energy field). Stay here for a while, breathing *qi* into your lower *dan tian*, sensing your breath with your hands.
3. Bring the left hand to the earthing position, palm facing the earth, hand sitting next to the lower hip. The energy pathway will then connect from the palm down the side of the leg to the earth. At the same time the right hand rises, palm facing the heavens, turning at the level of the face, until the back of the hand reaches and sits directly above the crown of the head, palm facing towards the heavens. The right arm is curved, the elbow soft. Remain in this position, and breathe for several steady breaths.
4. Allow the top right hand to unfurl, bringing it slowly to briefly meet the left hand at the lower *dan tian*.
5. Bring the right hand to the earthing position at the side of the hip, as the left hand rises, palm facing the heavens to begin with, turning at the level of the face until the arm lengthens and curves, with the palm facing the heavens and the arm extended directly above the crown. Remain in this position and breathe for several steady breaths.
6. Continue alternating, one hand to the heavens, one to the earth, until you achieve a sense of balance.
7. Draw arms towards the lower *dan tian*, and remain for a few minutes in the Holding the Ball position (palms beaming into and sitting on the periphery of the *lower dan tian*). Remain in this position, and breathe for several steady breaths.

step 1

step 2

step 3

step 4

step 5

step 6

Balancing Heaven and Earth 1-6

8. Bring both hands down to the earthing position, knees and shoulders soft and relaxed, to finish.

There are many more qigong movements I would love to share with you. I have posted some of these on the Healing InSight website. I recommend all of the above, plus the Crane for opening the heart and the Bone Marrow Cleanse, for boosting the immune system and supporting cell regeneration.

## Meditation

### Activating the Small Heavenly Circuit (Sometimes referred to as the Microcosmic Orbit)

The Small Heavenly Circuit meditation is a beautiful way to help bring energy flow back to the body through intention, attention, and breathwork. It activates the "superhighway" meridians (the Governing Vessel up the spine and the Conception Vessel down the front of the body), which helps increase energy, remove stagnation from certain areas in this circuit and transform the *jing*, or kidney essence, into *qi*, or energy flow, in the organ meridians. This is best practised after doing qigong gathering work in the lower *dan tian*, such as "holding the ball". See diagram for the circuit.

1. This meditation is best practised seated on a chair, but can be done standing.
2. Place the tip of the tongue on the roof of the mouth. This connects the two vessels to enable the circulating orbit to generate and move energy.
3. Imagine four balls of energy spinning in the lower *dan tian*, circling in a vertical manner, up the back, and down the front of this area, and allow this *qi* ball to expand or increase.
4. Imagine and feel the moon spinning in orbit around the earth, and the earth spinning in orbit around the sun. Everything, from the cosmos to the electrons in our cells, is spinning in orbit. Place your own orbit within the larger orbits around you.
5. As you breathe in, imagine a ball of *qi* travelling up the spine, over the top of the head, through the third eye, to the tip of the tongue.
6. As you breathe out, imagine the ball of *qi* travelling down the front of your body to the perineum.

7. With a gentle squeeze of the perineal muscles, direct the *qi* ball back up the spine again with the inward breath.

8. Repeat this circular orbit nine or 18 times. Then change direction, starting with the ball of *qi* in the lower *dan tian*, connecting with the macrocosmic orbit of the sun, and breathing up the front and down the back, maintaining a tip-of-the-tongue connection and squeezing the perineum to help direct the energy flow.

9. Optionally, add in a figure of eight orbit (the Large Heavenly Circuit) by following the ball of *qi* in the *dan tian* (up the back and down the front), then directing the energy flow in a figure of eight down the back of the legs to the feet/earth and back up the front of the legs to the perineum, up the spine, over the head, and down the front, down the back of the legs, and up the front of the legs to the perineum. Repeat nine or 18 times, then in the opposite direction nine or 18 times. This should help with energy coherence and health, create a vibrant field that helps protect against EMFs or outside energies, and boost energy levels!

The Small Heavenly Circuit

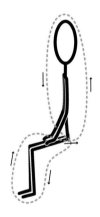

The Large Heavenly Circuit

# References

Burge, Brad. Press Release: "FDA Grants Breakthrough Therapy Designation for MDMA-Assisted Psychotherapy for PTSD, Agrees on Special Protocol Assessment for Phase 3 Trials" [Online]. Multidisciplinary Association for Psychic Studies. [Cited 26, August, 2017]. Available from https://maps.org/news/media/6786-press-release-fda-grants-breakthrough-therapy-designation-for-mdma-assisted-psychotherapy-for-ptsd,-agrees-on-special-protocol-assessment-for-phase-3-trials.

Chang, Stephen T. *The Complete System of Self-Healing, Internal Exercises.* San Francisco, CA: Tao Publishing, 1986.

Church, Dawson. *Mind to Matter: The Astonishing Science of How Your Brain Creates Material Reality.* Carlsbad, CA: Hay House, 2018.

———. *The Genie in Your Genes: Epigenetic Medicine and the New Biology of Intention.* Santa Rosa, CA: Energy Psychology Press, 2014.

Cohen, Kenneth. *The Way of Qigong: The Art and Science of Chinese Energy Healing.* Toronto, Canada: Random House, 1997.

Cosic, I., D. Cosic, and K.Lazar. 2015. "Is It Possible to Predict Electromagnetic Resonances in Proteins, DNA and RNA?" *EPJ Nonlinear Biomedical Physics, 3(1).* 5. Springer Open, https://epjnonlinearbiomedphys.springeropen.com.

Dispenza, J. *Becoming Supernatural: How Common People Are Doing the Uncommon.* Carlsbad, CA: Hay House, 2017.

Eden, Donna. *Energy Medicine: Balancing Your Body's Energy for Optimal Health, Joy and Vitality.* London: Piatkus Books, 2008.

Edition CNN. http://edition.cnn.com/2011/HEALTH/03/03/ep.seidler.cancer.mind.body/index.html. 2011.

Ellis, Richard. *Reiki and the Seven Chakras: Your Essential Guide.* London: Vermillion, 2002, pp.66-67.

———. *The Heart of Reiki.* UK: Self published, 2014.

Fannin, Jeffrey L., and Robert M. Williams. 2012. "Neuroscience Reveals the Whole-Brain State and Its Applications for International Business and Sustainable Success." *The International Journal of Management and Business,* 3, (1): 73–95.

Farez, Mauricio F., Ivan D. Mascanfroni, Santiago P. Mendez-Huergo, Ada Yeste, Gopal Murugaiyan, Lucien P. Garo, Marıa E. Balbuena Aguirre, Bonny Patel., Marıa C. Ysrraelit, Chen Zhu, Vijay K. Kuchroo, Gabriel A. Rabinovich, Francisco J. Quintana, and Jorge Correale. 2015. "Melatonin Contributes to the Seasonality of Multiple Sclerosis Relapses." *Cell. 162,* 1338–1352. Elsevier Inc. https://www.cell.com/cell/pdfExtended/S0092-8674(15)01038-7.

Fell, Jurgen, Nikolai Axmacher, and Sven Haupt. 2010. "From Alpha to Gamma: Electrophysiological Correlates of Meditation-Related States of Consciousness." *Medical Hypotheses, 75(2). 218-24.* https://www.sciencedirect.com/science/article/pii/S0306987710000903.

Fumoto, M., T. Oshima, K. Kamiya, H. Kikuchi, Y. Seki, X. Yu Nakatani, T. Sekiyama, I.Y. Sato-Suzuki, and H. Arita. 2010. "Ventral Prefrontal Cortex and Serotonergic System Activation During Pedaling Exercise Induces Negative Mood Improvement and Increased Alpha Band in EEG." *Behavioural Brain Research, 21(3).* 1–9.

Hamilton, David. *How Your Mind Can Heal Your Body.* London: Hay House, 2008.

Hebb, D. *The Organisation of Behaviour.* New York: John Wiley and Sons, 1949.

Heider-Rauter, Barbara. *The Power of the Infinity Symbol: Working with the Lemniscate for Ultimate Harmony and Balance.* Rochester, VT: Earth Dancer/Inner Traditions, 2018, pp 16–19.

Hicks, Esther, Jerry Hicks. *Ask and It Is Given: Learning to Manifest the Law of Attraction – The Teachings of Abraham.* London: Hay House, 2005.

Judith, Anodea. *Wheels of Life: The User's Guide to the Chakra System.* Woodbury, MN: Llewellyn New Age, 1987.

Jung, Carl. *On the Nature of the Psyche.* Oxford, UK: Routledge, 1969.

——. *The Undiscovered Self.* Oxford, UK: Routledge, 1958.

Killgore, William. D. S. and Deborah A. Yurgelun-Todd. 2007. "The Right-Hemisphere and Valence Hypotheses: Could They Both Be Right (and Sometimes Left)? *Social Cognitive and Affective Neuroscience.* 2(3): 240–250. Available from National Centre for Biotechnology Information: https://www.ncbi.nlm.nih.gov/pmc/articles/PMC2569811/. 2007.

Kim, Bong-Han. *Great Discovery in Biology and Medicine: Substance of Kyungrak.* Pyongyang, China: Foreign Languages Publishing House, 1962.

Lakhiani, Vishen. *The Code of the Extraordinary Mind: 10 Unconventional Laws to Redefine Your Life and Succeed on Your Own Terms.* New York: Rodale Wellness, 2016.

Lao Tzu. *Tao Te Ching*, translated by Gia-Fu Feng and Jane English. New York: Vintage Books, 1972.

Liberman, Jacob. *Light: Medicine of the Future*. Rochester, VT: Bear & Co., 1991, p32–128.

Lipton, Bruce. *The Biology of Belief: Unleashing the Power of Consciousness, Matter & Miracles*. London: Hay House, 2005.

Lipton, Bruce. Documentary *As Above—So Below: An Introduction to Fractal Evolution*. YouTube. https://youtube.com, 2005.

MacLean, Paul D. *The Triune Brain in Evolution: Role in Paleocerebral Functions*. New York: Plenum Press, 1990.

Malhotra, Samir, G. Sawhney, and P. Pandhi. 2004. "Neurology and Neurosurgery – The Therapeutic Potential of Melatonin: A Review of the Science." *MEDGENMED*. Medscape Psychiatry. [Cited 8 October, 2018]. Available from: https://medscape.com.

Massion, A.O., J. Teas, J.R.Hebert, M.D.Wertheimer, and J. Kabat-Zinn. "Meditation, Melatonin and Breast/Prostate Cancer: Hypothesis and Preliminary Data." *Medical Hypotheses*. 44(1), 39–46. Elsevier. Science Direct. https://www.sciencedirect.com/science/article/pii/0306987795902996?via%3Dihub. 1995.

McCraty, Rollin, Mike Atkinson, and T. Raymond Bradley. 2004. "Electrophysiological Evidence of Intuition: Part 1 – The Surprising Role of the Heart." *Journal of Alternative and Complementary Medicine*; 10(1): 133–143.

McFetridge, Grant, and Jacquelyn Aldana. *Peak States of Consciousness: Theory and Applications, Vol 1: Breakthrough Techniques for Exceptional Quality of Life*. Canada: The Institute for the Study of Peak States Press, 2004.

McLeod, Saul. "What Are the Most Interesting Ideas of Sigmund Freud?" Retrieved from https://www.simplypsychology.org/Sigmund-Freud.html. 2018.

McTaggart, Lynne. *The Intention Experiment: Use Your Thoughts to Change the World*. London: Harper Element, 2008.

McTaggart, Lynne. "The Intention Experiment" @ TCCHE - YouTube: https://www.youtube.com/watch?v=EU55kcXF0H0. 2015.

Mc Taggart, Lynne. *The Power of Eight: Harnessing the Miraculous Energies of a Small Group to Heal Others, Your Life and the World*. New York: Atria, 2017.

Morton, Brian. "Falser Words Were Never Spoken." *New York Times, 29th August, 2011*. Cited in: https://www.nytimes.com/2011/08/30/opinion/falser-words-were-never-spoken.html.

Moseley, J.B., N.P. Wray, D. Kuykendall, K.Willis, and G. Landon. 1996. "Arthroscopic Treatment of Osteoarthritis of the Knee: A Prospective, Randomized, Placebo-Controlled Trial. Results of a Pilot Study. *American Journal of Sports Medicine*, 24,1: pp. 28–34.

Moseley, J.B., K. O'Malley, N. Petersen, T. Menke, B. A. Brody, D. H. Kuykendall, J. C. Hollingsworth, C. Ashton, and N.P. Wray. 2002. "A Controlled Trial of Arthroscopic Surgery for Osteoarthritis of the Knee." *The New England Journal of Medicine*. 347:81–88.

O'Regan, Brenda, and Caryle Hirshberg. *Spontaneous Remission: An Annotated Bibliography*. Petaluma, CA: Institute of Noetic Sciences, 1993.

Pearsall Paul. *The Heart's Code: Tapping the Wisdom and Power of Our Heart Energy*. New York, Random House, 1998.

Pert, Candace B. *Molecules of Emotion: The Science Behind Mind-Body Medicine*. New York: Touchstone, 1999.

Purce, Jill. *The Mystic Spiral: Journey of the Soul*. London: Thames & Hudson, 1974. NOTE: Image on Throat Chakra card is a representation of Figure 62 in this book, entitled Mandala Fresco, Temple Court of the Fortress of Part Dzong, West Bhutan.

Reber A. *The Penguin Dictionary of Psychology*. London: Penguin, 1985.

Schlebusch, K., W. Maric-Oehler, and F.A. Popp. 2005. "Biophotonics in the Infrared Spectral Range Reveal Acupuncture Meridian Structure of the Body." *The Journal of Alternative and Complementary Medicine, 11(1)*. 171–173. Scribd. https://www.scribd.com/document/236442045/Biophotonics-in-the-Infrared-Spectral-Range-Reveal-Acupuncture.

Shatz, C.J. 1992. "The Developing Brain." *Scientific American, September 267(3)*. 60–7.

Szegedy-Maszak, M. 2005. "Mysteries of the Mind: Your Unconscious Is Making Your Everyday Decisions." *U.S. News & World Report*. Available from http://www.auburn.edu/~mitrege/ENGL2210/USNWR-mind.html.

Sheldrake, Rupert. 1987. *Beyond the Brain, Extended Minds*. The Scientific & Medical Network. https://explore.scimednet.org, 2017.

——. *Morphic Resonance: The Nature of Formative Causation*. South Paris, ME: Park Street Press, 2009.

——. "Part I – Mind, Memory, and Archetype: Morphic Resonance and the Collective Unconscious." *Psychological Perspectives*, 18(1) 9–25. Semantics Scholar. https://pdfs.semanticscholar.org.

——. *The Presence of the Past: Morphic Resonance and the Habits of Nature*. London: Icon Books, 2011.

——. *The Sense Of Being Stared At: And Other Aspects of the Extended Mind.* London: Arrow Books, 2004.

Tekutskaya, E., M. Barishev, M., and G. Ilchenko. 2015. "The Effect of a Low-Frequency Electromagnetic Field on DNA Molecules in Water Solutions." *Biophysics, 60(6).* 913.

Toshitaka, Mochizuki. 2000. *Reiki Iyashi No Te—Manos Curativas.* Spain: Kier. Cited in https://reiki.org/reikinews/rn960401.html.

Weiss, Suzannah. 2018. "How Badly Are You Messing Up Your Brain By Using Psychedelics?" [Online] Tonic. [30 March, 2018]. Available from: https://tonic.vice.com/en_us/article/59j97a/how-badly-are-you-messing-up-your-brain-by-using-psychedelics.

Williamson, Marianne. *A Return to Love: Reflections on the Principles of a Course in Miracles.* New York: Harper Collins, 1992, pp 190–191.

Yu, X., M. Fumoto, Y. Nakatani, T. Sekiyama, H. Kikuchi, Y. Seki, I. Sato-Suzuki, and H. Arita. 2011. "Activation of the Anterior Prefrontal Cortex and Serotonergic System Is Associated with Improvements in Mood and EEG Changes Induced by Zen Meditation Practice in Novices." *International Journal of Psychophysiology, 80(2),* 103–111.

## Further Information

Clara Apollo, Qigong Teacher Trainer: https://consciouslivingevents.co.uk

Electricsense: https://www.electricsense.com

Esther Hicks: www.abraham-hicks.com

Geneline therapy: http://www.hypnoshealing.com

Jill Purce: http://www.jillpurce.com

Jill Bolte Ted Talk: https://www.ted.com/talks/jill_bolte_taylor_s_powerful_stroke_of_insight

Richard Ellis: http://www.practicalreiki.com

The Emotional Freedom Technique: https://eft.mercola.com or, https://www.efttrainingcourses.net

The Lightning Process: https://lightningprocess.com

Psych-K: https://psych-k.com or, http://yearning4learning.co.uk

Theta Healing: https://www.thetahealing.com

What Doctors Don't Tell You: https://www.wddty.com

More information about the Healing InSight Method, app, and resources including details of workshops; retreats; and personal, practitioner, and teacher training can be found at http://www.healinginsight.co.uk

# Acknowledgements

Thank you sincerely to all of the people who have entrusted me with their deepest fears, hurts, and limitations. I respect and regard you more than you know. You have been my greatest teachers, from whom I have learnt so much. It was with you in mind that I wrote this book—clients past, present, and future—to give you the answers that you have been looking for. Ultimately, they are inside of you. This gift is the "how" to access these answers and, hopefully, the inspiration to try.

My loving partner Rob, I could not have done this without you. My technical, literary, and creative wizard—your contribution has extended beyond reasonable. You are such a treasure of a human being, and we are so blessed to have you in our lives. Thank you, heart and soul. I thank my three beautiful boys, Jackson, Benjy, and Phoenix, who inspire and drive me to be the best that I can be—I love you all so very much.

My thanks go out to Lucy Record, who handcrafted with love each of the beautiful scriptures on the card deck, and Jo Davey, the artist who brought my designs to life. I trust that you believe in yourself now, Jo! Your patience with me, willingness, positivity, and the end result are outstanding. Thank you also to Jenny, Rachel, Anna, Natalie, Lindsay, Allison, Richard, and Clara for your feedback and direction to get me through the last hurdle, to grandparents for babysitting whilst we were crafting this work, and to Sabine, my editorial director who has such tremendous grace, skill, integrity, and generosity.

Final thanks go to my parents. I love you so dearly. You have given everything endlessly. Without you, my soul would not have evolved and learnt the important lessons that it was here to share with the world. You have taught me that with love, trust, and focus, "all is possible". I have a life of love and purpose and am ever grateful to you both.

# About the Author

Photo by Rob Record

NIKKI GRESHAM-RECORD is one of the UK's leading spiritual healers, a Chartered Counselling Psychologist, Reiki and Qigong teacher. Whilst trained scientifically using evidence-based practice, her life experiences have taken her work outside of the box to incorporate energy psychology and healing methods. Having healed herself from the supposedly incurable Systemic Lupus Erythematosis, Nikki has used her professional background and her interest in both vibrational emotional healing and the power of belief to develop her Healing InSight Belief Change System.

She works with a broad client base on a one-to-one basis as well as facilitating workshops. Nikki lives with her family in Midhurst, West Sussex, UK. For more information visit her website: **www.healinginsight.co.uk**